PUBLIC ORGANIZATIONS AND POLICY

An Experiential Approach to Public Policy and Its Execution

David Bresnick, Director, Center for
Management Development and Organization Research
*Baruch School of Business and
Public Administration*
City University of New York

SCOTT, FORESMAN AND COMPANY
Glenview, Illinois
Dallas, Tex. Oakland, N.J. Palo Alto, Cal. Tucker, Ga. London, England

I dedicate this book
to my parents and my grandparents
who taught me to be suspect of government
and to work to make it better.

Library of Congress Cataloging in Publication Data

Bresnick, David
Public organizations and policy.

Includes index.
1. Public administration. 2. Policy sciences. I. Title.
JF1351.B663 350.007 81-14471
ISBN 0-673-16054-8 AACR2

ISBN: 0-673-16054-8

Printed in the United States of America.

2 3 4 5 6-KPF-88 87 86 85 84 83 82

CONTENTS

PREFACE vi

INTRODUCTION 1

What Are Public Organizations? 1

Roles in Public Organizations 2

The Variety of Public Organizations 5

Public and Private Corporations 8

The Political Dimension 10

Our Approach 14

SECTION I
UNDERSTANDING PUBLIC ORGANIZATIONS 19

MODULE 1 Motivating People, The Personnel Function 21

Introduction 21
"Circling to Nowhere" 23
Comment on Circling to Nowhere 25
Note on the Personnel Function 29
Selected Bibliography for Module 1 32

MODULE 2 Organizational Behavior: The Civil Service 34

Introduction 34
Understanding Organizational Behavior: The Civil Service in Action 34
"The Van Waters Case" 40
Comment on the Van Waters Case 41
Note on the Civil Service 46
Selected Bibliography for Module 2 56

MODULE 3 Managing Public Organizations, Supervision, and Leadership 57

Introduction 57
Roles and Game Playing 58
"SUPSUB: A Role Play" 59
Comment on SUPSUB 61
Note on Leadership Style 62
Selected Bibliography for Module 3 71

MODULE 4 Communications and Organizational Development 72

Introduction 72
Introduction to Team Building 72
Comments on Team Building 75
Introduction to Goal Communication 76
Note on Ongoing Communications 78
Introduction to External Communications 82
In-Basket Exercises 87
Comment on In-Basket Exercises 100
Note on Gathering Information 100
Selected Bibliography for Module 4 101

SECTION II
POLICY AND DECISION PROCESSES **103**

MODULE 5 Policy Development, Agenda Building, Interest Groups 108
Introduction 108
Policy Development 108
Agenda Building 110
Interest Groups 111
Agenda Building in the Policy Process 113
Agenda Building Exercise 114
Comments on the Agenda Building Exercise 115
Note on Influencing Agenda Building 115
Selected Bibliography for Module 5 118

MODULE 6 Policy Formation, Interest Aggregation, Accountability 120
Introduction 120
"POLFORM" 125
Comment on POLFORM 127
Note on Policymaking Roles, Accountability, and Rulemaking 128
"Conceptual Models and the Cuban Missile Crisis" 133
Selected Bibliography for Module 6 138

MODULE 7 Policy Implementation, Planning, Intergovernmental Relations 139
Introduction 139
Disenchantment with the Great Society 139
"ESEA: The Office of Education Administers a Law" 143
Comment on Implementing Title I 150
Note on Implementation Planning 151
Scenarios 155
Note on Obstacles to Implementation 158
Selected Bibliography for Module 7 162

SECTION III
TECHNIQUES OF POLICY ANALYSIS **163**

MODULE 8 Systems Analysis of Public Policy, Program and Performance Evaluation 167
Introduction 167
Systems Analysis and Operations Research 168
Outline of a Systems Analysis 170
Developing Alternative Policy Options 175
Choosing Criteria 177
Comment on Systems Analysis 178
Note on Program and Performance Evaluation 179
Selected Bibliography for Module 8 182

MODULE 9 Calculating the Impact of Policy, Benefit/Cost Analysis 183
Introduction 183
Benefit/Cost Analysis 185
"Downtown Parking Authority" 187
Comment on Downtown Parking Authority 190

A Note on Benefit/Cost Analysis and Other Quantitative Techniques 191
Criticisms of Benefit/Cost Analysis 196
Selected Bibliography for Module 9 197

MODULE 10 Less Formal Techniques for Predicting the Future, Social Indicators, Forecasting 199
Introduction 199
Scenarios 201
"CROSSPACT" 202
Comments on CROSSPACT 208
"The Delphi Method" 209
Comments on the Delphi Method 211
A Note on the Delphi Method 212
A Note on Social Indicators and Subjective Judgment 213
Selected Bibliography for Module 10 216

SECTION IV
PUTTING IT ALL TOGETHER **217**

MODULE 11 Public Budgeting: Organizational Activity and Policy Process 218
Introduction 218
"BUDGSIM" 224
Comment on BUDGSIM—Phase I 239
Comment on BUDGSIM—Phase II 243
On Budgeting and Other Things 244
Selected Bibliography for Module 11 247

INDEX 248

PREFACE

Underlying this book is the deeply held belief that public administration requires sound theory closely tied to administrative practice. The result is a book that eschews the distinctions sometimes made among public administration, public policy, and policy analysis. My belief is that one field easily spans these topics. I am convinced that introductory treatments should include all of these topics and that soon, if not already, most instructors will agree. I am also convinced that the relationship between theory and practice, particularly at the introductory level, can best be taught through experiential approaches, including case studies, role playing, exercises, and longer games. I also believe that students and instructors, once exposed to these methods, will be converted and that the days of the traditional textbook are numbered.

My perspective on the close relationship between theory and practice was nurtured during my graduate school days by the late Professor Wallace Sayre, who provided careful guidance in the preparation of my dissertation on the legislative aspects of school decentralization. While working at the New York City Board of Education, I came into contact with Harvey Sherman of the Port Authority of New York and New Jersey, who has provided helpful reactions to my writing over the years and who also represents this close connection of theory with practice.

In developing my approach to an understanding of public organizations within the larger framework of behavioral science, I owe an intellectual debt to Herbert Simon and his major work, *Administrative Behavior.* His text, *Public Administration* (1950), coauthored with Donald Smithburg and Victor Thompson, still strikes me as the outstanding example of a public administration text with a strong and viable theoretical base. Leonard Sayles, both through his writing, particularly *Managerial Behavior,* and his willing advice also has contributed to the behavioral orientation of my thinking about public organizations.

The chapters on the policy process show the strong influence of Charles Lindblom and Yehezkel Dror and their respective works, *The Policymaking Process* (and, of course, *A Strategy of Decision* with David Braybrooke) and *Public Policy Making Re-examined.* The chapters on policy analysis reflect the seminal work of E.S. Quade, *Systems Analysis Techniques for Planning-Programming-Budgeting,* and Charles Hitch and Roland McKean, *The Economics of Defense in the Nuclear Age.*

Without going into voluminous detail in any particular subject, I have attempted to review every major topic in the areas of public administration, public policy, and policy analysis and provide a coherent framework for tying them together. A student who has completed these materials will have had a thorough introduction to the field.

INTRODUCTION

WHAT ARE PUBLIC ORGANIZATIONS?

At one time most Americans could live their lives barely recognizing that government existed. That is no longer the case. Unless one chooses to live in one of a limited number of remote regions, government is a necessity. It has changed its character from the provider of occasional services to a major producer. In 1975 government accounted for approximately 40 percent of the total value of goods and services in this country.

Direct government employment today represents a substantial portion of total employment and government contract employment another major portion. Most of us are affected in many ways by government, including those who are unemployed.

Perhaps the most persistent presence of government is in its efforts to collect taxes on the things we buy, for the property we own or rent, and on the money we earn or inherit. Taxes are needed to support innumerable public organizations that provide a range of services. Yet tax collection represents a small part of government operations. At the local level government collects garbage, fights fires, and educates our youth. At the state level government builds highways, supports higher education, and provides recreation facilities. At the federal level government provides military support, provides funds for education, health and welfare, runs the currency system, and administers huge expanses of real estate referred to as the public lands. The federal and state governments also support the lesser levels of governments. While at times it seems that government has an insatiable appetite, the billions of dollars collected in taxes all can be accounted for in terms of the goods and services they provide.

These goods and services are spent by our legislators through government agencies sometimes referred to as the bureaucracy. But how can the legislators and the bureaucracy possibly spend so much money? The federal portion represents about two-thirds of the total costs — $602 billion in fiscal 1980. Surely some of that money could be saved and returned to reduce taxes! But while many citizens seek to lower government expenditures and many legislators try to reduce spending, the trend has been to higher and higher allocations.

Over the years, as governmental bureaucracy and budgets have grown, the government has taken on more tasks, leading to an increase in its scope. Even as citizens seek to reduce government spending, new demands continue to be made for increased services.

Let's reduce the bureaucracy and save the taxpayer money. Reducing the bureaucracy means reducing services, cutting salaries, or cutting the purchase of goods. Which alternative is most desirable?

In addition to the costs of government, its organization often causes consternation. Why do we need all that government red tape? Let's do away with bureaucracy! Even in the private sector organizations and organizational structures are subject to increasing criticism. Organizations, though, are man-made institutions. They facilitate tasks that individuals cannot accomplish single-handedly. More than ever, living in the world means living in and with organizations, and this is increasingly true in contemporary American society. More and more Americans will be working in and having contact with public organizations. What are these fascinating and complex organizations and how do they formulate policies that affect us all?

ROLES IN PUBLIC ORGANIZATIONS

Public organizations are people interacting in special ways. These ways are determined in large measure by individual behaviors, sometimes referred to as roles. A major part of the business of public organizations is establishing policy. Understanding the process of policy formation is critical to understanding the operation of public organizations. People who work in and with organizations also evaluate these policies and their impacts on society, utilizing the techniques of policy analysis.

People assuming roles, making policies, using acknowledged techniques of analysis, making public organizations work and affecting the lives of all of us — unless we understand how all this works, our chances for affecting the process will be minimal. But although understanding public organizations cannot ensure that our impact on them will be great, if we understand how they operate we will have a better chance of using them to make our lives happier.

Public organizations are cooperative efforts to achieve certain common goals. The most dramatic instance of group cooperation is in the conduct of war. Most national states trace their history to the need to protect their territorial unit from domination by another territorial unit. So the United States was formed in reaction to British domination.

While the conduct of war and the related area of foreign relations usually have been the first and most important tasks of national governments, local government has had a different orientation. People living in close proximity to one another have found that it often becomes useful and even necessary to cooperate in common tasks. Perhaps the most basic common functions in primitive tribes revolve around food gathering. As settlements grow, the necessity for a common approach to securing a water supply and disposing of wastes assumes top priority and requires common attention. Then, protection of private property through the creation of police and fire services and passing on the common cultural heritage through formal education soon become priority items.

In the United States this heritage of local governments providing for water supply and disposal, police and fire services, and education is strong. For example, an official board is created to allocate water according to rules about the sinking of wells. Or, where water is scarce, such as in the West, its allocation may develop in more elaborate ways. Where a settlement does not have adequate clean water, common aqueducts may be necessary. Where informal agreement is insufficient, groups will form an organization to oversee common activities, and these general purpose or special purpose associations are usually referred to as governments. Village, town, and city governments are examples of general purpose governments formed because the concentration of population has led to the desire to arrange common solutions to common problems.

In the United States, general purpose governmental institutions ordinarily are chartered by the state government, as are many general purpose units. Often these units enlist the help of volunteers. In many less populous areas throughout the country volunteer fire departments and emergency medical units exist, made up of citizens who donate their time.

Sometimes self-help groups, for example block associations, establish formal relationships with actual government agencies and take on quasi-governmental responsibilities.

The variety of public organizations is so great that there is almost assuredly a public organization in some part of the world that does virtually what every private organization does. In order, however, to limit the discussion of public organizations to manageable proportions, this book will deal with public organizations in the United States, emphasizing executive agencies and departments and their subdivisions, which carry out the main work of government. We will consider both federal and state agencies and departments as well as their local analogues and individual organizational units such as hospitals, schools, and recreation facilities that provide direct services.

Public organizations provide a vast array of services. They provide health services of all kinds, feed the old and the young, educate and train for employment, protect us from fire and crime, provide compensation for the damages caused by floods and other natural disasters, provide water, electric, and gas services, and run some railroads. In fact, they do everything that needs to be done and cannot or is not provided by private corporations.

They also intervene in many areas where private corporations provide services. Particularly where those services are affected by an important public interest and where competition among private corporations is minimal, government regulation becomes an important factor. Public regulatory agencies supervise utilities such as gas and electric companies, communications industries such as radio and television, and transportation industries such as the railroads, airlines, and truckers. Antitrust, environmental, and health and safety regulations affect most large corporations to some degree. Labor unions also are regulated.

Public organizations also affect the distribution of individual and group resources through tax policies, subsidies, and a variety of individual cash grant programs. When direct services or regulatory policies provide benefits to particular individuals or groups, they, too, affect the distribution of resources. Thus government programs may affect the existing distribution of resources among individuals and groups.

Public organizations, then, undertake activities that fall within one or more of the following categories:

1. direct services,
2. regulation, or
3. redistribution.

The use of these categories will help simplify analysis of the great variety of public organizations. As you become familiar with these organizations, you will learn to differentiate them and their activities.

While this book does not attempt to describe and analyze profit-making institutions of the private sector such as business corporations, some of the following discussions will be applicable to them. Nowadays the distinction between private business corporations and public government bureaus is not as clear as it used to be. It used to be thought that private businesses were totally free of government and that government never functioned in areas in which private enterprise operated. Schools in this country, for example, have come in two varieties, public and private. Although differences exist, particularly with respect to funding and student body composition, in most respects public and private schools are quite similar. Both are organized into class units, hire teachers and administrators of similar training, and rely upon curricula that are taught at the same schools of education and incorporated into the same textbooks. Recent developments in the health care industry that make hospitals more dependent upon funding may soon turn hospitals, by and large, into public organizations. Even today, many public hospitals are run by federal, state, or local governments. In most respects publicly administered hospitals are similar to private hospitals, although their funding may be very different. Nurses, doctors, and administrators tend to come from common professional schools and supplies and equipment are purchased from common commercial sources. Certain utilities such as water and power systems may be similar, whether run by private or public institutions. In some areas, then, the distinction between public and private organizations is minimal.

Certainly, however, in the United States private profit-making corporations still operate in many areas exclusively and distinctly. Profit and salary incentives, job insecurity, and the dangers of bankruptcy are some characteristics that make these organizations distinctive.

One of the objectives of this book is to deepen the student's understanding of the variety of public organizations. Sometimes overzealous critics of government refer to it as a gigantic, monolithic conspiracy against the simple people of the world. Nothing could be further from the truth. Government is merely people trying to accomplish common goals through specific forms of organization. What types of public organizations are there and how do they work?

THE VARIETY OF PUBLIC ORGANIZATIONS

If you approached a man or woman in the street and asked for an opinion about public organizations, he or she might look at you blankly and stare. But if you asked for views on government the person might harangue you for fifteen minutes and then ask what you meant by public organizations. Everybody has an opinion about government, but many of these opinions are based on very little thought or evidence. Indeed, government is approximately what we mean by public organizations, but not exactly.

The United States government is usually described as the three branches discussed in the Constitution: the executive, the legislature, and the judiciary. The legislature is responsible for making laws, the executive for enforcing laws, and the judiciary for interpreting laws. You will see later on how the notion of policymaking is used to develop a more systematic view of governmental activity. For the time being we will examine the variety of public organizations. Within the American governmental system state and local governments roughly mirror the federal government with a separation of powers among the legislature, executive, and judiciary.

While some commentators on public administration omit legislative and judicial institutions from consideration, they are included here as public organizations. Examples will usually focus on agencies directly responsible to the executive branch, but legislatures, courts, and their supporting units are also public organizations. In fact, in recent years the increasing realization that problems of administration confront courts and legislatures has given rise to a new emphasis on judicial and legislative administration.

The structure of legislatures is certainly very different from the executive. While legislatures, at least formally, have a large number of equal, elected members, the executive is organized hierarchically with a single elected individual in charge. At the federal level judges in the district courts, courts of appeals, and United State Supreme Court all are appointed. Legislatures are different from elected executives in that they are concerned almost exclusively with broad policy and formulate such policy, at least formally, by collective voting. This does not mean, however, that a small number of individuals, or for that matter one very skilled individual, may not dominate any particular legislature. Judicial institutions are different in that they are concerned with making decision in individual cases rather than promulgating general policies. Decisions are usually made by single individuals, although collective decision making is often practiced at the higher appellate levels. Increasing attention to the problems of backlog and delay in some courts has encouraged efforts to improve judicial administration. A new breed of public servant, the court administrator, has been created to cope with these problems.

By far the most numerous organizations, however, and surely those most commonly referred to as the bureaucracy, are the agencies and departments of government subordinate to the elected executive. At the federal level these include the departments of State, Treasury, Defense, Justice, Interior, Agriculture, Commerce, Labor, Health and Human Services, Housing and Urban Development, and Transportation, in addition to the newly created departments of Energy and Education. These departments are directly responsible to the president, who appoints (and may fire at any time) their heads, the department secretaries. Each of these departments has a varying number of employees organized into subunits. The departments are represented in each of the ten federal regions of the United States.

States have their own executive departments, which vary from state to state. Most states have departments that provide these major services at the state level: education, both higher and lower; highways; welfare; and health and hospitals. At the local level, since the scope of services varies so greatly from government to government, the departments also vary. Most city governments have police and fire departments. Education is usually controlled by an independent board of education. Welfare and related social services are ordinarily county functions.

In the United States, the president, the governors, and the mayors appoint the heads of major departments. It is the president's responsibility to appoint each of the secretaries and assistant secretaries of each department. Considerable variation exists in the method of appointing officials to head state departments. At the state level many of the major departments are headed by individuals who are elected independently of the chief executive or by appointed boards. Such arrangements diminish the authority of the chief executive.

In addition to the departments that report directly to the elected executive at the federal level, a large number of other agencies, commissions, and public corporations exists. Perhaps the most important and well known are the independent regulatory commissions, which are strongly influenced by Congress. Examples are the Civil Aeronautics Board, the Federal Communications Commission, the Federal Maritime Commission, the Federal Power Commission, and the Federal Reserve Board. Other independent agencies, such as the Central Intelligence Agency, the General Services Administration, the National Aeronautics and Space Administration, and the Veterans Administration, are important and powerful public organizations. Foundations and institutes such as the National Science Foundation and the National Institutes of Health perform important research functions at the federal level. Government corporations such as the Federal Deposit Insurance Corporation, the Tennessee Valley Authority, and the Panama Canal Company are other variants of public organizations. Others include the Administrative Conference of the United States, the Migratory Bird Conservation Committee, the Corporation for Public Broadcasting, the Advisory Commission on Intergovernmental Relations, and the Appalachian Regional Commission.

At the federal level the creation of independent regulatory commissions has had a critical impact on national political institutions. These organizations have a special relationship with Congress, which makes them less dependent upon the president. When President Carter proposed merging the Federal Power Commission (FPC) with the newly created Energy Department he was rebuffed by a Congress that preferred to maintain its existing, greater authority over the FPC.

Many states have followed the lead of the national government and have created independent regulatory commissions, especially to oversee the utility industries. A further complication at the state level is the existence of independently elected executives, such as attorneys general and comptrollers. In some cases, states elect boards of education, which are responsible for the statewide education program. In other cases such boards may be appointed by the governor. One state, New York, has a board of regents, in effect the statewide board of education, which is elected by joint vote of the state legislature.

PUBLIC AND PRIVATE CORPORATIONS

Part of the rationale for creating agencies independent of the elected executive is the feeling that certain governmental functions should be insulated from the ordinary political processes in which agencies are directly responsible to the elected officials. Independent regulatory commissions, it is argued, are not making governmental or political decisions, but basically are deciding about administrative matters not related to the general problems of government. While the view that independent regulatory agencies are concerned with nonpolitical matters has been disputed, it also has been made with respect to other public organizations. Public corporations have developed in part based upon a desire to shield these organizations from the political process. It is argued that they are carrying out essentially nonpolitical functions.

The removal of the post office as a department of government is an excellent example of this argument in action. The post office, it was argued, basically performed a function that should not be subject to political considerations and should be run by professional managers who understand post office operations. It is really more like a private business than a general governmental function. Why has the post office continually operated at a loss if it can be run efficiently as a private business? How different is it from the telephone service, gas and electric service, or for that matter, United Parcel, a private corporation that delivers packages all over the country.

Can you think of any example of public corporations or authorities that operate in your part of the country? Are you familiar with the Tennessee Valley Authority or the Port Authority of New York and New Jersey? These are public organizations created by legislation and are not directly responsible to an elected executive. They are concerned with providing services of a particular kind, on a monopoly basis. Do you think it would be better to have private utilities doing these tasks?

In addition to the independence that a public corporation or authority has from the elected executive, it has the capability of raising capital by floating bond issues, in much the same way as a private company. This ability is another reason for the creation of such authorities and has been particularly important in the area of urban renewal.

Even though public corporations and authorities have independent charters, which minimize the intervention of executive and legislative leaders, they are run by boards or individuals appointed by the elected executive or some public official. They may also depend upon the elected executive and legislature for revenues, even though part of their revenues is often obtained independently of government.

The public corporations and authorities are designed to take advantage of the autonomy of private organizations from government authority. Yet they maintain a critical link to government in that their governing bodies are selected by government officials, usually the elected executive. As a result major policy decisions often become infused with a public dimension. While the appointing official or officials may be restrained from immediately replacing recalcitrant officials appointed for a term of years, in the long run these corporations find it difficult to resist the demands of political leaders.

This power of ultimate appointment usually is accompanied by fiscal and personnel powers that reflect public goals. Money policies may be determined in a public forum and often public subsidies will be applied, or the resources of the organization will be directed, toward certain public purposes. Personnel policies, even if independent of the comprehensive civil service system, often will maintain characteristics of merit selection and advancement on the basis of examinations.

As the personnel and fiscal policies of independent agencies, authorities, and public corporations diverge from those of general governmental agencies, their similarities with private organizations may increase.

Still, the basic distinction between public and private organizations remains. Private organizations are free to pursue private profit without accountability, except to the stockholders. Public organizations are held accountable at every step to the government officials who have created them and to the public they serve. Public organizations are dependent upon elected executives and legislatures for their authority, for their top appointments, and for their revenue sources. Even those public organizations that generate some of their own revenue and are insulated from the direct supervision of elected executives ultimately are engaged in this process of gathering and strengthening their support with the governmental elite, those individuals with authority to make important decisions. These public organizations operate in a special environment, which often leads to the resigned evaluation: "That poor fellow can't run his organization; he's got to do what the politicians tell him to do."

Public organizations must be run for the common good, not in the interests of the ownership or management. This means that decisions having an impact on the public are subject to review and influence by government officials. It is the genesis of the feeling that political influence permeates public organizations.

THE POLITICAL DIMENSION

Political influence over organizational activity is a much misunderstood phenomenon. To some critics, any time the operations of some hospital, school, profit-making institution, or government bureau are subject to the control of elected or high-level appointed officials, condemnation is appropriate. When the government official intervening is a party leader such intervention is considered even worse. And when political leaders respond to local citizen groups or special interests they may be disparaged as politicians without backbone.

Political influence is not necessarily bad, even though it may make an organization's operations more difficult. When political influence is aimed at protecting the larger interests of the community, it may be performing a valuable service. Needless intervention in the affairs of any individual or organization should be condemned. But intervention to protect the interests of the larger society is the basic function of the political system, whether acting to protect the environment, to enforce safety and health standards, or to provide commonly needed services. At present, political intervention affects all organizations. We are merely talking about a matter of degree.

Of course public organizations are much more vulnerable to political influence from elected officials than private organizations. Indeed, this vulnerability is an important distinguishing characteristic of public organizations. Private corporations may court public goodwill and promote good customer relations, but for a public organization the cultivation of clientele and constituency groups and major political figures is an item of top priority, second to none. This means that the public executive is often even more outwardly oriented than his or her private counterpart, and an understanding of the political environment is even more critical to a successful career.

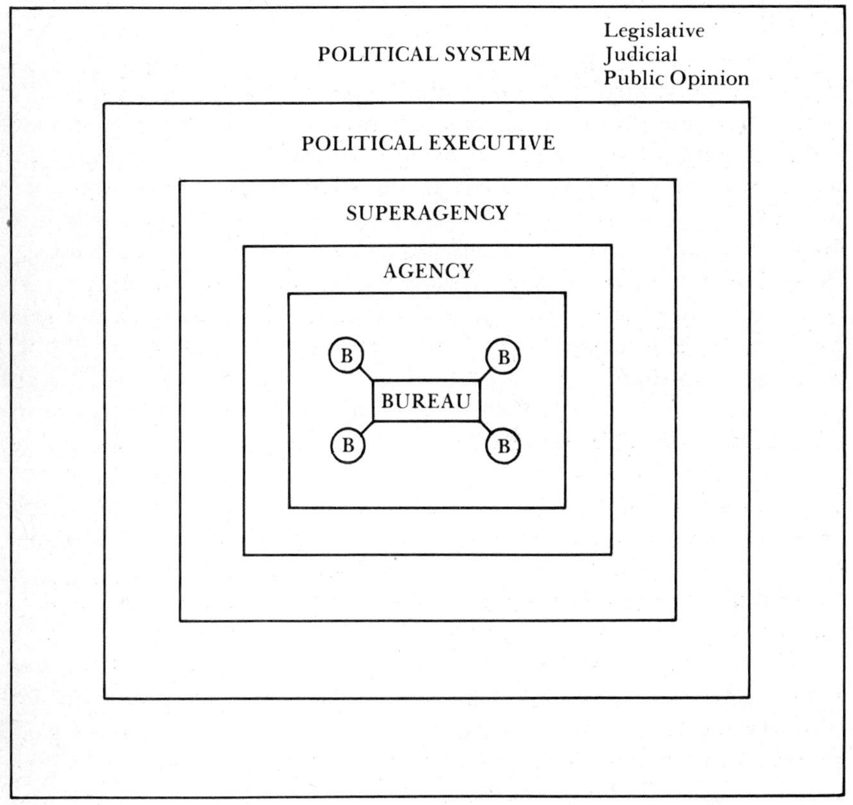

Setting of an Administrative Game

The setting of public organizational activity is described schematically in the accompanying figure. It places the individual at the center of a bureau, inside an agency, contained in a superagency, which is responsible to the political executive who operates within the political system, which is embedded in the social system. Bureaus are public organizations, subunits of larger public organizations referred to as agencies. Superagencies or departments contain several agencies. They are responsible to elected executives: at the local level, the mayor or his or her equivalent; at the state level, the governor; and at the federal level, the president. The political executive must operate within the larger political system, which includes other levels of executive government, the judiciary, the legislature, and independent agencies. Legislators and elected executives must be particularly solicitous of public opinion or they may find themselves voted out of office.

While private organizations, too, must cope with the political and social systems, the direct dependence of public organizations upon elected officials defines a large part of their peculiarity. Public organizations, you will remember, are created to carry out social purposes. These social purposes are defined in the first instance by elected governmental officials responding to the demands of public opinion and influential opinion leaders. In order to ensure that public organizations indeed carry out their intended purposes, accountability relationships develop between public organizations and elected officials. The elected official may hire and fire top agency personnel at will. Both the executive and the legislature will use their budgetary powers to deny monies to those agencies that are not performing well or properly and to support those agencies that are best executing their programs. Legislatures frequently will hold hearings to examine agency performance and executives will conduct their own investigations. Audits conducted by the elected executive or independently elected comptrollers, at the state and local level, will provide a measure of agency performance. At the federal level the General Accounting Office, an arm of Congress, performs similar audits. The Office of Management and Budget similarly performs such analyses for the president.

The ultimate accountability of public organizations, of course, is to the people, who speak at election day by voting out those elected officials whose performance they do not like. It is this relationship among the public, elected officials, and public organizations that constitutes the accountability relationship. Public organizations must respond to their dependence on public opinion, legislatures, and elected executives.

Just as private organizations constantly must be concerned that they earn enough profit to allow them to continue in operation, government bureaus and the larger units within which they operate must constantly attend to their survival. This depends upon their ability to maintain support from the individuals in control of resources. When that support becomes questionable, the survival of the bureau also comes into question. Thus in recent years such venerable institutions as the Federal Bureau of Investigation and the Central Intelligence Agency have been threatened with radical surgery and reorganization. Congressional members in particular have suggested that these executive agencies are not functioning well and need to be changed.

One way that public organizations survive and prosper is by building support among clientele groups that benefit from the services they provide. This base of support can be very important when the agency seeks more resources from the legislature or the executive.

An example of one of the most highly developed clientele networks is that benefiting from public education. Parent associations, which are organizations of clientele on a school-by-school basis, provide an important base of support for the public organizations that carry out education — the schools. When the schools seek more funds from the executive or the legislature they can count on the parents to write letters and testify at hearings about the need for more services for children. Those who have been through the public school system or who have had children in the system provide a potent base of clientele support groups when the school system seeks to survive and prosper. Do you know of any other groups that are important in helping the public school system? Are you familiar with the American Federation of Teachers and the National Education Association, two national organizations of teachers?

The public school system provides services for a large percentage of the children in this country, as well as for many adults through adult education programs. Can you think of any other agencies that provide services? How do the services provided by the police, fire, and sanitation departments differ from those provided by the educational system? Which bureaucracy has greater support from clientele groups? Are prisoners powerful allies when the corrections department attempts to secure monies from the state legislature? What is the clientele group associated with the welfare department?

The welfare bureaucracy, unlike the educational bureaucracy, administers a large system of individual grants that redistribute monies to those in need. While the welfare department provides supplemental services to welfare recipients, the greatest share of the money passing through the welfare system goes directly to individuals. Do grant programs develop support among clientele groups? What is the role of public employees and their organizations in supporting the grant programs they administer? Other examples of grant programs are subsidies for agricultural crops, veterans benefits, and supplemental security income for the aged. What clientele groups would support each of these programs? How do clientele groups support such programs?

The third category distinguished above is government regulatory programs. Regulatory agencies are charged with representing the public and ensuring that those regulated serve the interests of all citizens. In such situations, why would groups being regulated seek to influence government policy? Do you see how these groups might become powerful allies to the agencies in their own efforts for organizational survival? What will happen to the public interest if government agencies become too dependent on these groups?

If properly cultivated, relationships with constituency or clientele groups can mean the difference between drought and prosperity for public organizations. These groups are most directly affected by specific organizations and most willing to devote time and resources either to bolster the organization or to undermine it.

In order to survive and prosper, public organizations often create their own field of forces, in which affected individuals and groups form an alliance with the organizations for mutual protection. This development has particularly affected the independent regulatory commissions. Recent controversy surrounding the Food and Drug Administration has centered on the alleged cozy relationship between the regulators and the regulated.

This tendency of public organizations to increase their own power and bolster their own position is related to the concept of bureaucratic autonomy. As organizations become more powerful and seek to control their own environment, they strive toward bureaucratic autonomy, minimizing the influence of other public organizations, particularly the elected executive. As agencies obtain such autonomy, however, an important issue relating to their accountability is raised. If they are independent of the political executive, elected by all the people, what mechanisms ensure that they are carrying out public purposes and not the narrow interests of their own clientele groups, or, in fact, their narrower bureaucratic interests of survival and growth? This issue was posed during the 1960s when the alleged insulation of large city bureaucracies led to demands for increased citizen control and decentralization to ensure accountability of the bureaucracies to the public.

While the dependence of public organizations upon top governmental officials for their authority, top appointments, and revenues make them distinctive, they nonetheless are like private organizations in that they confront the same basic tasks of defining their goals, creating an organizational structure for accomplishing those goals, and creating an environment in which the members of the organization are encouraged to work cooperatively and effectively in pursuing organizational goals. In this sense public and private organizations are similar. Yet the types of goals they pursue and the methods they use may be very different.

OUR APPROACH

Learning about public organizations is different from learning about mathematics or philosophy. It is much more like learning how to run a business. The study of public organizations and policy, or public administration, as it has been more traditionally called, is a practical science. It aims at helping people who function within or around public organizations understand what is happening there and learn how to manage these organizations better.

Reading about public organizations is one way of getting to understand them better. Another way is by participating in their operation — learning by doing. This book is aimed at facilitating classroom learning about public organizations. For the most part it discusses these organizations, but it also uses experiential devices to create situations similar to those that might be encountered in a real-life public organization. These devices, if properly used, can be an asset in increasing your understanding of public administration. They provide a next best experience for those who have never worked in a public organization and will allow those who have had public organization experience to build upon that foundation to achieve greater understanding.

Public organizations can be studied from a pure research point of view with the emphasis on developing a formal body of theory and knowledge. The orientation of this book is much more practical. It aims to transmit knowledge about public organizations, including how they work and how to function within them. This book is a primer for would-be bureaucrats or, for that matter, antibureaucrats. It seeks to explore the relationships between individuals who are part of public organizations and those who must deal with them. It also explores the policymaking process and deals with some specific techniques of policy analysis.

Public organizations are sometimes characterized as unknowable or subjected to simple clichés. This book seeks to avoid both excesses.

In a classic treatment of some of the myths about public organizations, Harvey Sherman, the Deputy Executive Director of the Port Authority of New York and New Jersey and one of the wisest practitioners in the nonprivate sector, insists that *It All Depends.* Indeed, easy answers to complex questions too often ignore the complexities that make the situation interesting. But *It All Depends,* if taken too literally, suggests that nothing can be said about public organizations and the individuals who make them work. Such is definitely not the case. While the level of theory about public organizations, like that of private organizations, is not as advanced as one might hope, we do know a lot about public organizations and how to make them work.

This book represents a distinctive approach to understanding public organizations and policy. It is divided into four sections. The first section develops an understanding of what public organizations are and how they harness individual efforts toward social goals. The second section focuses on the most salient aspect of public organizational activity: policymaking, the process by which rules are made governing social behavior. The third section investigates approaches and tools for analyzing policies with particular emphasis on the assessment of their impacts. A final section reviews and integrates the first three sections by considering public budgeting as an example of organizational activity of a policymaking nature which incorporates analytical tools for impact assessment.

Each section consists of a series of learning modules, with the exception of Section IV, which is a self-contained module. The term *learning modules* has been chosen because within each module at least one experiential exercise, case study, role play, or simulation game has been integrated into the standard text.

Module 1 begins by posing the central dilemma of public organizational activity: How can individuals working in public organizations bring about the social goals imposed upon them by the political system? In "Circling to Nowhere," a brief case study, the student is asked to analyze the failure of a minority internship program. Two basic lessons emerge from that case: that to understand administrative activity is to understand the roles and goals of the individuals engaged in organizational activity, and that a central concern of the participant in public organizational activity is how to organize and motivate the other participants. Module 1 ends with a discussion of recent developments in the theory of motivation and the description of the personnel function as a specialized approach to the utilization of human resources in achieving organizational effectiveness.

Module 2 begins with an overview of conceptual approaches to the study of organizations, including Weber's concept of bureaucracy, Taylor's approach to scientific management, and subsequent developments in the observational approach, leading to the development of the human relations approach. To illustrate, the concepts from the Van Waters case are provided. Finally, the concept of the civil service, introduced in the Van Waters case, is described at the end of the module.

Module 3, "Managing Public Organizations," focuses on the management function in public organizations. A role play juxtaposes the supervisor and the subordinate in a public organizational setting. Supervisory and subordinate role orientations are investigated through experiential interactions with individuals exhibiting differing role orientations. The textual material then elaborates on the concept of role and discusses some of the literature relating to effective supervision and leadership. A final section describes management by objectives as one approach to effective management that focuses on the effective communication of organizational goals.

The final module of Section I focuses on communications. A series of exercises are used to introduce team building as an approach to developing communication at the work group level. Next, communication of organizational goals is considered, and ongoing communications within public organizations are described. External communications are considered in terms of the needs for public organizations to receive information and to provide information to the outside world. Skills in communications involving these various aspects are developed through the use of an in-basket exercise.

Section II begins with an overview of the policy process in four basic phases: policy development, policy formation, policy implementation, and policy revision. Module 5 considers policy development. Distinguishing several different approaches to the understanding of policy development through the use of a structured game, the student experiences the process of agenda building. Two stages in policy development are discussed: raising an issue onto the public agenda so that a response becomes assured, and raising that issue onto the agenda of some institutional context, such as a legislature or a political executive, for decision making. A final note on influencing agenda building describes how individuals other than the institutional decision makers affect the development of public policy.

Module 6 concentrates on policy formation, the process by which institutional decision makers arrive at some specific policy that is committed to writing and formally adopted. After the concept of policymaking is introduced and applied to the full range of public organizations, the student is asked to participate in a generalized decision-making group to experience firsthand the process of policy formation. A final note describes the role conflicts that policymakers may confront and the various limitations upon the policymaking processes, including the institutional procedures, the customs and amenities, and the dynamics of coalition formation.

The next stage, policy implementation, is considered in Module 7. The difficulties of implementation of policy are discussed and investigated through several planning exercises. This allows for the introduction of the concept of planning and a smooth transition to the next section, which focuses on analytic techniques in the policy process.

Section III begins by integrating the theory of the public interest, approaches to decision-making analysis, and the place of knowledge into an overview of rational techniques in policy analysis. Module 8 describes the systems approach to the analysis of public policy. Each of the major steps in a classic systems analysis are described: specifying objectives, defining alternatives, calculating impacts, and assessing alternatives. The student is asked to use these steps in the analysis of some familiar policy. A note on analytic techniques suggests that similar approaches can be brought to bear on organizational activities.

Module 9 provides an example of a typical systems analysis using a benefit cost approach. The case of the "Downtown Parking Authority" is used to illustrate how benefits and costs can be calculated. A note at the end of the module suggests further applications for benefit cost techniques.

Less formal techniques for predicting the future are the subject of

Module 10. Analytic techniques, it is shown, need not be as precise as benefit cost analysis, and two less formal techniques are described that help policymakers predict future policy impacts. A final note on social indicators reviews the place of analysis and data in public policymaking.

The final section of the book allows students to integrate and apply the learned insights to arrive at an understanding of the budget process and the mastery of budgeting skills. The budget process is explained as both an organizational phenomenon and a policy process, which requires the use of analytic techniques such as benefit cost analysis.

In the course of this book you will have an opportunity to sample our knowledge about public organizations, the process of policymaking, and the techniques of policy analysis. To the extent possible, go beyond the reading. Undertake the suggested case analyses, participate in the suggested games, and try your hand at the exercises. Think of yourself not as the master of some esoteric body of knowledge but as a practitioner of the art and science of administration. Mastering the professional skills of a public administrator is a process of learning by doing. You now have an opportunity to begin.

SECTION I

UNDERSTANDING PUBLIC ORGANIZATIONS

Public organizations are composed of people attempting to achieve common goals. The police officer, fire fighter, teacher, and welfare worker are all individuals working toward ends defined by the larger society and articulated by elected government officials. But how do these individuals achieve the purposes of government? The smallest building block of public organizations is the work group, composed of individuals who are in more or less constant contact with one another. A work group might be a fire engine company, a police detail, a casework supervisor and the caseworkers being supervised, or an academic department in a school. The size of the work group affects its activities.

The central advantage of organizations is that groups of individuals working through coordinated efforts are able to accomplish more than individuals working independently. What makes people work together? How is dedication to organizational goals encouraged? Why should individuals pursue group goals when they can pursue their self-interest? The answers to these questions as applied to public organizations form the bulk of what constitutes traditional public administration studies.

In the next four modules these questions will be considered from several perspectives. Module 1, starting with the case study "Circling to Nowhere," confronts the dilemma of the individual caught in an organizational situation that appears insoluble. The technique of situational analysis is used to draw attention to the analytic importance of roles and goals. Moving beyond the individual to an understanding of role behavior associated with positions in organizations develops students' understanding of organizational behavior. The importance of human motivation and management of human resources is also stressed. These concepts lead naturally to a consideration of the personnel function.

The Van Waters case, a more complicated example of situational analysis, becomes the point of departure for distinguishing between supervisory and subordinate roles within the public bureaucracy. Situational analysis depends to a large extent on an understanding of organizations. Weber's conceptualization of bureaucracies as purposeful organizations is introduced in conjunction with contemporary treatment of organizational behavior and its roots in scientific management, and the observational method. Finally, since the Van Waters case hinges upon an application of the civil service law respecting the right to hearings and appeals, it is used as an example of how civil service regulations impinge upon the operation of public organizations.

Once the concepts of bureaucracy and the civil service have been introduced, the third module considers management and leadership in public organizations in greater detail. A role play involving supervisory and subordinate behavior is used to provide an experiential base for investigating the interaction of different role orientations among supervisors and subordinates.

The final module investigates communications within organizations. Both external and internal, and formal and informal communications are considered. An in-basket exercise is used to develop communication skills.

After learning these concepts of public organizational behavior, you will be prepared to study the processes of policy development, formulation, implementation, revision, and analysis.

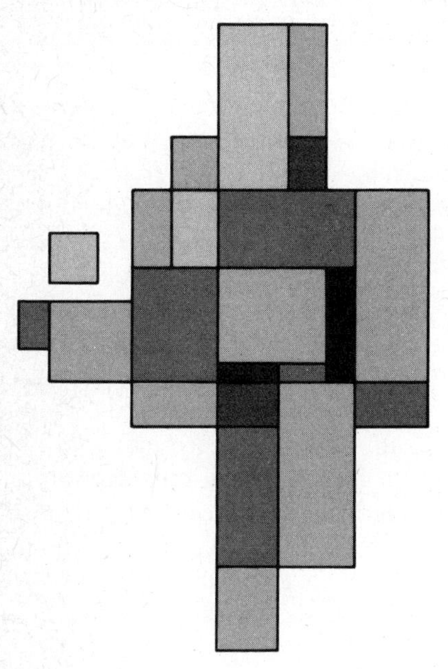

MODULE 1

Motivating People, The Personnel Function

INTRODUCTION

Public organizations are composed of people working together to carry out social goals determined by governmental institutions. What makes the teacher teach, the police officer patrol, and the fire fighter battle fires? Motivation in public sector organizations may be more difficult and complicated than motivation in private organizations. Have you ever condemned the government bureaucrat who seems unmoved by your arguments and plods along in his or her own way? Yet most government bureaucrats do their jobs most of the time. But why?

Do government bureaucrats fear that unless they do their jobs they will be fired? Are they likely to receive money bonuses if they do good jobs? Recently in an unusual ceremony the mayor of New York City gave cash awards to several workers who had outstanding attendance records. Almost all of them, when asked why their attendance records had been so outstanding, despite liberal allowances for sick leave, told of their feelings that their work was important and that they were doing a job that needed to be done.

Government bureaucrats, then, are similar to other individuals in our society. They work because they have adopted the habit of work. They perform most consistently when they believe that what they are doing is important and worthwhile.

An understanding of the sources of individual behavior is a prerequisite to an understanding of public organizations. One of the most comprehensive thinkers and most widely accepted writers about human motivation is the late Abraham Maslow. Maslow argued that human needs could be categorized in an hierarchical fashion, so that as each level of needs became satisfied a new level commanded the individual's attention. Physiological needs are the first that require attention: hunger, thirst, and sex. Next come safety needs: security, stability, dependency, protection, and the need for structure and order. Once physiological and safety needs are met, the individual strives for belonging and love. Next are the esteem needs, which include the desire for strength, achievement, mastery and competence and in addition prestige, status, fame, glory, dignity, and appreciation. Even if all these needs are met, according to Maslow, individuals will develop uneasiness and dissatisfaction unless they are doing what they are best suited for. This need to be true to one's own nature Maslow called the need for self-actualization. Maslow's approach, recognizing the variety of needs, is generally accepted, although his specification of the hierarchy of needs is often criticized.

It should be noted, however, that even Maslow recognized that the hierarchy of needs was not applicable to every individual. The hierarchy of needs has been used to reinforce the views of those students of human behavior who reject the carrot-and-stick approach to understanding human motivation. They argue that even if at one time humans were basically motivated by greed and fear, most workers today are reasonably secure and are more concerned with higher level needs.

Herzberg, Mausner, and Snyderman, in their classic study, *Motivation to Work,* found confirmation for the importance of self-actualization in job satisfaction. After interviewing 200 engineers and accountants, they found distinctively different responses to questions about what made these workers unhappy about their jobs. The factors that led to positive job attitudes satisfied the individual's need for self-actualization. It was only by performing the task that the individual reinforced his or her aspirations. On the other hand, the factors that related to avoidance of unhappiness were those involving the context of the job: supervision, interpersonal relations, physical working conditions, salary, benefits, job security, and policies. These findings led the authors to suggest greater emphasis on structuring jobs to foster individual satisfaction and greater care in the selection of individuals for jobs.

In slightly different form, Chris Argyris, in *Personality and Organization,* also suggests that higher level needs motivate individuals and that these needs are stymied by the structure of organizations. Argyris calls for the redesign of organizations to eliminate the constant loss of energy as individuals seek to adapt to a structure that frustrates their needs for self-actualization. Warren Bennis, in *Changing Organizations,* makes a similar plea in his call for planned organizational change.

The theory of motivation, then, recognizes a whole range of human needs. Extra money or a smile or a pat on the back will not suffice to motivate an individual. Motivation is based on an understanding of a particular individual's needs and the organizational context in which he or she is operating. A person's pattern of response is learned in the course of a lifetime. To modify that response pattern is a laborious undertaking. In this sense, then, motivation requires both an understanding of the individual and an understanding of the organizational setting.

As you read the case below, "Circling to Nowhere," consider the problems of individual motivation as they affect Mrs. Brensley and Tommie Dixon. But consider, also, the organizational context. As Argyris argues, the two can best be understood together.

After you have read the case study, determine what you think is its central theme. Discuss this question with others; they may have very different ideas. Is it about a new administrator trying to make a success of a new job? Is it about an old-line supervisor resisting intrusions upon everyday routines? Is it a situation of ethnic conflict within a bureaucratic setting? The ways in which individuals perceive bureaucratic events have an important impact on the business of public organizations. These perceptions are molded by individual experiences and ways of looking at the world. An important part of a person's ability to live successfully in a bureaucracy is to understand how others perceive common events. You should strive to develop this understanding. Studying public administration helps develop a framework for viewing the events that you experience.

Working in organizations, especially public ones, sometimes can be exceedingly frustrating. Sometimes it seems as though an individual is "caught in the bureaucracy" and can't make any headway. That's why the following excerpt is entitled "Circling to Nowhere." Dan Thompson, a new personnel training officer, is having little success in the new internship program he is running. As you read the case study of Thompson's attempt to launch the Summer Employee Program (SEP), think about the ways in which you might have done things differently. To what extent is the problem discussed peculiar to public organizations?

Circling to Nowhere*

Dan Thompson, a new personnel training officer at a subregional office in a large agency, is assigned staff responsibility for the Summer Employee Program (SEP). Dan is pleased in two senses. He likes the idea behind SEP, and he appreciates the confidence that his superiors apparently have in him so soon after his arrival on the job.

---

*Robert T. Golembiewski and Michael White, eds. "Circling to Nowhere," in *Cases in Public Management* (Chicago: Rand McNally, 1976), pp. 30–32.

SEP has two purposes. It is designed to provide minority group youths with a meaningful work experience, and it also provides them with an opportunity to earn money for college.

Dan hears rumors that SEP is poorly run, and that it is not really worth getting excited about. But he decides he will judge from his own experience. If SEP fails, moreover, it will not be for lack of his effort. He gives it all he has — too much, to judge from the teasing comments of coworkers. A typical work request to Dan, for example, usually is followed by the mildly sarcastic, "If you can tear yourself away from SEP, of course."

The first order of business is to get enough supervisors, preferably volunteers, to provide guidance for the anticipated fifteen SEP employees, mostly blacks. Dan calls a group meeting of the supervisors. At this meeting, six supervisors finally volunteer.

Dan enthusiastically sets up a development program for the SEP employees and trains the supervisors. Their attendance is good at the training sessions, and he hopes their enthusiasm will increase when the SEP employees arrive. The summer program is off to a running start, he believes.

After only six weeks, however, seven of the original fifteen students quit the program. Most explain that they can earn more money elsewhere.

Today Dan is notified that Tommie Dixon is also threatening to quit his job. Tommie was hired to work in the engineering department as a draftsman. Dan feels that losing this young man will be a real loss to the organization, major evidence that SEP is not succeeding even with motivated and highly talented youngsters.

Mrs. Brensley, Tommie's supervisor, comes in to see Dan. She says: "Tommie is going to quit and I am glad. Just as I expected, he is the most lackadaisical employee I've seen. I guess they don't know any better. He plods around when given work and, worse than that, he is late pretty often. Why don't you talk to him and straighten him out?"

Dan goes to see Tommie, and finds that he is not very talkative. "In the beginning I was doing drafting work," he finally admitted, "and it was great. But later I was only given Xerox work. My supervisor does not like me, and has to hunt work for me as if it were her personal white woman's burden. I don't really need to come in on time, do I? After all, what's the big important job that can't wait?"

Dan sees the light. He charges back to Mrs. Brensley, filling her in on all the latest theories about meaningful work and its relation to motivation. She does not want to be enlightened about behavioral research, however. Mrs. Brensley states: "I didn't ask for Tommie, and I did not want him. I can keep female clerk-typists busy, but not a male. But my supervisor said we had to take two females and one male. Can I help it if his drafting work only lasted half the summer?"

Dan approaches Mrs. Brensley's supervisor. "Well, that really is interesting," the supervisor responds, "seeing as how you personnel people cram this program down our teeth. And then you expect us to love it. You set these damn quotas. I could care less about your problems."

The problem has come full circle, right back to personnel. Dan recounts the wages of compulsion to his boss, and then listens to the explanation. "For years, Dan, we tried a strictly voluntary approach, but when we did there was no program because there were no volunteers. So, finally, because our Washington office is under great pressure from the Civil Service Commission to implement SEP, the quota system came about. The real problem is a motivational one, and people like Mrs. Brensley really ought to want to do the right thing."

Dan slowly plods back to his desk, which nicely frames Tommie's resignation. Dan's shoulders slump. He wonders, "Why knock myself out? Next year I'll do just enough to comply with what Washington wants. People don't like to be forced, but that's too bad. I have the feeling that the supervisors are racists anyway, especially people like Mrs. Brensley. Somebody else can try to break the vicious cycle."

Directions:
You are Dan and have had a chance to recover from the fact that "your program" has failed. You notice that no one blames you for the failure, as you expected might and should happen. No one even says, "Nice try." "I told you so, but you wouldn't listen," is more the message.

You have time to think ahead to next year's SEP. Decide on a strategy for yourself.

COMMENT ON "CIRCLING TO NOWHERE"

Contextual analysis is critical to your success in public organizations. It is a central skill of successful public and private managers. To what extent do you understand the basic issues of the case study? To help you analyze the case, see if you can isolate some specific roles that individuals are playing. Conceiving of administrative activity as the interaction of individuals assuming roles and pursuing specific goals will be helpful as you develop skills in contextual analysis.

Who are the major actors in "Circling to Nowhere"? What are they trying to accomplish? How do they pursue their goals?

Dan Thompson, Mrs. Brensley, and Tommie Dixon, although individuals coping with real situations, are also limited by their roles and the roles of others. Dan Thompson is a new personnel officer, Mrs. Brensley is an experienced supervisor, and Tommie is an inexperienced intern. Classifying individuals in this way is describing the roles they assume. A role is a picture of behavior, which raises expectations about future actions.

A large part of your success in working with public organizations will be determined by your ability to play your role and to understand the roles of others. A role is a fancy and more precise term for a job. Often a job is described by the organization in a formal, written job description that an individual may receive when beginning a job. Other times the job description may be developed jointly between the employee and the employer.

A role is an expected pattern of behavior. In order to perform a job or a role you must learn what behavior is expected of you. Similarly, when you learn to anticipate the behavior of other organizational members you are learning the roles of others with whom you must interact.

Roles are important because they help us to understand public organizations and anticipate how people will act. A cluster of roles that interact on a regular basis is often referred to as a work group, the basic building block of complex organizations. The work group is made up of individuals who are in more or less constant contact. Each unit or division in a public organization may include several work groups. Whenever an individual like Dan Thompson begins to work for the government or any other organization he must accept limitations on behavior, which raise expectations in others familiar with that particular role.

What kinds of behavior do you anticipate in a new personnel officer, an experienced supervisor, and a fledgling intern? A new personnel officer might have difficulties in establishing relationships with supervisors who are more experienced than he. A new personnel officer might also be eager to accomplish his first assignment in a satisfactory way. An old-line supervisor might resent the intrusion of a new personnel officer and might find a new intern more trouble than help. A new intern might lack confidence and feel not needed or wanted in an ongoing organization.

What would be the significance of the ethnic backgrounds of the individuals in this case? Did you notice that SEP was a program designed to provide "minority group youths with a meaningful work experience"? How would this ethnic dimension affect the interactions of the major actors?

Look back now at the figure in the Introduction, which describes the environment of public organizations. Notice that a public organization is contained in the political system, which itself is contained in the social system. The mediating effects of the political system make public organizations particularly sensitive to social problems. For example, the importance of race relations and the demands of previously deprived ethnic groups assume particular importance in the public sector.

Why did Dan Thompson and his bureau become involved in the SEP program? Why not have a strictly volunteer program? When Dan in frustration seeks some explanation from his supervisor he is told that the strictly volunteer program never worked. SEP came about because the agency headquarters in Washington, under pressure from the United States Civil Service Commission, ordered a mandatory intern program. In other words, Dan's boss was merely carrying out the orders of superiors in Washington. But why did the Washington-based agency adopt such a program? It was responding to pressure from the Civil Service Commission, which in turn got its orders from the president and the Congress. So political pressures were being brought to bear on Dan's bureau.

The accountability of Dan's bureau to the president and Congress, in this instance through the Civil Service Commission, is one of the outstanding characteristics of public organizations. While divisions of national corporations may also be responsible to their headquarters, they do not have to respond directly to the president and Congress in the same way. While there is a federal agency, the Equal Employment Opportunities Commission, that encourages private corporations to undertake such affirmative action programs, their relationship is very different from and considerably weaker than that of the Civil Service Commission to federal government agencies.

The Summer Employment Program (SEP) is an attempt by government to respond to a social problem – the plight of black and Hispanic citizens. Does it constitute unjustifiable political interference in the operation of government bureaus or the legitimate furtherance of important social goals?

Roles in public organizations ordinarily are task oriented. Individuals pursue goals and objectives. They seek to accomplish their own goals as well as those of the organizations and groups with which they work. This goal-oriented dimension of individual and group behavior has important consequences for understanding how public organizations operate. You must be aware of your own goals and those of other individuals in order to understand how public organizations function.

What were Tommie's goals? Dan's goals? Mrs. Brensley's goals?

Individual	**Goals**
Tommie Dixon	learn, earn, secure future job
Dan Thompson	run a successful program
Mrs. Brensley	avoid disruption of routine work

Can you think of other goals? Are these individual goals compatible? How can individuals ensure that their goals will be accomplished? The desire to attain specific goals provides a stake for individuals participating in social situations. They have something to lose or to gain, which is determined by the way they interact with other individuals. This stake provides an element of risk. Current choices are rewarded by furthering goals. Mistakes mean lost opportunities and the possible success of others with incompatible goals. The ambiguities of this situation give rise to both cooperative and competitive elements. As individuals attempt to achieve their own goals a gamelike situation develops.

"Circling to Nowhere" is a case study, a picture of reality about the administration of public organizations, and has a gamelike quality to it. Actors or players pursue goals while constrained by certain roles and rules that define their patterns of behavior. A case study, since it is based upon a sequence of events that has occurred, can form the basis of a game, but does not actually constitute a game itself. A game is an abstraction and can be played again and again by individuals assuming the same roles and subject to the same rules as they pursue goals.

If we focus on the intern aspects of the game we might define an "Intern Game" based on "Circling to Nowhere." The central roles would be the intern, the program developer, and the line supervisors who are responsible for the work of the interns. If you were the program developer in the intern game, how would you handle the intern program? If you were the intern, what attitude toward the supervisor would you take? If you were the intern, do you think you'd make it to the end of summer? Why? Which goals would be most important to you?

A game may be defined as a structured interaction of individuals assuming roles and pursuing goals according to certain rules. Does this concept of game contradict your own associations with the word *game?* How would you have defined a game before analyzing this short case?

Most people would be inclined to say that a game is a form of play. Hopscotch, Monopoly, and baseball come to mind. Do their outcomes have effects on people's lives? The salaries baseball players earn depend upon their performances. Gambling is game with often serious consequences for the participants. Eric Berne, in his book *Games People Play,* discusses the way in which personal relationships can be hampered by counterproductive games.

Make-believe games allow individuals to practice skills needed for participating in the real world without risking real consequences. Spring exhibition games do not affect the individual and group records of baseball players and teams. Participating in the intern game described above would not have the serious consequences for you that the actual play of the intern game did for Dan Thompson, Mrs. Brensley, and Tommie Dixon.

When games are played in a classroom or another artificial situation they allow individuals to learn without the consequences of participation in the real world. To be useful, however, games must approximate or simulate reality. As you proceed through the modules that follow, you will have an opportunity to participate in games that will help you master situations you may face when you work in public organizations. These games will allow you to experience firsthand what public organizations are and the dilemmas with which workers are confronted.

Learning through gaming or "gaming the public policy process," is a way of uniting physical and mental activity. Embodying the ancient Greek ideal of the union of thought and action, gaming provides an approach to learning which both actively involves the learner and includes reflection on experience. As you participate in these learning experiences you will be developing skills and experiences to apply to real life situations. The ability to perform well in public organizations depends upon theoretical knowledge, but knowledge that can be applied to a variety of practical experiences.

A large element of your success will depend upon your ability to understand the competitive nature of the group situation. But in order to achieve your own goals you must be not only a good competitor, but a good cooperator as well. Can you develop a strategy that will allow the other participants to achieve their goals while you reach your goal?

In order to participate in the gaming process you must be creative and sometimes suspend your own sense of reality. Such an ability is useful in the real world also, for the suspension of the present allows you to create for the future. Be sure to remember that your overall need is to cope with the real world of unwieldy, unresponsive, and frustrating activity in public organizations.

Gaming, more than other approaches to learning, depends upon your own efforts. If you let yourself become involved in the games presented in this book you will find that you can have experiences that closely approximate real life situations. You will learn why the complexitites of public organizations are so frustrating and disheartening, yet you will also learn ways to work with organizations to achieve your own goals. You will experience the satisfaction of creatively using an organization rather than being carried from task to task without sense or direction.

Like Dan Thompson, you will often experience the feeling of "circling to nowhere" when you work in public organizations. But unlike Dan, you will have the advantage of having experienced some of these situations before your response really counts.

NOTE ON THE PERSONNEL FUNCTION

Why did Dan Thompson assume the responsibility for the SEP program? SEP was an internship program and, as such, part of the broader training function of the agency. Often training is carried out by a specialized personnel office within an agency. What is a personnel office and why do agencies have them?

While the effective utilization of people is a pervasive management function, separate personnel offices often develop to focus on special tasks. As governments have grown larger and as individual bureaus expand, the need for a specialized personnel office increases. Often the routine paperwork associated with hiring, maintaining, and terminating employees becomes the first function of a specialized personnel office. But other aspects soon develop. Personnel officers become responsible for providing services to employees and prospective employees that will encourage them to join the organization, contribute to it, and develop personally. They attempt to nurture the basic resource of the organization: its workers.

Sometimes personnel is referred to as a staff function since it services other parts of the organization rather than working directly for the goals of the organization. Individuals providing services to others are often referred to as part of the line organization. This distinction between line and staff functions is often useful, though sometimes it may be difficult to make. The personnel function is concerned with providing services to the employees of an organization. When you apply for a job you will probably go to the personnel office. When you want to inquire about your health coverage you will go to the personnel office. When you want to find out why you didn't receive a raise you might go to the personnel office. And when you retire, the personnel office will take care of your pension arrangements.

A personnel office is an example of specialization in large organizations. Since organizations are made up of many individuals, substantial resources are devoted to the effective utilization of human resources. Some of these organizational efforts become routinized and concentrated within the personnel office.

Ordinarily the personnel office will serve the top management in a support or staff capacity. By providing services within the organization the personnel office becomes a potential mechanism for the exercise of the control function by top management. Thus the formulation and execution of personnel policies, particularly those involved in hiring, termination, and personnel evaluation, may be valuable levers for executive control over agency personnel.

The functions performed by a personnel office will vary from agency to agency. Agencies of less than 100 employees usually cannot afford to designate special personnel offices, but must be content with an individual who includes personnel matters as part of other responsibilities. The larger the agency, the larger and more comprehensive in scope the personnel office tends to be. Let's examine some of the typical functions of a personnel office attached to a public organization.

Perhaps the most basic and uniformly observed function of the government personnel office is the maintenance of employee records. Because government bureaucracy depends upon written records, there is a need for maintaining records of employees that include such matters as dates of services, particular characteristics, performance on the job, and salary rates. The need for establishing a permanent identity for government workers by providing a written record of their activities results in specialized personnel offices where these records can be maintained. An important element of these official records is their confidentiality and the personnel office is ordinarily charged with formulating policies to protect this confidentiality.

As the personnel function within an agency enlarges, the office begins to function as a support mechanism for top management in dealing with employees. As such it becomes involved in the formulation of agency-wide policies in the area of employee relations. Depending upon the confidence top management has in the personnel office, it may become actively involved in basic questions involving employee motivation and human resource management within the organization.

Often the personnel office is responsible for compiling a handbook of rules and regulations governing the treatment of employees. These handbooks may incorporate matters established by law and through collective bargaining agreements with public employee unions.

The third major function of the personnel office is the establishment, maintenance, and modification of the staffing system. Government agencies maintain comprehensive lists of job classifications. The personnel office usually establishes these classifications in accordance with the requirements of law and is responsible for altering them when necessary. In order to carry out this function efficiently, the personnel office must assess the needs of the organization and the relationship of position classifications to these needs. In carrying out this function the personnel office will work closely with top management.

A fourth function of the personnel office is the recruitment of personnel. In some instances this may involve only the formal posting of openings, while in other instances it may involve active recruiting trips, interviewing, and actual decisions about whom to hire. The personnel office is usually given the responsibility of ensuring conformity with legal requirements.

Staff development is another function of personnel offices. This function varies greatly from office to office. In some instances it may involve only the processing of papers regarding current status and benefits such as sick leave. In others it involves active counseling about an individual's status and benefits in the organization. In its fullest development this function involves active involvement with individual employees regarding their personal development. It may include training responsibilities and individual counseling regarding current performance and future expectations. It may range from formal processing of evaluation reports to active participation in the assessment process.

Finally, the personnel office becomes involved in the separation of the employee from the organization. Again the activities range widely. They may involve simply the processing of termination papers or active counseling regarding alternative work or retirement possibilities.

No exact formula can describe the functions of all personnel offices.

Depending on the organization, personnel offices serve employees differently. Some are essentially record depositories, keeping files on individuals and providing routine services such as credit checks, job references, and payroll. Other offices have a much wider scope of operation, stressing personal development and encouraging attendance at training sessions. While some personnel departments organize and staff such sessions themselves, others facilitate attendance at such sessions outside of the work setting. Either through information dissemination or direct subsidy, individuals are encouraged to participate in such programs.

Personnel-related functions are often provided by public sector unions. While unions continue to concentrate on negotiating salaries, public sector unions have stressed the importance of working conditions and fringe benefits. In fact, they have been so successful in obtaining fringe benefits, including pensions and health benefits, that they are being criticized as contributing to the high costs of government today.

Unions often work closely with personnel offices by informing members of their rights regarding working conditions, health benefits, and retirement rights. Unions provide an additional service in establishing mechanisms for the employee to contest decisions regarding benefits, working conditions, and job security. In such public service jobs as teaching, where job security may become the object of considerable controversy, unions will often provide legal assistance to employees contesting dismissal or failure to be granted tenure.

Personnel functions often spill over into the regular work group. Supervisors, for example, may determine which employees will be offered opportunities for special training and development. While records of such matters as ratings will usually be maintained in personnel offices, the rating process is generally part of the supervisory process. Organizations that function effectively jealously guard their human resources. While the personnel office has a special role to play in assisting employees, effective organizations devote a substantial proportion of their efforts to nurturing their human resources.

Public personnel systems in the United States are greatly influenced by the civil service system, which is an attempt to provide a framework for an effective personnel system within government. The next module focuses on the operation of the civil service system and its effects on the use of human resources.

SELECTED BIBLIOGRAPHY FOR MODULE 1

ARGYRIS, CHRIS. *Personality and Organization.* New York: Harper and Row, 1957.

BENNIS, WARREN. *Changing Organizations.* New York: McGraw-Hill, 1966.

BERNE, ERIC. *Games People Play.* New York: Grove Press, 1964.

GUETZKOW, HAROLD; KOTTER, PHILIP, and SCHULTZ, RANDALL, *Simulation in Social and Administrative Science.* Englewood Cliffs: Prentice-Hall, 1972.

HERZBERG, FREDERICK; MAUSNER, BERNARD, and SNYDERMAN, BARBARA BLOCK. *Motivation to Work.* New York: John Wiley, 1959.

LAUFFER, ARMAND. *The Aim of the Game.* Gamed Simulations, 1973.

MASLOW, ABRAHAM. *Motivation and Personality.* New York: Harper and Row, 1970.

MCGREGOR, DOUGLAS. *The Human Side of Enterprise.* New York: McGraw-Hill, 1960.

ROETHLISBERGER, FRITZ, and DICKSON, WILLIAM. *Management and the Worker.* Cambridge: Harvard University Press, 1939.

SHERMAN, HARVEY. *It All Depends.* University: University of Alabama Press, 1966.

SIMON, HERBERT. *Administrative Behavior.* New York: The Free Press, 1945.

STAHL, O. GLENN. *Public Personnel Administration.* New York: Harper and Row, 1971.

TAYLOR, FREDERICK. *Scientific Management.* New York: Harper, 1911.

WARNER, W. LLOYD, *et al. The American Federal Executive.* New Haven: Yale University Press, 1963.

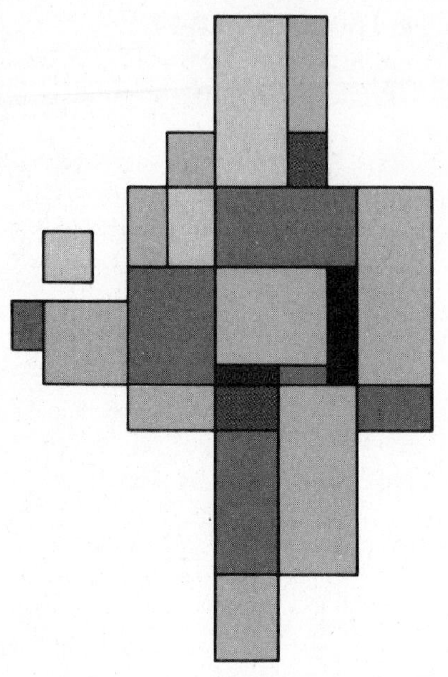

MODULE 2

Organizational Behavior: The Civil Service

INTRODUCTION

"Circling to Nowhere" is an experience that individuals involved in organizations often feel. Trying to realize your own goals within organizations can be frustrating. Understanding individuals' motivations and the interactions of their roles is an important part of understanding organizational behavior. Organization theory attempts to understand how organizations function and how to make them function better. It is the conceptual underpinnings of a realistic knowledge of organizational behavior and is a prerequisite to effective situational analysis.

The basic building block of organizations is the work group, a number of individuals exercising particular roles who are in more or less constant contact. A complex organization consists of work groups related to one another through an organizational structure, which may be expressed in a formal chart of the authority relationships among individuals within the various work groups. These relationships often form a pyramid, whose pinnacle is the top executive and whose base is those individuals to whom no one else reports.

UNDERSTANDING ORGANIZATIONAL BEHAVIOR: THE CIVIL SERVICE IN ACTION

The importance of hierarchical authority patterns in organizing purposeful organizations has been long recognized. Primitive tribes ordinarily were ruled by a chief and often had a more elaborate authority structure that included one or more intermediate levels. The early city-states, nation-states, and empires usually had one leader and other intermediate groups, while the Roman republic was headed for a period of time by a triumvirate.

During the late nineteenth and early twentieth centuries, largely as a result of industrialization and urbanization, bureaucratic organizations became more prominent. Three men, the Frenchman Henri Fayol, the German Max Weber, and the American Frederick Taylor, began studying these organizations. Although the most prominent examples were found in business and government, Weber pointed out that political parties and certain religious groups also exhibited similar bureaucratic characteristics.

Weber observed that as industrialization became the dominant mode in contemporary society it brought with it a form of organization that exhibited a new type of hierarchical authority, based on legal and rational elements. This new type of organization, referred to by Weber as a bureaucracy, progressed beyond the more primitive types of authority, which he identified as traditional and charismatic. Traditional authority was usually based upon birthright, as exemplified by kings and queens and feudal lords and ladies. Charismatic authority was based upon an individual's ability to command authority through personal magnetism. Popular war heroes are a good example. But bureaucracy, according to Weber, had a sounder basis for authority: the existence of rational rules governing its operation and leading to fairness and effectiveness.

In order to characterize existing bureaucracies and to provide a model toward which these organizations should strive, Weber set forth a conceptualization of an ideal bureaucratic organization. Although existing bureaucracies did not necessarily possess all the qualities of the ideal, according to Weber it represented the most complete, and rational, functioning model.

Weber's conception of model bureaucracies consisted of the following characteristics:

1. Their scope and operations are incorporated into formal rules.
2. Their operations conform to general rules, which are stable, exhaustive, and can be learned.
3. Their routines are based upon written documents, which are maintained by clerks.
4. They are governed by a strict system of hierarchical supervision and control.
5. Individuals making up the bureaucracy require thorough and expert training, reflecting the specialization of roles.
6. These individuals must devote their full and primary attention to their jobs.

Let's consider each of these characteristics in turn.

Their scope and operations are incorporated into formal rules. Most bureaucratic organizations are governed by a legal document setting forth their scope of operations and powers. Articles of incorporation perform this function for business corporations, and laws, sometimes referred to as charters, set forth the powers and responsibilities of state and local governmental agencies. These documents provide some limitations upon the operations of these organizations and allow aggrieved individuals to seek a remedy in the courts or elsewhere when the organizations have exceeded their powers. The entire area of administrative law is concerned with individual and corporate rights against governmental agencies that act outside their authority.

Their operations conform to general rules, which are stable, exhaustive, and can be learned. In addition to their operating charters, bureaucratic organizations are governed by exhaustive rules. City governments, for example, while operating under their charters, are also subject to state laws and their own laws, which are adopted by local legislative bodies. Business corporations are subject to a panoply of federal, state, and local laws, in addition to their own corporate bylaws and regulations. These rules are generally written and subject to regular formal procedures of change. They tend to remain stable over time.

Their routines are based upon written documents, which are maintained by clerks. The everyday operations of business and government are based upon procedures that are often committed to writing. The enormous amount of paperwork that bureaucracies develop is a reflection of this characteristic. Clerks become essential to bureaucratic operations, introducing patterns of consistency and regularity.

They are governed by a strict system of hierarchical supervision and control. In order to allow for central coordination and direction by the leaders of the organization, a strict system of hierarchical control is created. Hierarchy allows for the coordination of disparate individuals and the direction of individual energy toward the common organizational goals. Authority within a bureaucracy is based neither on tradition nor on charisma, but on the rational pursuit of common goals and acceptance of organizational relationships independent of the particular individuals functioning in these roles.

Individuals making up the bureaucracy require thorough and expert training, reflecting the specialization of roles. In addition to the regularity of bureaucratic organizations, the division of labor into simple and repeatable tasks is a major asset. It allows for recruitment and training of specialists who, given their training and experience, perform difficult and complex tasks with relative ease. The encouragement of specialization is a major strength of bureaucratic organizations, but also creates problems relating to integrating individuals of diverse backgrounds and experience.

These individuals must devote their full and primary attention to their jobs. Bureaucratic organizations depend upon numbers of individuals working together at complex tasks. In order to harness individual effort, they demand complete absorption in work. They replace traditional and charismatic loyalty with loyalty based upon rational integration into an operating whole.

Bureaucracy, which was chosen by Weber as a neutral term to refer to purposeful organizations, is sometimes used to represent the perversion of some of the characteristics of these organizations. Sometimes *bureaucracy* is used as a synonym for the triumph of one of these attributes of bureaucracy over the purposes of organization itself. When the rules governing the operation of organizations become so complex that they are difficult for individuals to follow, we refer to them as *bureaucratic red tape.* Have you ever moved from line to line in a government office, for example, the motor vehicle bureau, attempting to follow the procedures, and experiencing the feeling that the complicated procedures were keeping you from getting your license? Have you ever attempted to pinpoint responsibility for your not receiving a government paycheck, only to learn, after calling ten offices and visiting five more, that you still won't be paid?

While Weber is known for his description of the bureaucratic model, Frederick Taylor and Henri Fayol were more concerned with developing techniques for improving the operation of bureaucratic organizations. Taylor spurred the development of the scientific management movement in the United States and abroad. Taylorism, as his approach is sometimes labeled, stressed ways of doing tasks more efficiently. It focused on the division of labor within organizations and sought to find ways of doing specific aspects of a job more quickly. This tendency to capitalize on specialization and the division of labor gave rise to such techniques as time and motion studies and job analysis. Time and motion studies attempt to determine the way a particular task, for example, the typing of letters, can be carried out with the least expenditure of time and effort. Job analysis seeks to ensure that particular individuals are spending their time on tasks that are most efficiently done together and that are directly related to organizational goals. Job analysis may suggest new divisions of labor and responsibility to maximize the efforts of employees working in related fields. Closely related to these techniques are work simplification studies, which attempt to analyze how to break down complex tasks into simpler ones and eliminate unnecessary operations.

To apply these techniques, as well as others, some organizations have created special management analysis units. Other organizations hire outside consultant groups to undertake such analyses for them. The application of these techniques has become a regular part of the operation of bureaucratic organizations.

The work of Fayol, as developed by Luther Gulick, led to another effort to improve organizational management. In *Papers on the Science of Administration,* Gulick and others attempted to set forth guiding principles for effective management. The volume deals with such principles as the unity of command — that each individual should be responsible to only one supervisor; the span of control — that a supervisor should have a specified number of individuals, often five, reporting to him or her; and the distinction between staff and line. However, Herbert Simon has criticized this approach for displaying little actual knowledge about the operation of organizations and offering little guidance.

If the application of scientific management approaches and principles of administration has been criticized for failing to offer comprehensive theories and for its limited applicability, another profound criticism has come from a different source. They have failed, in the view of some, to sufficiently appreciate the importance of human motivation in determining organizational behavior and effectiveness. Chris Argyris, one of those associated with the human relations approach, emphasized, in *Personality and Organization,* that organizations are made up of individuals and must take into account their needs. Argyris goes so far as to suggest that the hierarchical basis of authority needs to be altered drastically. He has been joined by others, including Warren Bennis, who predicted in *Changing Organizations* that the end of bureaucratic organization was in sight:

> The burden of this book rests upon the premise that this form of organization [bureaucratic] is becoming less and less effective, that it is hopelessly out of joint with contemporary realities, and that new shapes, patterns, and models — currently recessive — are emerging which promise drastic changes in the conduct of the corporation and in managerial practices in general. So within the next twenty-five to fifty years, we should all be witness to, and participate in, the end of bureaucracy and the rise of new social systems better able to cope with twentieth century demands. [p. 4]

Even though bureaucratic organizations do not seem in imminent danger of extinction, the insights of the human relations school and its emphasis on individual behavior rather than organizational principles are important. The human relations approach traces its origin to an important aspect of Taylor's scientific management, its stress on the observational approach. According to Taylor, in order to improve an organization, one must first observe it. Different approaches should be tested to achieve the greatest efficiency. This observational or empirical orientation is perhaps an even more basic contribution of scientific management than the specific techniques and principles discussed above.

The observational orientation was the stimulus for a series of experiments undertaken by Elton Mayo and his student assistant, F. J. Roethlisberger (who himself became an important scholar), at Western Electric's Hawthorne (Illinois) state plant beginning in 1927. These experiments, which drew upon the scientific management approach, sought to investigate the effects of better working conditions, such as brighter lighting and longer rest periods, on the productivity of workers. In the course of these experiments, Mayo noticed that it was often difficult to assess the impact of particular changes in the environment because workers seemed to respond to the expectations of the experimenters themselves. If workers believed that a change had been introduced and that they were expected to perform better, their performance might improve simply because of these expectations. This finding highlighted the importance of worker motivation and stimulated a new line of thought in attempts to increase organizational performance. Instead of streamlining the process of work, the human relations approach seeks to motivate individuals.

If the structure of organizations is basically a reflection of their need to reach their goals, they must take into account the ways in which people respond. Should they provide for the maximum control and surveillance of individual workers or should they emphasize autonomy and self-motivation? While the answer to this question cannot be determined once and for all, and surely each organization must be judged in terms of its specific purposes and the individuals making it up, different views of human behavior and the bases of human motivation result in different approaches to the proper structure for organizations.

The link between individual motivation and organizational structure is very well illustrated in the distinction that Douglas McGregor makes between Theory X and Theory Y. According to McGregor, organizations based upon Theory X stress hierarchy and the need for close and continuing supervision of employees. They believe that people will best respond to organizational goals when they receive direct and immediate incentives for proper behavior, based upon continuing monitoring. Organizations based upon Theory Y, however, stress recognizing human development needs and relying upon self-motivation, based upon long-run commitments to organization goals.

The controversy that McGregor characterizes as the choice between Theory X and Theory Y has been a continuing concern of organizational theorists. Recently, *Public Administration Review,* the journal of the American Society for Public Administration, carried an exchange between Herbert Simon and Chris Argyris that continues this dialogue. Argyris defends the human relations tradition, while Simon emphasizes the importance of hierarchy in addressing human motivational needs. In reflecting upon the role of hierarchy as an attribute of bureaucracy, try to separate the need for hierarchy in existing bureaucracies from the possibility or desirability of changing the current reliance on it.

Differences as to the importance of hierarchy in organizations influence the way people operate in organizations. Such differences are manifest in the relationship between Commissioner McDowell and Superintendent Van Waters, the principal actors in the Van Waters case. The Van Waters case opens with the appointment of a new commissioner of corrections in the state of Massachusetts and discusses his developing relationship with one of his subordinates, the superintendent of Framingham Prison. As you read this case you will see how differing concepts of hierarchy and human motivation affect the perceptions of individuals and intrude upon their organizational relationships. This controversy, which centers around the problems of a corrections institution, raises critical issues about how public organizations operate and how people affect their operations.

The Van Waters case is the story of how real bureaucrats acted. It is meant to provide further basis for your understanding of how public bureaucracies work. As you read the case, think about how you would have acted as commissioner of corrections or superintendent of Framingham.

The Van Waters Case*

THE COMMISSIONER DECIDES TO ACT

When a new and little-known department head distrusts an experienced and famous subordinate and disapproves of her policies, but can lawfully remove her only for "just cause," what happens? That is the subject of this study.† The events related here excited thousands of people in Massachusetts in 1948 and

†In this study, a number of inmates and former inmates of the reformatory are given wholly fictitious names. No person having any such name is known to the author, the editor, or the publisher; and if any person exists who does have any such name, she is obviously not the inmate or former inmate mentioned herein.

*Thomas Eliot, "Van Waters Case," Inter-University Case Program, Case No. 22, pp. 1, 6–8. Box 229, Syracuse, N.Y. 13210.

1949. The commissioner of correction, Elliott E. McDowell, clashed with the superintendent of the State Reformatory for Women, Miriam Van Waters, and, in an atmosphere of controversy and sensational publicity, made a series of decisions, which largely determined the nature and the outcome of the conflict.

The struggle, however, was influenced not only by the commissioner's official decisions but by his theory of the administrator's function, by his methods of dealing with his staff, and by the interplay of personalities. What might have been a fairly routine administrative problem became, instead, a fighting issue in which the decent reputation of the state itself was at stake.

The chief actors in the case were McDowell, Van Waters, and Frank A. Dwyer, Jr., deputy commissioner under McDowell.

McDowell, a graduate of Massachusetts Institute of Technology, was by profession a construction engineer. As such he had worked on the building of Norfolk State Prison Colony (for male offenders), and then for fourteen years had directed the "prison industries" program at that institution. He was elevated to the commissionership of the Department of Correction in 1948. In speech and appearance, he gave the impression of being unaffected and direct, a good fellow and a good citizen. He had a heroic record in the first World War, and afterwards maintained a very active interest in veterans' organizations. His onetime deputy described him as "having more intestinal fortitude than any man I ever knew."

Van Waters was one of the best-known penologists in the country. Professionally trained at the University of Oregon and Clark University, she had served as superintendent of the Juvenile Court Detention Home and referee of the Juvenile Court in Los Angeles, as president of the National Conference of Social Work, and as the Wickersham Commission's specialist on juvenile delinquency. After she became head of the reformatory at Framingham, Massachusetts, in 1932, her reputation continued to grow. She wrote several books; she was appointed as the one woman member of a United States delegation to a United Nations body studying delinquency; she was awarded the annual medal of the United Prison Association "for meritorious service." In speech articulate and precise, in appearance short, erect, and dignified, she had a natural histrionic talent, which added to the impact of her personality. She was the kind of disciplined, quietly forceful person who makes some bitter enemies and wins many devoted admirers.

Dwyer was a "self-made man" and conscious of that fact. He had been a member of the state police force, but when his friend Charles F. Hurley became governor of Massachusetts in 1937, Dwyer served as one of his aides and found time to study law. He was admitted to the bar, but never practiced, for when Hurley was leaving office a place was found for Dwyer in the Department of Correction. Dark, earnest, and intense, Dwyer was a man of strong emotions and strong convictions, a believer in the observance of strict rules of conduct and compliance with the letter of the law.

COMMENT ON THE VAN WATERS CASE

Having read the background of the Van Waters case, how would you characterize McDowell, Van Waters, and Dwyer? Can you foresee possible conflicts developing among their own personal goals? A role was defined earlier as the expected pattern of behavior associated with an individual because of his or her position in an organization. Write a paragraph describing the roles of commissioner, assistant to the commissioner, and superintendent of Framingham.

Why might the new commissioner be concerned with establishing his authority over Superintendent Van Waters? What measures might he take to accomplish this?

Suppose Commissioner McDowell wanted to remove Superintendent Van Waters. What measures might he take to bring about her removal? What obstacles might make such an action difficult? What might Superintendent Van Waters do to fight her removal? Now, continue reading the Van Waters case.

The Van Waters Case (continued)

Early on the morning of February 28, without any advance notice to Van Waters, McDowell and Dwyer drove to Framingham. It was Saturday and Van Waters's secretary was off duty. The commissioner and his deputy suddenly appeared and demanded all outstanding day work contracts. They were not favorably impressed when Van Waters and her assistant superintendent took some time to find copies of all of these contracts in the files, and they were surprised that there was no contract with Seiler [a restaurant owner]. (The contract had been made with Seiler's Wellesley manager personally.)

Then, as abruptly as they arrived, McDowell and Dwyer departed. They went to Seiler's restaurant and explained to the manager that his employment of inmates was illegal because the work was not "domestic service." From the restaurant McDowell telephoned Seiler, making the same explanation. "We left," he said later, "with everybody satisfied about the termination."

There were three other small but revealing factors in this incident. When they visited the restaurant McDowell and Dwyer insisted on being shown the payroll records and examined the recorded deductions. Dwyer's distrust of the indenture system extended to its financial operation; he had heard critics refer to it as "penal servitude" and he was suspicious.

Second, on the day that the governor's office called the commissioner about Seiler's, one of the department staff mentioned to him that the manager of Seiler's restaurant in Wellesley had a criminal record. If, in McDowell's eyes, it was dubious policy to employ exconvicts as reformatory officers, it was worse to indenture female prisoners to exconvicts outside of the reformatory gates. As his controversy with Van Waters developed, McDowell did not forget that she had permitted inmates to work for a man with a record — even though the manager had been "going straight" for many years, had earned a good reputation in Wellesley, and might well have been considered to be a good example of successful rehabilitation by the Commonwealth. Nor did the commissioner hesitate to expose the facts about the exconvict, who thereupon left town.

Third, while McDowell was waiting for the contracts to be gathered at the reformatory, Van Waters spoke to him. She later testified: "I asked Commissioner McDowell to return soon as there were urgent matters of policy I wished to discuss with him in private — because although I did not say this to my commissioner, my reason for needing to see him in private was that Mr. Dwyer's attitude toward me was so belligerently hostile and scornful that I could not present problems of policy effectively to the commissioner in Mr. Dwyer's presence."

McDowell responded to Van Waters's invitation by spending most of March 8 at Framingham without Dwyer. The chief subject Van Waters wished to discuss with him was a major one at the reformatory — the treatment and release of alcoholics. Under Massachusetts law alcoholics were given an indeterminate sentence with a one-year maximum; the commissioner of correction had authority to release them at any time during that one year. In the case of male alcoholics at Norfolk, release was customary at the end of six months, and sometimes it happened earlier. But for Framingham inmates there had been no six-months custom. Van Waters said that the alcoholic women "should wait until the institution authorities thought they should be released." This was because she had embarked on a vigorous program to help them, using the services of a special clinic at a Boston hospital and encouraging the growth of an Alcoholics Anonymous chapter at the reformatory. Automatic release at the end of six months might, in some cases, interrupt real progress toward rehabilitation. Hence her desire for a flexible system.

The commissioner had a friendly talk with her as they strolled around the grounds. He consented to her request that he should release alcoholics only on her recommendation, at least for the time being. But this was the last time that the commissioner and the superintendent ever talked together alone.

On April 7 McDowell and his department's business agent stopped briefly at the reformatory to instruct Van Waters about the desired procedure for submitting applications for indenture contracts. Van Waters had often sent to previous commissioners, for their signatures, contracts already signed by the prospective employer. Now, however, McDowell decided to have applications signed by the prospective employer and submitted to him by the superintendent. The applicant would then be examined by one of his staff before any final contract was drawn up.

Only nine days later, however, McDowell departed from this new procedure by initiating an indenture contract, signing it in blank, and forwarding it to Van Waters with instructions that an inmate was to be indentured immediately to Mrs. J. Alan Hodder. This housewife had employed indentured inmates before, and her husband was a member of the state legislature.

McDowell made one more friendly visit to Framingham that spring. That was on the annual Prison Industry Day, when he spoke to an assembly of inmates. *Harmony News,* the inmates' newspaper, reported him as saying that he didn't have much experience with women offenders but that the institution existed to better the condition of the inmates and that he would do everything possible to accomplish this end.

But as spring came the seeds of controversy were sprouting fast. The *Boston American* was smoldering after its series of articles on Framingham. It was willing to give the commissioner a little time, but only a little. McDowell may have been thinking merely about the employment of exconvicts, indenture irregularities, and the coddling of alcoholics when, that April, he said at a United Prison Association luncheon that he intended to "straighten things out" at Framingham. Apparently he hoped to move slowly and steadily toward the establishment of a regime there that would conform strictly to the statutes, with adequate security and none of the "favoritism" alleged by the *American.* But his hand was forced, or so he seemed to believe. In early May he ordered an investigation of the reformatory, and by so doing plunged his administration into a highly charged emotional maelstrom.

COMMENTS ON THE VAN WATERS CASE (CONTINUED)

McDowell ordered Dwyer to undertake the investigation beginning on May 4. The focus of the investigation was the death the preceding November of an inmate named Antonette A. DiBenedetto who was found hanging in her room shortly after lunch. The girl's parents did not believe that she had been a suicide and pressed their case through their state senator, Michael LoPresti, who contacted the *American.* Although two previous investigations had confirmed the suicide, after McDowell took office the case was once again pressed.

After receiving some corroboration of an early rumor that the dead inmate had been beaten the prior day by a homosexual lover and uncovering possible evidence of widespread homosexuality involving both inmates and staff, Dwyer devoted the entire month of May to an extensive investigation, questioning fifty-three inmates and former inmates and twenty-three members of the reformatory staff, including Van Waters herself. Meanwhile Dwyer was discussing his investigation with McDowell on an almost daily basis. While concurring in the earlier suicide findings, he also reported that he found conditions not conducive to proper management at Framingham. Such conditions included: (1) privileges to inmates; (2) condoning of homosexuality; (3) violations of rules and regulations; (4) violations of the indenture statute; and (5) employment of exconvicts.

On the basis of Dwyer's findings, McDowell issued a directive, which he personally delivered to Framingham, although Van Waters was not present to receive it. That directive effectively reversed policies that had been pursued at the reformatory for nearly forty years. It terminated those contracts indenturing inmates to the superintendent and other reformatory officers. It directed that no more outings would be permitted. It forbade the superintendent to allow former inmates to visit the institution voluntarily. It ordered her to refuse admission to "voluntary" inebriates. It required her to send to the commissioner a variety of information. And finally it ordered her to comply with all rules and regulations issued in 1923 as amended in 1926. Van Waters responded to the directive and complied with it. McDowell then waited while legislative hearings began. He felt he had accomplished his immediate goals: he had established his authority as commissioner, insisted on strict compliance with the law, and eliminated special privileges for inmates.

Seven months elapsed between the date of McDowell's directive to Van Waters and her removal. According to the commissioner, his hand was forced. He delayed in order not to interfere with an impending legislative probe; he acted because he was under violent attack and had to move, virtually, in self-defense. On June 9, Senator LoPresti filed a resolution to establish a special commission to "make an immediate and thorough investigation of the conduct of the Reformatory for Women." Meanwhile Van Waters's friends created an organization, "The Friends of the Framingham Reformatory," to marshal support for her. Her appearance before the legislative hearing became a mock trial of Miriam Van Waters, and she conducted herself impressively. McDowell, who sat in the audience and witnessed the superb performance, might have been warned that in any public hearing following her removal, Miriam Van Waters would be a potent and dangerous antagonist. Nonetheless, by December 16, 1948, McDowell decided to remove Van Waters and had detailed charges drawn up, to which she responded.

Van Waters, exercising her prerogatives under the Civil Service regulations, requested a public hearing, at which McDowell served as the hearing officer. The hearing lasted eighteen days and the transcript of the record, exclusive of exhibits, fills 2,257 pages. Van Waters was a powerful witness and dominated the hearing during the time she testified. She became a popular figure in the media as well as in the hearing room, which was filled with her supporters. Despite this, McDowell decided to uphold his own decision. Van Waters formally appealed to the governor, who promptly selected a three-member impartial commission whose decision under the law would be final.

The prestigious commission unanimously held that no "just cause" had been shown for removal and therefore ordered Van Waters restored to her former position. The commission found that:

1. Brief trips away from the reformatory were a clearly planned part of the rehabilitation program and could not constitute cause for reprimand.
2. Private manufacturing at the reformatory had been arranged for by Commissioner Doyle and Van Waters's part in it "was at most an irregularity (and we are not sure it was that)."
3. The charges concerning homosexuality were wholly unproven.
4. The use of keys by inmates until late 1947 did violate the rules, but it was approved by a former commissioner, and did not constitute just cause for removal.
5. Van Waters sought faithfully to comply with the directive of June 4, except for the excusable use of a bathroom key by an inmate.
6. No law or rule forbade the employment of prior inmates and in fact it might be a constructive influence on the reformatory.
7. The indenture system was approved and the responsibility of former commissioners.

8. Insufficient evidence was produced of understaffing the night shift.
9. Although some employees worked outside their classification, if this were a ground for removal every responsible officer of the Commonwealth would be liable to dismissal.

Miriam Van Waters returned to Framingham as superintendent in 1949 after a three-month suspension. According to her obituary in the *New York Times* (19 January 1974), "she went on to serve in her position until 1957, although many of her reforms were not restored."

What is your assessment of the fairness of the hearings provided under Massachusetts state law? The procedures that provide for removal of employees only where there is "just cause" are part of the basic protections that have come to be known as the civil service system, protecting government employees from arbitrary action.

Do you think government employees should be entitled to their jobs until retirement so long as they have not provided just cause for being removed from office? What is the impact of such measures on the organization of government bureaus? Does it encourage stability or rigidity?

Under what circumstances can employees lose their jobs? What happens when government bureaus are eliminated or funds are insufficient to pay government employees?

What are the ways that individuals are promoted in the public service? How do individuals enter the civil service?

NOTE ON THE CIVIL SERVICE

Government is the largest employer in the country, carrying out an incredible diversity of tasks. Making the large and diverse bureaucracy work is an enormous job, which depends upon the quality, timing, and organization of large numbers of government employees. Where do those people come from? How should they be selected? Who should be promoted? How much compensation should these workers receive?

These problems confront any organization, but are especially complicated for government. If you or I decide to organize a business or a club, we can go out and recruit our friends or the best qualified people. If the organization can compete successfully with similar organizations, it will survive. Otherwise, it will collapse and new organizations will replace it. In government, however, decisions to create organizations are based upon an assessment of public need. If the organization fails, this public need will not be met; no other organization will develop spontaneously to fill it. Furthermore, if you hire your own friends, other citizens might complain that they too should have a chance to compete for these public jobs.

Public organizations are faced with an additional dilemma. Since elected officials change office every two or four years, each time government changes the newly elected officials might be tempted to place their own supporters in public jobs. Since the costs of running for office are high, the temptation to use jobs to repay favors is great. In the absence of other rules, public bureaucracies would probably see a comprehensive housecleaning after each election. In fact, public attention to such a massive housecleaning during the presidency of Andrew Jackson gave rise to demands for an end to the spoils system and the creation of a career civil service. The term *spoils system* refers to the saying, "To the victor belong the spoils." Jackson was accused of putting his friends on the public payroll.

The Pendleton Act and Development of the Civil Service

Such massive dislocation is thought to inhibit the effective operation of public agencies. It runs counter to the operation of bureaucracies that require regular procedures and expertise. To solve this problem of constant change, with its attendant dangers of favoritism and lack of expertise, the civil service system was created. While every government throughout history has been forced to wrestle with this problem of creating a cadre of government employees who know their jobs, are committed to their jobs, and receive job permanence, the British civil service system is a model that has been emulated worldwide. This was the system chosen by the United States. Congress, reeling from the criticism of Andrew Jackson's presidency, and thirty years of political and incompetent appointments, passed the Pendleton Act of 1883, creating the Federal Civil Service. No action was taken in the Senate on the Pendleton bill until Garfield's assassination and the Republican reversals in the Congressional elections of 1882 produced fears within the Republican party of massive loss of jobs if they should lose the election of 1884.

The Pendleton Act incorporated three basic features borrowed from the British civil service: the use of competitive entrance examinations; job security, incuding the abolition of removal for political reasons; and the political neutrality of the civil servant. It avoided, however, another feature of the British civil service — the concept of a closed career system in which entry is at the lowest levels only.

According to the Pendleton Act, about 10 percent of federal jobs were placed within the competitive service. Provisions were made for the extension of the competitive service by act of the president and, as Table 2 – 1 indicates, that has been exercised periodically. The last major addition to the civil service pool was that of 70,000 postmasters and rural letter carriers by President Nixon.

TABLE 2 – 1 Merit Systems

Year	Number of Employees in Civil Service	Number Under General Merit System	Number Under Special Merit Systems	Percentage Under Merit System
1884	131,200	13,800	—	10.5
1900	208,000	94,900	—	45.6
1930	580,500	462,100	—	79.6
1950	1,934,000	1,641,900	—	84.9
1970	3,000,000	2,565,000	110,000	89.1

Merit systems have developed at the state level both through emulation and by the requirement of the Social Security Act of 1940 that federal funds for employment security, welfare, health, and other grant programs must be administered by state agencies operating under merit systems. Thus in every state at least a major portion of state employment is under the merit system. By 1970, thirty-four states had adopted statewide systems of merit. Similarly, large cities have mostly adopted such systems.

The Federal Civil Service System Today

The federal civil service is an enormous system, encompassing the great majority of jobs filled by the federal government and its agencies, including more than 2½ million employees, a geographic spread of 50 states and 125 foreign countries, and an occupational diversity representing just about every significant profession. Although in some ways the federal government represents a loose aggregation of very different public organizations, for some purposes it acts as a single employer. The United States Civil Service Commission for many years was its guiding authority, taking its direction from the president and Congress. Most important phases of personnel administration are based upon laws of general applicability, though specific laws govern some specific categories of workers, such as postal employees, foreign service officers, and manual workers. In addition to the laws passed by Congress were executive orders and instructions issued by the Civil Service Commission.

The centralization of authority in the Civil Service Commission was fed by tradition as well as budget and appropriation processes. But since the days of the New Deal, the trend has been to decentralize federal personnel operations away from the Civil Service Commission. In 1938, following the recommendations of the Brownlow Committee, President Roosevelt ordered all departments and agencies to establish personnel offices. An important event in this decentralization process was the Classification Act of 1949, which vested in the departments and agencies full authority and responsibility for evaluating and classifying jobs, according to standards promulgated by the Civil Service Commission and subject to periodic postaudit. Today, the bulk of personnel work is performed by the operating agencies and a large proportion is done in field offices away from Washington.

Through the years the Civil Service Commission adopted many different functions. Frederick Mosher characterized some of the conflicts in these diverse functions:

> The U.S. Civil Service Commission exemplifies both the dilemma and a stalwart effort to perform effectively in all these capacities. It continues to draft and pronounce, for management, the standards and ground rules for personnel administration. Its chairman, under one of his several hats, is the President's principal adviser on personnel policy and, paradoxically, on political appointments. The commission is the initiator of most new employee benefit programs and the administrator of several. It is the leader of programs to eliminate discrimination in employment against minority groups, against women, and against the handicapped. It is the guide and monitor of employee relations programs and the place of final appeal from certain kinds of adverse action — a role which calls for neutrality and objectivity. Finally, it continues to be the principal guardian of the older merit principles — open and equal competition, position classification, equal pay for equal work, etc. Whether or how long the Commission can successfully maintain this four-directional posture is questionable. (pp. 194 – 5).

The dilemma that Mosher describes has been somewhat ameliorated by the recent division of the Civil Service Commission's functions with separate organizations created for the maintenance of the merit system, the Office of Personnel Management (OPM), and for appeal of alleged misuses of the system, the Merit Systems Protection Board (MSPB).

The operational responsibilities of these two agencies were set forth in the Civil Service Reform Act of 1978 (CSRA). The act restated the fundamental merit principles of the civil service while increasing management's ability to reward performance by linking performance appraisal systems to personnel actions. Laws for taking action against employees for unacceptable performance and misconduct were revised. Steps also were taken to encourage affirmative action for women, minorities, and disabled veterans. A system of merit pay for supervisors and managers in grades GS-13 through GS-15 was established, as was the Senior Executive Service (SES). The act also authorized research and demonstration projects and established the labor relations program of the federal service on a statutory basis.

OPM is responsible for managing the federal work force. It administers the civil service system, prepares civil service rules, and acts to promote an efficient civil service. It recommends policies relating to selection, promotion, and retention of employees. It also conducts studies and research into methods of improving personnel management and operates the classification system.

The Merit System

The functions of hearing and adjudicating employees' appeals are delegated to the Merit Systems Protection Board. CSRA allows employees to choose between appealing adverse actions to MSPB or under the agencies' negotiated grievance procedures, if the employees are members of the bargaining units and the grievance procedures cover the area being appealed. In appeals to MSPB, the burden of proof is on the agency that took the action. However, if an employee is appealing an agency's actions based on alleged harmful procedural error, prohibited personnel practices, or a decision that was not in accordance with law, the burden of proof to show harmful error is on the employee. As a practical matter, prior to CSRA, agencies found it very difficult to develop the quantity of evidence needed to remove unproductive employees and, as a result, very few employees were removed. Now an agency can remove an employee or reduce his or her grade if it can present substantial evidence to support its decision that the employee has failed to meet the performance standards for one or more critical job elements, regardless of how well he or she performed other elements of the job. It would appear that removal will be a more frequent occurrence.

The major aspects of the merit system as it operates at the federal level, and for the most part at the state and local levels, include the following: (1) entrance and promotion on the basis of competitive examination; (2) classification according to systemwide principles based upon comparability of responsibilities and pay; (3) job security and promotion of career service; and (4) insulation from the political process.

From the beginning the civil service system has focused its energy on recruitment and selection of federal personnel. In recent years, the government has announced an average of more than 200,000 examinations per year and processed nearly two million applications. The procedure to be followed in open, competitive examinations is standard: (1) examinations are scheduled at the request of agencies; (2) examinations are announced; (3) applications are reviewed for eligibility; (4) examinations are given for those eligible; (5) eligible registers are set up in rank order on the basis of examination scores; (6) the top three names on the list are certified in response to an agency request; (7) the agency selects one out of the top three certified.

While the open, competitive system has its defenders, who point to its fairness and efficiency in identifying qualified personnel, critics argue that it is cumbersome, ignores important personality factors, and is not very useful in predicting on-the-job performance. In response to some of these criticisms, the Civil Service Commission has moved to decentralize administration of the examinations, thus greatly diminishing the delay factor. In certain jobs that are continually in demand, such as typing and stenography, continuously open examinations allow for application, examination, and appointment all in the same day. Another modification is the unassembled examination, which rates applicants for professional and specialized positions on the basis of educational credentials, prior experience, evidences of achievement, and letters of recommendation. Selective certification allows agencies to request candidates who have particular qualifications for a particular job from general civil service registers.

While open, competitive qualifying examinations are often used in the civil service system for promotion, the federal civil service is attempting to increase the discretion of management in the use of promotions. In addition to these factors, education, training, and performance on the job may be used. The tendency to use seniority as a basis for promotion is generally frowned upon and not used with the federal civil service.

If the system of competitive examination is a major boost to selection and promotion on the basis of merit and equity, what is to prevent individuals in different agencies or different regions of the country from receiving very different pay for comparable jobs? As the federal civil service system developed during the early part of the twentieth century, disparities in salary and rank among individuals performing comparable jobs became widespread. The result was the Classification Act of 1923, later amended by the Classification Act of 1949. These acts have established a system of positions and classes of positions that establish comparability in pay and rank for similar jobs throughout the civil service. The Civil Service Commission is responsible for the overall establishment of the system of position classification, although individual agencies and departments classify individual positions, subject to a postaudit by the Civil Service Commission.

Efforts at position classifications have focused on the issue of comparability, with the need to clarify job responsibilities associated with specific positions playing a secondary role. Position classification within the federal civil service falls within a series of governmental service classifications ranging from GS-1 to GS-18. Table 2 – 2 provides specific details of the system.

Career Civil Servants — Advantages and Problems

An important part of the civil service in its rejection of the spoils system was the establishment of a career service, made up of individuals who would provide continuity in the running of government. The concept of a career service requires methods for retaining individuals within government. Beginning in 1934 under the leadership of Commissioner Leonard White, the Civil Service Commission made a special effort to bolster its general management capability through the systematic recruitment of college graduates. The most recent variations of this theme are the Professional Advancement in Career Education (PACE) exam, the newly established program of presidential interns, and work study programs at the federal level.

In the development of the federal civil service, the British concept of the closed system, in which entry was limited to the lower levels, was explicitly rejected. In fact, recently the injection of new top management with each four-year presidential election has been criticized. In the absence of a closed system, the federal civil service has had to work harder to encourage career civil servants. In a closed system the rewards of promotion are retained for those staying with the system and provide a powerful mechanism for encouraging loyalty and longevity. Where the higher positions are open to individuals from without the service, the incentives for moving back and forth between the public and private systems is increased. In some instances this back and forth mobility creates considerable problems of conflict of interest. Since the government is involved in many contracting and granting activities, private organizations may seek to place their own employees in government jobs to increase their chances of receiving government contracts and grants. They also may seek to employ individuals with recent experience and contacts in government. Of course the possibilities of outright bribes or subtle bribery exists when a private company currying favor may make promises of future employment to helpful government bureaucrats. In a more subtle way this same problem exists in those areas where government agencies regulate private companies. Incentives exist for moving back and forth between government and private companies that may not be in the best interest of the public.

The advantages of attracting former government bureaucrats into

TABLE 2 – 2 Federal Salaries by General Schedule (GS) Levels, Each with Ten Within-Grade Step Increase (Schedule 1 — The General Schedule)

	STEPS									
	1	2	3	4	5	6	7	8	9	10
GS-1	$ 7,960	$ 8,225	$ 8,490	$ 8,755	$ 9,020	$ 9,175	$ 9,437	$ 9,699	$ 9,712	$ 9,954
2	8,951	9,163	9,459	9,712	9,820	10,109	10,398	10,687	10,976	11,265
3	9,766	10,092	10,418	10,744	11,070	11,396	11,722	12,048	12,374	12,700
4	10,963	11,328	11,693	12,058	12,423	12,788	13,153	13,518	13,883	14,248
5	12,266	12,675	13,084	13,493	13,902	14,311	14,720	15,129	15,538	15,974
6	13,672	14,128	14,584	15,040	15,496	15,952	16,408	16,864	17,320	17,776
7	15,193	15,699	16,205	16,711	17,217	17,723	18,229	18,735	19,241	19,747
8	16,826	17,387	17,948	18,509	19,070	19,631	20,192	20,753	21,314	21,875
9	18,585	19,205	19,825	20,445	21,065	21,685	22,305	22,925	23,545	24,165
10	20,467	21,149	21,831	22,513	23,195	23,877	24,559	25,241	25,923	26,605
11	22,486	23,236	23,986	24,736	25,486	26,236	26,986	27,736	28,486	29,236
12	26,951	27,849	28,747	29,645	30,543	31,441	32,339	33,237	34,135	35,033
13	32,048	33,116	34,184	35,252	36,320	37,388	38,456	39,524	40,592	41,660
14	37,871	39,133	40,395	41,657	42,919	44,181	45,443	46,705	47,967	49,229
15	44,547	46,032	47,517	49,002	50,487	51,972	53,457	54,942	56,427	57,912
16	52,247	53,989	55,731	57,473	59,215	60,957	62,699	64,441	66,183	
17	61,204	63,244	65,284	67,324	69,364					
18	71,734									

SOURCE: Office of Personnel Management

private industry and the consequent depletion of the federal civil service are becoming more critical as goverment regulation of private companies expands. It forces government to be more conscious of pay comparability with the private sector. To the extent that the civil service remains an open system with frequent movement back and forth, pay comparability is critical if the government is to retain competent staff and not become just a dumping ground for those individuals who are not successful in the private sector.

Within the United States, particularly at the federal level, the career civil service tends to function quite well. In recent years, however, in part due to the pressures described above, questions have been raised about the ability of the federal government to retain individuals at the highest levels, including that of assistant secretary, which traditionally has been an appointed office. Recent suggestions for reform of the civil service contain measures to strengthen the managerial service at the highest levels.

Title IV of CSRA created the Senior Executive Service (SES) based on "rank in the person" instead of "rank in the position." SES covers positions classifiable as GS-16, -17, and -18 and executive levels IV and V (or their equivalents). SES is designed to provide a cadre of high-level executives who are retained and promoted on the basis of merit and who are mobile among the various federal agencies. Greater accountability will result from a system of appraisal based upon actual performance, with rewards of merit pay increases and promotions.

Since the origins of the federal civil service were deeply affected by a reaction to the spoils system, whereby politically successful candidates regarded adherents by providing them with jobs, the separation of the civil service from political patronage has been a basic concern. In fact, the ideology of the civil service at one time was reinforced by the accepted distinction bewteen politics and administration. As the distinction has broken down, however, the rationale for separation of the civil service from the political processes has been weakened.

While it is easy to condemn elected officials for placing unqualified adherents into public jobs, it is less difficult to criticize their need to bring with them into government loyal lieutenants who will be able to translate their policies into action. In fact, elected officials' success often depends in large measure upon the subordinates they appoint. But while the need for political executives to be able to appoint individuals is well recognized, the dangers of the spoils system remain. Moreover, the constant rotation of the top management of city, state, and federal governments may cause considerable dislocation in the operation of government. In the view of a prominent private sector executive who served in a top capacity in New York City government, the single greatest lack in

New York City government was the absence of a top-level, dedicated, committed management. At the federal level recent calls for greater flexibility in the higher levels is directed in part to the penetration of the career service to even the highest levels of assistant secretary which are now political appointments which evidence almost complete turnover from administration to administration.

The intersection of the civil service with politics, evident in higher appointments, occurs also at the lowest levels. In addition to low-level political patronage jobs, which existed until recently in the Postal Service and which still exist in many states, for example in the highway departments, and which have been a continuing phenomenon at the local level, a broader questions may be raised as to the right of civil servants to participate in politics.

The federal Hatch Act prohibits federal employees from engaging in overt political involvement. At the state and local levels employees have tended to become involved in politics in a variety of ways. As public employees have become unionized in recent years, their use of the political process has become more sophisticated and more frequent. At the federal level, the Hatch Act has been revised after considerable lobbying in Congress.

Government employees point out with some justification that given the large number of citizens now involved in government, to deny them political involvement is to deny basic political rights to a large proportion of the population. This argument has been successfully made and restrictions have been eased. The further definition of the boundaries between legitimate political activity and the compromise of the neutrality of the civil service will probably receive increasing attention in the years ahead.

Major issues today remain unresolved. Written competitive examinations are being attacked as unrelated to job requirements. Affirmative action is needed to promote black and Hispanic minorities, who over the past three years have achieved remarkable access to lower-level jobs. The tension between public accountability and insulation from political pressures remains.

The operation of the civil service system places certain important constraints upon public organizations. Yet despite its harshest critics, who have sometimes referred to the "meritless" civil service, it has been a mechanism for providing secure and equitable employment for a large portion of the work force. Its system of protection of employee rights provides dignity and fairness. If it has gone overboard and tied the hands of management in making changes and providing performance incentives, this may be more an expression of the desire to avoid political interference in the hiring and promotion process than anything else. Given the competing demands on a system of public sector employment, if we didn't have the civil service we'd have to invent something pretty close to it.

SELECTED BIBLIOGRAPHY FOR MODULE 2

ARGYRIS, CHRIS. *Personality and Organization.* New York: Harper & Row, 1957.

———"Some Limits of Rational Man Theory," *PAR* 33 (1973): 253.

BENNIS, WARREN. *Changing Organizations.* New York: McGraw-Hill, 1966.

BLAU, PETER. *Bureaucracy in Modern Society.* New York: Random House, 1956.

FAYOL, HENRI. *Industrial and General Management.* London: Pitman, 1916.

GERTH, H.H., and MILLS, C. WRIGHT. *From Max Weber.* New York: Oxford University Press, 1958.

GULICK, LUTHER, AND URWICK, LYNDALL, eds. *Papers on the Science of Administration.* New York: Institute of Public Administration, Columbia University, 1937.

MARCH, JAMES, and SIMON, HERBERT. *Organizations.* New York: Wiley, 1958.

MCGREGOR, DOUGLAS. *The Human Side of Enterprise.* New York: McGraw-Hill, 1960.

MOSHER, FREDERICK. *Democracy and the Public Service.* New York: Oxford University Press, 1968.

ROETHLISBERGER, FRITZ, and DICKSON, W. J. *Management and the Worker.* Boston: Harvard University Press, 1939.

SIMON, HERBERT. *Administrative Behavior.* New York: Free Press, 1945.

———"Organizational Man: Rational or Self-Actualizing." *PAR* 33 (1973): 346.

STANLEY, DAVID; MANN, DEAN; and DOIG, JAMESON. *Men Who Govern.* Washington, D.C.: Brookings Institution, 1968.

TAYLOR, FREDERICK. *Principles of Scientific Management.* New York: Harper and Brothers, 1911.

THOMPSON, VICTOR. *Bureaucracy and the Modern World.* Morristown, N.J.: General Learning Press, 1976.

VAN RIPER, PAUL. *History of the United States Civil Service.* New York: Harper and Row, 1958.

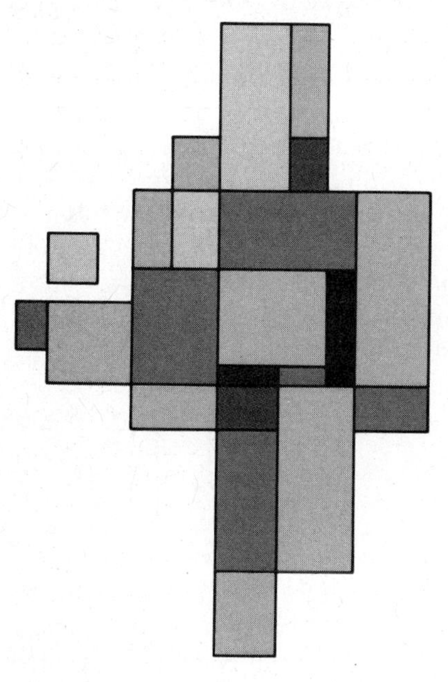

MODULE 3

Managing Public Organizations, Supervision, and Leadership

INTRODUCTION

Since, in bureaucratic organizations, authority is defined in hierarchical terms, each member of the organization knows his or her supervisors and subordinates. Working successfully in public organizations depends on understanding and adapting to these authority relationships. As an individual you may sometimes experience difficulty in understanding where an organization is heading and in molding that organization. Or, you may feel that your own goals and those of the organization are at loggerheads. Unless you understand the authority structure of the organization, you cannot exercise much influence upon its direction. (It may be that even if you understand the authority structure you will not have a great impact, but that is another matter.) Would you rather work in an organization that emphasizes the importance of authority relationships or in one that deemphasizes such relationships? Would your position in the hierarchy change your views about how best to structure authority?

Since bureaucracies have a hierarchical structure, a good deal of time and effort is spent in superior-subordinate interaction. Yet time also is spent relating to individuals at the same level in the hierarchy. One of the most pervasive aspects of the Van Waters case was the interaction between Van Waters, the subordinate, and McDowell, the supervisor. To a large extent the case focused on defining this relationship. The firing of Van Waters was an indication of the inability of individuals to establish a satisfactory superior-subordinate relationship. The superior-subordinate roles dominating this case may also be characterized more specifically. McDowell's role was that of state correction commissioner and Van Waters's role that of the superintendent of a reformatory. Since a role is a way of generalizing about the behavior of individuals, when you are told that Miriam Van Waters is the superintendent of Framingham, you know something about her activities. You can predict to some extent what she will be doing. You know that she will be in a supervisory relationship with many individuals and a subordinate role with a few individuals.

ROLES AND GAME PLAYING

A role is a characteristic pattern of behavior associated with an organizational position. One way of ensuring that individuals carry out the roles to which they have been assigned is through the use of job descriptions. A job description is a series of tasks that an individual is expected to fulfill in the performance of a particular job. Job descriptions may range from the very general to the very specific. The nature of a job description will depend upon the organizational requirements and the approaches that the individuals in an organization have toward their jobs. The use of job descriptions can clarify the responsibilities of individuals in an organization and improve communications among them. However, the development and use of job descriptions also can be the source of considerable organizational tension. Since they define an individual's tasks, they can provide the occasion for reevaluation of a person's status within the organization.

When individuals are applying for new jobs, job descriptions can give them an overview of the requirements. Using such descriptions can be an effective technique for increasing communication within the organization about tasks and responsibilities.

Role is an important concept, because it reduces the uncertainty of living in public organizations. Situational analysis, as described in Module 1, depends to a large extent on the ability to identify role behavior and to predict how individuals will react in given circumstances. Although this is particularly important when you are eager to please your boss, it is also important in many other organizational situations. Your perceptions of how others are playing their roles will influence your own conduct and determine whether you can successfully anticipate their behavior.

Eric Berne suggests that we play games all the time, by assuming roles and reacting to the roles of others, but sometimes these roles become counterproductive by getting in the way of effective interpersonal communication. Anne Rosen, in an article in *Supervisory Management* entitled "Games Subordinates Play," illustrates how these games can interfere with the operation of organizations. She characterizes one game as IDTT (I'll Do Only What You Tell Me To) in which a subordinate refuses to do anything except that which is directly assigned. Have you ever played that game, as either a subordinate or a superior?

One of the ways to minimize such distracting games and promote constructive organizational behavior is by sharpening your perceptions of superior-subordinate relations. These relations are central to organizational success. They are affected by the ways in which individuals perceive one another.

Common misperceptions can easily undermine the effectiveness of the organization. For example, a study of supervisors and subordinates revealed that while 80 percent of the supervisors claimed that they gave recognition to subordinates, in the form of pats on the back and sincere and thorough praise, only 14 percent of the subordinates recognized that such praise was being given. Accurate role perceptions increasingly form the basis of effective interaction. Indeed, organizations are increasingly making extra efforts to improve the communications process and sensitize their members to the need for accurate mutual perceptions. The field of organizational development devotes a substantial part of its attention to designing organizations and processes to foster accurate communications and perceptions. This will be discussed more fully in the next module.

In order to sensitize yourself to the nuances of superior-subordinate relations, you will now take part in a role-playing exercise. Such exercises are a regular part of training efforts in many modern organizations. This particular role play focuses on the understanding of different supervisory and subordinate role orientations — styles of behavior associated with particular roles — and their interactions.

SUPSUB: A ROLE PLAY

Those participating in the role play will be divided into two groups: supervisors and subordinates. The subordinates are caseworkers with the local department of welfare. A caseworker's job is to provide services to welfare recipients by helping them with problems that arise in their social situation and in their relationships with the welfare system. Caseworkers provide both field services and consultations at the welfare center. Often a welfare caseworker is an individual with some social work experience. Some of you may be familiar with caseworkers in the real world who have different responsibilities. Try to remember that to play this game you need to use your imagination and remove yourself from your own experiences. A role play reflects the real world, but may be different from the world with which you are familiar.

The supervisor is responsible for the activities of approximately fifteen caseworkers. The duties include monitoring the work of the caseworkers, ensuring that work is done correctly, and providing assistance with difficult cases. Supervisors usually have a minimum of three years' experience as a caseworker and a master's degree in social work.

Presently, caseworkers spend one-half of their time assisting recipients with their problems, one-quarter of their time making field visits, and one-quarter making reports. Supervisors spend all their time at the offices ensuring a smooth flow of work and acting as mediators in case of conflict between recipients and caseworkers.

Recently an article has appeared in a statewide newspaper which indicates that "widespread" idling and "unreasonable" self-imposed work limits are hampering the productivity of employees at welfare centers. Recipients are forced to wait two or more hours before being seen. In response to this report the commissioner of welfare has ordered all supervisors to meet with their subordinates to review the progress of their work. The commissioner says that he will not tolerate a self-imposed limit of five clients per day and that the average work load must be set instead at eight clients per day.

Meetings are scheduled between each caseworker and his or her supervisor to develop a plan for increasing productivity from the current five daily visits to eight daily visits. You and your colleague will have fifteen minutes to arrive at a written plan of action to accomplish this.

What type of role orientation would you naturally tend to have in playing the role of caseworker or caseworker supervisor? How would you convince your superior or subordinate of the justice of your demands?

Although a variety of role orientations are possible, for the purpose of this role play you will be assigned one of the following six orientations:

Supervisor–Coercive: This type of supervisor tends to emphasize the hierarchical characteristic of organizations. Subordinates are expected to accept the authority of their supervisors. The coercive supervisor believes his or her function is to formulate policy, which should be followed with minimal questioning. Failure of subordinates to accept the direction of supervisors is looked upon as insubordination and a threat to the organization.

Supervisor–Persuasive: The persuasive supervisor is directive, like the coercive supervisor. However, while the subordinate is expected to follow the supervisor's suggestions, this supervisor seeks to persuade, rather than order. He or she is willing to undertake to convince subordinates of the advisability of a particular course of action, but expects subordinates to implement policies once they are understood.

Supervisor–Participative: The participative supervisor views the task of supervision as one of mutual decision making and implementation. Commitment to organizational goals is built through individual commitment to a plan of action developed in conjunction with employees. Hierarchy is deemphasized and greater attention is given to motivation of the employees.

Subordinate–Eager: The eager subordinate is sometimes ambitious and sometimes subservient, but always eager to please. The ideal is to follow the wishes of the superior. The eager subordinate assiduously seeks to learn the supervisor's desires and then to convince the supervisor that they will be followed.

Subordinate–Autonomous: The autonomous subordinate is an independent individual who does what he or she believes to be right. Such a subordinate has many suggestions, expects them to be followed, and thrives in an independent sphere of operation. Often the autonomous employee is a professional with a sense of expertise and competence developed from prior training and experience.

Subordinate–Minimal: The minimal employee is interested in structuring the job to involve the least time, energy, and commitment. This employee seeks to avoid conflict with the supervisor as well as work, and is open to suggestions only so long as he or she sees a way of avoiding extra work and commitment. 

Try to understand and adopt the role orientation to which you are assigned. In the series of two or three role plays that you will carry out, try to be explicit in portraying your assigned role. Be dramatic! While participating in this role play you will not be told which of the orientations your opposite number is assigned. As you interact, try to understand your opponent's orientation and adjust your style to be most effective. Never forget your own orientation, however, and always remain consistent with it.

COMMENT ON SUPSUB

At the end of the allotted time period you will be expected to submit a written conference report signed by both parties, explaining how the case load is to be increased from five to eight cases per day. Then write a paragraph explaining what devices you used to portray your role orientation. Were you successful in your role, and if so, why? To what extent did your role orientation limit your success with your particular adversary? Have you ever encountered someone of your own or your adversary's role orientation in a real-life situation? Which combination of orientations would you say were best and least able to carry out the assigned task?

Everyone falls into patterns of behavior when interacting with others. These patterns of behavior often constitute roles and role orientations of readily identifiable sorts. Roles are important because they ensure that individuals will be doing tasks assigned to them and expected by others. A large part of operating in public bureaucracies is understanding your role and carrying it out in line with others' expectations, particularly those who determine your success and advancement within the organization.

Role orientations are to a large extent the result of individual reactions to a particular role situation. Depending upon background and experience, individuals naturally will react differently to being placed in a new role. The way they create roles through their adoption of specific role orientations shapes the character of the organization. When considering the general role orientations presented above —

supervisor-coercive	subordinate-eager
supervisor-persuasive	subordinate-autonomous
supervisor-participative	subordinate-minimal

— individual differences can seem insignificant. By selecting these particular orientations, others are deemphasized. Furthermore, it probably will be apparent that no one really pursues only one orientation all the time; rather, people switch from one to another.

Yet it is true, too, that unless you are able to categorize the behavior of others, it is more difficult to respond to it appropriately. Could you develop a different scheme of role orientations to capture more accurately the nuances of human behavior in the situation just posed for discussion?

NOTE ON LEADERSHIP STYLE

In an interesting analysis of leadership style, Robert Tannenbaum and Warren Schmidt attempt to help supervisors choose a role orientation. They describe how an earlier consensus that successful executives were individuals who are intelligent, imaginative, inspiring, and accurate decision makers has given way to a recognition of the importance of motivating people. They see the modern executive as torn between the desire to be "strong" yet "permissive," inspiring the support of the others in the organization. They claim that managers must be able to pursue a variety of styles, depending upon the circumstances, the nature of the problem, and the individuals with whom they are working.

The accompanying figure illustrates the dilemmas confronting the modern manager in attempting to reconcile the need for asserting authority with the need for permitting employees freedom. Tannenbaum and Schmidt suggest that leadership styles fall on a continuum dependent upon the relative mix of these two elements.

Continuum of Leadership Behavior

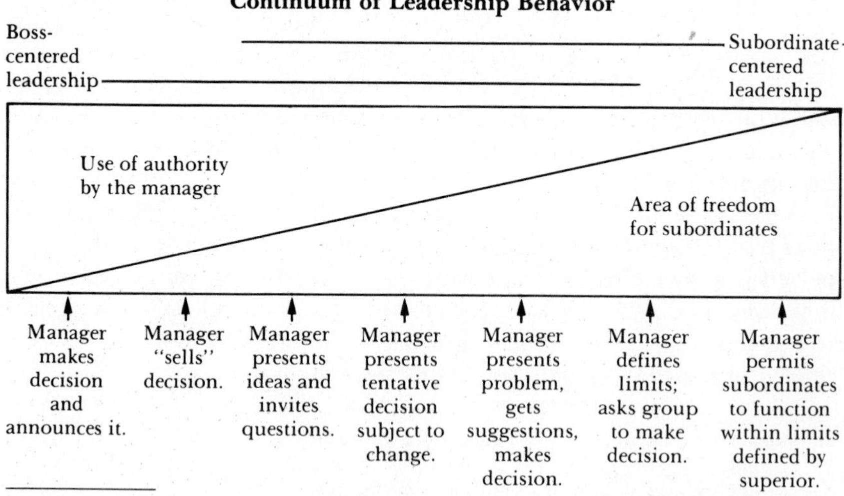

SOURCE: Reprinted by permission of the Harvard Business Review. Exhibit from "How to choose a leadership pattern," by Robert Tannenbaum and Warren H. Schmidt (March – April 1958).

At which point in the continuum did you or your adversary fall, as you played your role? Describe a job you have held and state where your supervisor was along the continuum. Where would you have preferred him or her to be?

Stressing the need for adaptability, Tannenbaum and Schmidt argue that leadership style depends upon the forces in the supervisor, the forces in the subordinates, and the forces in the situation. How did these three sets of forces influence the outcome of the role play in which you participated?

Because the superior-subordinate relationship is so important for hierarchical organizations, it has been the object of extensive investigation and discussion. The supervisor, in particular, has received considerable attention, as it is clear that the supervisor ordinarily has great influence in organization activity.

Theories of supervision are of course dependent upon theories of how people behave and, in particular, their reactions in organizational situations. As discussed in Module 1, contemporary theories of motivation stress the importance of the higher motivations of individuals and their needs for self-actualization. Organization theory has responded by deemphasizing hierarchical authority, sometimes as in the work of Warren Bennis, predicting an end to hierarchical organization. These developments were discussed in Module 2.

Similarly, theories of supervision stress the need for supervisors to take into account this new conception of employee behavior. Rensis Likert, a researcher who has focused on the study of leadership, in *New Patterns of Management,* a pioneering book that reviews the considerable literature on supervisory behavior, heralds the move from job-centered supervision to employee-centered supervision. He argues that contemporary developments in American society are reflected in the attitudes of employees, who are less willing to accept pressure and close supervision than they previously were. Likert sees a growing demand for freedom in schools, homes, communities, and the work place. This is a broad cultural trend bolstered by higher levels of education and an increasing concern with individual mental health. Another factor is the increasing dependence of business on technologically sophisticated professionals who demand recognition of their autonomy.

According to Likert, the traditional job-centered view of supervision relied on a number of principles of management, which included:

1. Break the total operation into simple components.
2. Develop the best way to carry out each of the components or tasks.
3. Hire people with aptitudes and skills to perform the tasks.

4. Train people to perform their tasks in the specified best way.
5. Supervise work to see that tasks are performed using specified procedures at an acceptable rate.
6. Use incentives where feasible in the form of individual or group piece rates.

This job-centered view relied heavily on that approach to scientific management focusing on the division of labor. It is also akin to the Theory X approach identified by Douglas McGregor. In extensive survey research, Likert found that supervisors who based their activity on this concept of management were in charge of units producing at a low rather than at a high level. But supervisors with the best records of performance focused their primary attention on the human aspects of their subordinates' problems and on endeavoring to build effective work groups with high performance goals. These supervisors he labeled "employee-centered."

Supervisors who had the most favorable and cooperative attitudes in their work groups displayed the following characteristics:

1. The supervisor is perceived by the subordinate as supportive, friendly, just. He or she shows confidence in the integrity, ability, and motivations of subordinates and has high expectations of performance. He or she devotes considerable resources to ensuring that the subordinate is well trained and coached.
2. The supervisor pays considerable attention to planning and scheduling work to be done and providing adequate support, including technical competence where work has not been highly standardized.
3. The supervisor develops his or her subordinates into a working team with high group loyalty by using participation and other kinds of group leadership practices.

Likert then concluded that effective supervision requires that organizational processes must ensure that each member will view the experience as supportive, while building and maintaining a sense of personal worth and importance. This includes the full use of human potential through the effective functioning of each person as a member of one or more work groups that have a high degree of group loyalty, effective skills or interaction, and high performance goals.

Understanding Management

The importance of supervisory-subordinate relationships in the operation of public organizations is an expression of the centrality of authority relationships. Yet Leonard Sayles cautions against the view that the primary purpose of the manager or administrator is transmitting orders downward to subordinates. More comprehensive theories of management reflect an increasing recognition that authority relationships tend to be more complex than those expressed by simple pyramidal organization charts. According to Sayles in *Managerial Behavior,* the primary purpose of the manager is to maintain the regularity or the sequential pattern of one or more of the work processes underlying the division of labor. He suggests that an understanding of organizations must proceed bottom upward and that, indeed, organizations should be built in this way. So long as an individual can complete a task or series of tasks there is no need for an organization. But once division of labor and specialization occur, mechanisms are required to coordinate and integrate the activities of the people making up the work system. Comprehensive theories of the management process emphasize the importance of the work group as the building block of organizations. Consequently it is the manager's relationship to work groups that is *central* to understanding the management function, rather than the individual supervisor-subordinate relationship. This perspective suggests a more workable notational system for classifying managerial behavior, based on a threefold division of activities into external work flows, leadership, and monitoring.

External Work Flows

External work flows are to a large extent interactions with other managers. In complex organizations lateral relationships are often plentiful. Sayles divides external work flows into:

(1) work flow relationships,
(2) trading relationships,
(3) service relationships,
(4) advisory relationships,
(5) auditing relationships, and
(6) innovation relationships.

External work flows take on a particular importance in public organizations. The setting of these organizations in a political environment means that all relationships outside the work group have the potential for involving a wide range of constituency groups, public opinion, executive, legislative, and judicial actors. The budgeting process is a good example of a work flow that within public organizations becomes highly politicized through the involvement of a variety of actors.

Trading relationships are particularly characteristic of public organizations. Since organizational survival is less tied to such objective measures as profit and loss, the struggle for support among other public organizations becomes highly charged. That is one of the reasons public sector managers sometimes feel so discouraged. The price of obtaining cooperation from other units may mean an endless process of bargaining as the units attempt to use their position in the work flow as way of bolstering their own position. Service organizations may amass considerable power, and they may exact support as a price for providing some service.

Advisory relationships are a pervasive aspect of public organizations and often include advisory groups outside the regular bureaucratic process. The tradition of lay intervention in governmental processes is great, and advisory groups often become critical in determining the fate of public organizations. Advisory groups often perform important functions for higher level executives whose responsibilities may be far reaching and who may require extensive outside advice. Policy-oriented analysis units, which have become a frequent accompaniment of executive activity, are another manifestation of advisory groups.

Auditing functions are an increasingly important component in public organizations. Financial auditing procedures have been built into state and local government through the creation of comptrollers, who are often elected independently of the chief executive and who are responsible for the auditing function. At the federal level the General Accounting Office performs the auditing function under congressional aegis. Legislatures perform what is termed the *oversight function,* which is an instance of auditing. More and more the fiscal auditors are assuming a role as program auditors, inquiring not only that money is spent for the purpose enunciated, but that it is spent effectively.

This tendency to extend fiscal processes to include substantive auditing has also been the tendency in budgeting. The Office of Management and Budget at the federal level, which has been imitated at the state and local levels, has become an important center of auditing activity, providing the elected executive with a central auditing capability.

At the federal level the increased expenditures for programs implemented at the state and local levels have increased the need for auditing. Often independent evaluators are hired to provide this dimension.

Along with the auditing function, specialized units concerned with organizational change and innovation develop. Sometimes these are institutionalized, like budget units and policy analysis units. President Carter established a number of ad hoc units to undertake reorganization studies. Often commissions or special study groups undertake this function in the public sector.

Leadership

Most writings about management and supervision focus on the second major group of management activities directed toward securing a group response from subordinates, which we refer to as leadership. In addition to its internal focus, leadership differs from the regulation of external work flows in that it is directed at group response as opposed to the one-on-one relationship that frequently characterizes external flow relationships. In theory, intragroup contacts among subordinates should be self-maintaining. But in the real world, the friction of external change frequently interferes. The assertion of leadership is required to maintain the sequential pattern of work flow.

Leadership may be analyzed into three components: direction, response, and representation. Giving direction is ordinarily associated with change. Relying upon monitoring processes, the manager detects that planned relationships and processes are not being maintained or that external circumstances have changed. The manager responds with direction, which requires a good deal of skill in application. Studies of leadership focus on the approaches that can be best utilized. Perhaps the single most important principle of giving direction is that it must result in action. However, the leader who leads best does not give the most orders. Skilled leadership requires adjusting the quantity of initiative to the situation.

To maintain receptivity to direction, the leader must be responsive to the group members. One of the most universal concerns of subordinates is being heard by the boss. Subordinates need an appeals procedure, help from the leader, assurances as to their position and security, and mutual exchanges of favors, concessions, or bargains, which give them some control over their work environment. The manager must be careful, however, to avoid an imbalance of contacts with particular work group members, to avoid undercutting lieutenants, and to avoid discouraging decision-making initiatives by subordinates.

Finally, leadership entails representation of work group needs before other organizational managers. Many times the leader cannot resolve a problem without calling upon others within the organization. This may require the concurrence of those over whom the leader has no authority or those who are at a higher level. Failure to provide representation undermines group effectiveness and may result in the failure of the group to obtain its fair share of resources.

Leadership style is of course dependent upon one's views of human motivation. Yet clearly the predominant image of the leader as the individual who gives orders and sees that they are enforced — the command view of the leader as the individual who gives orders and sees that they are enforced — the command view of leadership — is no longer accepted.

While different leadership styles are recognized as appropriate to different circumstances, the choice will rest on judgment and predisposition. The relative weight of motivation through incentives (what has been referred to as the carrot-and-stick approach) and motivation through self-actualization will affect individual leadership styles.

Chester Barnard, in his classic book *The Functions of the Executive,* equates management with the maintenance of a system of cooperative effort, anticipating Sayles's basic view. His views stress the importance of providing a system of communication, promoting essential efforts, and formulating and defining purpose. This latter function in particular does not play a prominent part in Sayles's approach. Yet to many observers of organizations the definition of purpose and the definition of organizational goals is a peculiar and vital function of leadership. It is generally, though, attributed to the higher levels.

The need for leadership, according to Philip Selznick, is no longer restricted to the political statesmen who function at the highest level of government. The growth of independent, powerful government agencies that are largely self-governing, along with institutions of industry, politics, education, and other fields that command considerable resources, has greatly increased the need for organizational leadership. Such leadership, Selznick argues, must extend beyond the efficient use of organizational resources to include the making of critical decisions and the exercise of institutional leadership. The higher the level of administration, the more complex decisions become. The logic of efficiency gives way as the characteristics of lower-level organizations with clearly defined operating responsibilities, limited discretion, set communication patterns, and a certain command structure, become less important. Leadership transforms an organization into an institution, embodying the desired aims and standards.

A leader may be defined as someone who coordinates organizational efforts toward the realization of organizational goals. In bureaucratic organizations, leaders are usually identified within the formal structure as supervisors. At times, however, individuals will assume leadership responsibilities not formally given to them. Organizations that can capitalize on such informal leadership have a built-in advantage over more rigid organizations that discourage leadership among those not formally designated as such.

Monitoring

As the manager regulates external work flows and exercises leadership within the work group, a constant process of evaluation takes place. The manager reads reports, observes activities within and outside his or her own department, and talks with subordinates. The manager's job is to achieve both stability and change, which allows for constant readjustment to externally and internally caused disturbances.

A total monitoring and control system should include:

1. an accurate conceptualization of the work processes to be monitored;

2. operational methods to check, monitor, and appraise these processes;
3. criteria for evaluating the significance of observations;
4. a description of short-range remedial actions;
5. criteria for identifying recurring problems;
6. methods of introducing long-term corrections through organizational change.

In obtaining information for control purposes the manager can rely upon contacts he or she initiates, contacts initiated to him or her, observation, and review of numerical records. Statistical checks must not be omitted. The manager must balance the need to avoid an overcommitment of time to monitoring with the need to obtain data that actually identify situations requiring intervention. The inherent variation in the technological and human system should determine the frequency of checks being made. The manager seeks to identify the points where disorganization, breakdown, or disintegration is occurring, in order to intervene to return the system to normal equilibrium.

This control function of management is stressed in most executive training courses, and in many ways is the most challenging aspect of the manager's task. The line between gathering information and spying on subordinates may be a thin one at times. Yet the need to encourage workers as opposed to creating an atmosphere of fear and resistance is critical.

One of the classic studies of monitoring in a somewhat specialized public organization is Herbert Kaufman's study of forest rangers. He inquired into the mechanism for monitoring forest rangers, who spend substantial portions of their time by themselves in the woods. Their solitary existence obviously makes monitoring their activities quite difficult. Yet the Forest Service hit upon a system that Kaufman found to be quite successful. It requires rangers to keep detailed logs of their daily activities. These logs provide the service with a record of rangers' accomplishments and serve as a successful method of motivation and monitoring. Supervisors can discuss these logs with personnel and make changes. Furthermore, on the basis of some personal contacts and internal consistency, the logs provide the basis for checking up on rangers' activities.

An example of a more direct method of monitoring, and one that has generated considerable opposition from employees, is the method that the Internal Revenue Service (IRS) uses to check up on agents making field audits of business operations. Because of the dangers of collusion and malingering on the part of individuals operating on their own, the IRS actually sends observers into the field to check up on field auditors. Can you think of any alternative to such a spy network?

In a more recent study, *Administrative Feedback,* Kaufman looks more systematically at this problem of monitoring subordinate behavior from the perspectives of a number of federal agencies. He investigates the mechanisms of administrative feedback and the flow of information about the organization from the field to central headquarters in a number of federal agencies.

Management by Objectives. Recent approaches to the control function stress performance evaluation, setting an explicit procedure for the evaluation of individual performance of subordinates by supervisors. While relying on the distinction between subordinates and supervisors and thereby stressing traditional authority relationships, these approaches also recognize the need for mutual involvement in the setting of personal goals between the supervisor and subordinate. A particular variety of performance evaluation is the approach referred to as *management by objectives,* or MBO.

Management by objectives is an interesting attempt to capitalize on the new participative management approach. It is both a prescription for undertaking certain specific measures and a broad approach to emphasizing certain aspects of the management process. In three significant ways it goes beyond goal definition and evaluation that have long been part of standard management practices. First, it requires an explicit periodic procedure for setting organizational goals as well as individual objectives for all personnel. Second, it requires periodic meetings between supervisor and subordinate to check on progress. Last, it requires individual evaluation in terms of objectives set at the beginning of the time period. MBO gained widespread acceptance in the private sector after the mid-fifties and has more recently achieved prominence in the public sector. Peter Drucker's *The Practice of Management* provided a major impetus to this movement.

While the specific details and terminology of MBO systems differ, the following set of definitions will give you an idea of how it works:

1. *Goal:* A continuous purpose that provides a sense of direction
2. *Objective:* A measurable, desired result to be accomplished within a specified time period
3. *Strategy:* An action designed to assist in meeting the objective
4. *Task:* An activity that is part of a strategy

After consultation, broad goals are promulgated at the highest level of the organization and translated down to the lower levels until they reach the smallest work units. Goals for individual work units form the basis for the development of specific objectives for each supervisor within that unit. Then subordinates formulate their objectives based upon their supervisor's objectives.

MBO is an approach to the systematic communication of organizational goals and individual objectives, while reinforcing intraorganizational communication. While it has been hailed as an effective management technique in both the private and public sectors, indications are that its implementation is no panacea. It can be a useful tool for motivating employees, but it can also be misused to increase the formal procedures of an organization without contributing to the attainment of group goals.

A large element of successful management is the pattern of communications in an organization. The next module concentrates on communications and organizational development.

SELECTED BIBLIOGRAPHY FOR MODULE 3

BARNARD, CHESTER. *The Functions of the Executive.* Cambridge: Harvard University Press, 1938.

BERNE, ERIC. *Games People Play.* New York: Grove Press, 1964.

DRUCKER, PETER. *The Practice of Management.* New York: Harper and Row, 1954.

KAUFMAN, HERBERT. *The Forest Ranger.* Baltimore: Johns Hopkins University Press, 1960.

———. *Administrative Feedback.* Washington, D.C.: Brookings Institution, 1973.

LIKERT, RENSIS. *New Patterns of Management.* New York: McGraw-Hill, 1961.

MINTZBERG, HENRY. *The Nature of Managerial Work.* New York: Harper and Row, 1973.

ROSEN, ANNE. "Games Subordinates Play." *Supervisory Management* (1972): 1 – 8.

SAYLES, LEONARD. *Managerial Behavior.* New York: McGraw-Hill, 1964.

———. *Leadership: What Effective Managers Really Do . . . And How They Do It.* New York: McGraw-Hill, 1979.

SELZNICK, PHILIP. *Leadership in Administration.* New York: Harper and Row, 1957.

TANNENBAUM, R., and SCHMIDT, W. H., "How to Choose a Leadership Pattern." *Harvard Business Review* 36 (1958): 95 – 101.

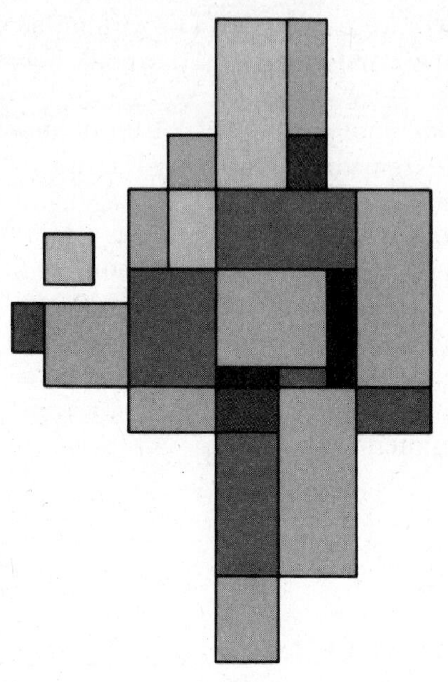

MODULE 4

Communications and Organizational Development

INTRODUCTION

Chester Barnard identified effective communications as the first task of the executive. Communications involve mutual understanding, the exchange of information, and the development of common goals.

Public organization, much more than private ones, are dependent upon their environment for survival and prosperity. Unless the outside world, including higher levels of the bureaucracy, clientele groups, responsible elected officials, and the general public, know what the organization is doing, an agency's continued existence may be in jeopardy.

Before concerning ourselves with external communications between the organization and its environment, let's consider *communications within the organization.* Think back to the Van Waters case. To what extent did the difficulties between McDowell and Van Waters result from a basic inability to communicate? Common action depends upon continuous communication. Unless individuals can communicate about organizational purposes and about the details of everyday activities, the organization will not be very effective.

INTRODUCTION TO TEAM BUILDING

Communication among individuals as individuals and as members of a group is recognized as an increasingly important component of effective organization. While such communication at the work group level is extremely important among individuals who have continuing contact (for example, in a supervisor-subordinate relationship), it is also important throughout the work group and the larger organization. An important part of this communication involves the development of a spirit of cooperation, similar to the "team spirit" that sports teams seek so assiduously. This spirit depends upon sociability and informal communications among group members.

The National Training Laboratory (NTL) in Bethel, Maine has a national reputation for helping individuals, including many top public and private management personnel, learn how to work better in small group situations. Sensitivity and T-group training, as these approaches are called, depend in large part upon building informal communications and feedback among group members. Feelings of ease and trust, which allow individuals to cooperate rather than work at cross purposes, develop from effective communication.

The National Training Laboratory began its first program of basic skill training groups during the summer of 1947. It was based upon developments in small group laboratory training and sensitivity training and later adopted the shortened reference term of T-group training. This recognition that the skills of operating in small groups could be learned and applied to work groups in everyday life has spawned the field of organizational development.

Organizational development (OD) is a broad approach to training and change in organizations that recognizes both individual needs and their relationship to the larger organization. OD usually involves the intervention of outside trainers to facilitate internal communications and feedback among group members. This diagnostic and learning approach has become a popular technique for improving the operation of public and private organizations.

At times small group approaches are criticized as being overindulgent. Many management specialists prefer to emphasize the development of "hard" management skills such as systems analysis. Others point out that focusing on interpersonal problems can exacerbate them. Some variants of small group approaches using physical contact have been criticized as "touchy, feely" exercises that contribute little to organizational coordination. While, no doubt, abuses of this training concept occur, establishing effective personal communication among group members is undoubtedly an important part of increasing work group effectiveness.

Building a work group is a process that ordinarily takes a long period of time. It is a central focus of supervisory responsibility and leadership skill. Coordination of group activity and motivation of individual members are two central aspects of management activity. But team building depends upon everyone in the group making an effort to work together and understand the other members. Organizations often try to help their members gain greater sensitivity to group dynamics, using exercises aimed at building group cohesion and communications. The following exercises are aimed at team building.

Exercise 1* — Triad Formation

Usually, when you begin working in a public organization, unless you are part of a new unit, you are thrust into a work group that has an ongoing history. Chances are that you will have little opportunity to define the relationships within the work group. In this exercise you will have the opportunity to participate in the formation of a work group to perform certain tasks and exercises. How would you bring together a group of people who are not well acquainted with one another?

Our group selection process will have two aspects: a method for randomly selecting individuals into groups, and a method for ensuring that individuals do not select their friends and acquaintances.

Each person will be given the number 1, 2, or 3. Then all the 1s, 2s, and 3s will form into groups in different corners of the room. Now each individual given the designation 1 will be asked to choose a partner from group 2 with whom he or she is least acquainted. The dyad formed by this step will then, after consultation, select a member of group 3 who is unknown to both. Some adjustment may be necessary if the groups choosing last are well acquainted with all the individuals not yet selected.

What are the grounds for selection? Which is more important — skills, personality, or appearance? Which do you have more information about?

Exercise 2 — Interpersonal Communication and Perception

Now, in each of the groups, person 3 will give a self-description, providing as much detail as possible, but taking no more than three minutes. Person 2 follows, then person 1. Then 2 and 1 will tell 3 what they heard. Similarly, 1 and 3 will tell 2 what they heard, and 2 and 3 will tell 1 what they heard.

Now a group discussion will take place about the outcome of Exercise 2. Were there any lapses of communication? Communication involves active interaction among all those involved. For a group to become cohesive and productive, the members must be aware of one another and understand one another. It helps if they can be forthright and trusting

---

*Exercises 1, 2, and 3 are based upon suggestions in J. William Pfeiffer and John E. Jones, *A Handbook of Structured Experiences for Human Relations Training*, vol. 1 (Iowa City, IA: University Associates, 1969, 1972), Exercises 1 and 2.

with one another, too. How far do you feel you could trust your group members? Would you allow them to babysit for your child or younger brother or sister? Would you allow them to use your car? Would you lend them your class notes for a day on which they were absent? Would you loan them $5? How much money would you loan them?

Exercise 3 — Groups of Six

Now each group of three will discuss which other group of three they would like to join to form a group of six. They will then invite another group to join them. Such an invitation may be declined. The last two remaining groups will form a group of six. If a triad remains, its members will be distributed among the existing groups of six.

What were some of the criteria used to select the remaining group members? Did the deliberate choice process of group creation build greater commitment and cohesivenesss than a strictly random process?

COMMENTS ON TEAM BUILDING

While team-building techniques are especially useful at the work group level, they also can be utilized within larger units. Interpersonal communications within the bureau, agency, and department as well as within the government are important. For example, often the merit principles of the civil service have been used as an excuse for refusing to recognize that public organizations require more than competent individuals. They need workers who know one another, enjoy one another, and understand one another. Otherwise, they cannot function as integrated units.

Business organizations have recognized this need and nurture it by providing opportunities for structured and unstructured interaction. Many companies organize retreats and conferences for employees to meet with one another. They encourage social events and many even supply free or reduced membership in country clubs to facilitate off-the-job interaction.

Unfortunately, public organizations spend considerably fewer resources in building interpersonal relations. In part they are hampered by the constraints of a cost-conscious public that often views conferences, meetings, and retreats as little more than padding of the public payroll. In part it is a failure to go beyond the concept of individual competence implicit in the civil service system.

Attention to communication among members of public organizations outside of the work group has nonetheless been on the rise. Because such organizations tend to be large and their central and field offices are often separated by great distances, they encounter a special problem of promoting communication and a sense of group identification. The impersonality of a bureaucracy that has offices throughout the country, as most federal departments do, presents a very real problem. The tendency to have uniform personnel practices that avoid special monetary and promotional rewards may hamper development of organizational commitment. The difficulty of fostering communications among the members of large nationwide, statewide, or even citywide bureaucracies is a major problem of public organizations and exacerbates the problem of morale development.

People like to know the people with whom they work, but unfortunately this becomes difficult in federal and state bureaucracies and even large city bureaucracies. Large private organizations in part deal with this problem by arranging for considerable regional mobility, at least on the part of top executives. But movement among regions for federal or state officials is less usual.

Nor have substitutes for face-to-face communication been effectively introduced in public organizations. Travel among different areas is considered a frill in times of limited agency budgets. Informal get-togethers or retreats are looked upon as suspect by the public, sometimes with justification. One development with considerable potential is the Federal Telecommunications System, which provides inexpensive telephone contact. Since its installation in 1965, it has greatly facilitated informal communication among federal personnel.

Communications among personnel within public organizations could benefit from greater resources. Unfortunately, the importance of communication in promoting organizational effectiveness has not yet been adequately recognized.

INTRODUCTION TO GOAL COMMUNICATION

Another area of communications that has received considerable attention in recent years relates to the goals of the organization. The social service supervisor in SUPSUB sought to communicate to the caseworker the organization's need for greater productivity. What would have been the best way of doing this? Should the supervisor have sent a copy of the memo stating this to the caseworkers under his or her supervision? Should a meeting have been called to discuss the memo? Or did the supervisor proceed correctly by working out the best plans with each individual?

One strength of management by objectives, the technique described in the last module, as a tool of supervision is that it requires communication between the supervisor and subordinate on a regular basis. Each supervisor works with each subordinate to set specific objectives for some time period, usually one year. These objectives derive from the organizational goals. This provides a systematic approach to communicating organizational goals and translating them into personal objectives. It is a tool in facilitating communication of goals within the organization and impressing them upon all members. Remember, communication is not enough, but it is a good start.

Management by objectives in both private and public organizations recognizes that communicating organizational goals to members and ensuring action consonant with them is a major part of running an organization effectively. But it can be dangerous to view that process of communication as inevitably moving from top to bottom. If a job of management is to motivate people, it is much easier if the people to be motivated are convinced that the goals of the organization are appropriate and worthwhile. Lower-level employees should be involved in goal-setting for the organization. Otherwise, goals may be developed that are incompatible with the training and orientation of the members of the organization. In any event, their involvement in goal-setting will help build their commitment. If time is available, go back to SUPSUB. Try it once more. To what extent were you able to improve your communication of the goals you wished to accomplish as supervisor? Is communication sufficient to accomplish these goals?

An example of the difficulties that can arise when communication of goals is incomplete is a situation involving management training of personnel in a large city's department of parks. A session was arranged to help implement a new program that was operating within the overall goals of the department. The new program involved a rating system for determining when a park was clean and in repair. As part of an effort to explain how the new rating system was related to the overall organizational goals, the department's previously articulated goals were set forth: to maintain clean parks, and to maintain parks with working facilities, such as park benches, playgrounds, and drinking fountains. The new system would allow top management to compare the cleanliness and repair of parks throughout the city.

Lower-level employees immediately began asking hard questions about the new rating system. They reserved their strongest criticism for the statement of organizational goals. They wanted to know why they had not been involved in its development. "If we go along with this system," they said, "we will be undermining what we consider to be a major goal of the department. We want the parks to look nice and inviting — aesthetically pleasing. If all we do is clean up papers and repair benches, we are not achieving our most important purpose."

Are you surprised to see that organizational goals were developed without communication with the lower levels of the organization? How would prior communication have altered receptivity to the new training program? Can you see why MBO encourages employee involvement in goal development?

The difficulty of arriving at goal agreement in public organizations depends upon the nature of the area and the level of abstraction. In some areas, value orientations may have a very marked effect on goal orientations of individuals.

Several years ago, the federal government decided that the administration of the welfare system should be changed to allow clerks rather than social workers to issue the checks. This introduced into the welfare bureaucracy a new group of workers, clerks, with major responsibility for issuing checks. Can you see the possibility that the perspectives of the clerks might be different from that of social workers? Many of the professional social workers viewed welfare as a minimal system to help the needy. Many of the clerks were more inclined to the view of the general public that welfare costs too much and is subject to abuse by people who should be paid as little as possible to discourage freeloading. Do you see how these different views of the goals of the system might lead to different consequences? Who was right?

An important part of leadership or management skill is gaining commitment to the goals of the organization. Obstacles are personal beliefs, professional training, and broader value orientations. Do you think that the students in this class have similar goals for this course in public organizations?

Exercise 4 – Ranking Goals

Try this exercise: bring to the next class a list of your three most important goals in taking this course, ranked in order of importance. While you're at it, consider an example of broader public policy focusing on our public welfare system. What, in your estimation, is the most important goal of the welfare system? In both cases, *please do not discuss your own views* with other members of the class.

In class, attempt to arrive at a common list of three course goals or one goal for the public welfare system within a ten-minute period. Compare the results of different groups. Would it be easy to obtain a general agreement? To what extent did group discussions bring about an agreement? Can you think of any other ways of gaining group consensus on goals? Must everyone agree on all goals all the time in order for a public organization to function? What are the consequences of goal disagreement?

NOTE ON ONGOING COMMUNICATIONS

Since the purpose of organization is to capitalize on the efforts of many, it is important that these efforts benefit from mutual reinforcement. A feeling of group togetherness and pursuit of common goals are important beginnings, but a public organization cannot function effectively without ongoing communications about organizational activity.

A group of fire fighters do not want to waste time raising ladders to trapped individuals while others are leading them to safety through the building. Police officers do not want to risk a car crash while converging from different directions on a one-way street to catch a fleeing suspected bank robber. Local welfare officials in two different sections of one city do not want to be paying benefits to the same person who is collecting benefits in two other cities while fully employed and paying withholding taxes to the federal government. It may make little sense to construct new highways in a metropolitan area that is attempting to encourage the use of mass transit.

Public organizations depend upon communication to avoid needless conflict. In an organization where common agreement on goals exists and relationships among individuals are cordial, informal communication about organizational matters will flow naturally. A group of fire fighters will reach informal agreements as to the procedures to follow, how to inform other members of the crew about decisions, and who should make spot decisions in an emergency. Similarly, police officers working in the same precinct will have arrived at such agreements. In fact, the need for split-second decisions to avoid conflict is part of the reason that police and fire departments tend to adopt strict hierarchical authority structures, often patterned on military bureaucracies. The need for communication and decision helps structure informal cooperation into formal structures and procedures.

Communication Networks — Formal and Informal

Every work group relies upon a variety of communication networks, both formal and informal. Communication is the essence of group activity, since it is the basis for common action. Unless group members communicate, they cannot act together. Since organizations are people working together, communications take the form that people prefer and find natural. Informal communications take precedence because they flow from the development of personal relationships. Informal communications have the added advantage of maintaining greater independence for individual action. Formal communication tends to be written down, becoming a permanent part of the group life. It tends to place limits on individual behavior. Bureaucratic organizations, as we have learned previously, are in part characterized by the formalization of the communication process. This tension between the individual desire to maintain informal communications and the organizational need for a formal communication network creates continuing conflict in organizations.

Communication in public organizations that involves more than the immediate work group tends to take on a more formal character. Although informal communications will exist in which individuals of different work groups communicate on an informal basis, formal communication tends to play a more important part. The sociability that characterizes many work groups and that is an important stimulus for informal communications tends to diminish in the larger organization. Informal relationships that are maintained tend to be nurtured particularly for their informational value. Individuals at different levels in the organization realize that informal contacts are important in providing a steady stream of information about the organization. These supplement formal communications, which may not necessarily reflect what is really going on because of their written, permanent, accessible form.

Formal communications, as part of a permanent record, are often quite accessible. Sometimes access to formal reports can be limited, especially when they are part of an intelligence function by which some part of the organization is concerned with gathering sensitive information. In this instance, a system of clearances will be established to decide who should have access to what information.

Public organizations often favor formal communications because they are written, permanent, and accessible. Such characteristics greatly facilitate public scrutiny. An outgrowth of this tendency is the recent emphasis on freedom of information laws, which give citizens the right to obtain copies of government records. The so-called sunshine laws, requiring public bodies to meet in sessions open to public view, is further evidence of this. Does the tendency of public organizations to favor written and accessible communications have any undesirable consequences? Is it possible to completely do away with informal communications in public bureaucracies? Would it be a good idea to do so?

Formal procedures, which become part of organizational practice, are usually committed to writing, and are made legitimate by the command structure of the bureaucracy, have many advantages over informal procedures. They become part of the regular practices of the bureaucracy, to be followed on a routine basis. However, they also tend to make the bureaucratic structure rigid.

Informal communication has great advantages in generating more spontaneous action, allowing for greater flexibility and increasing the responsibility of individual members of the organization. But it requires closer relationships within the group and is often impractical in larger organizations. Also, it makes tracking particular decisions much more difficult. The preference in public organizations is for formal communications patterns, but informal ones will always exist. And often they are more important in determining what an organization and its members actually do.

Formal communication patterns are often closely related to the authority structure of the organization. For purposes of monitoring and controlling subordinate behavior, supervisors often require a flow of communications. These communications include reports of activities and clearances on documents. These formal procedures are a way of keeping the upper levels of the organization apprised of activities at the lower level and ensuring that individual organizational members are not making contradictory decisions.

The need for one level of the bureaucracy to know what another level is doing or for the central headquarters to know what the field officers are doing is a compelling one in public organizations. The federal government, in particular, has many agencies with headquarters in Washington, D.C. and field offices in many parts of the country. How can the central headquarters know what is happening in the field offices? You may recognize this as part of the more general management problem of monitoring what is happening in the organization. Herbert Kaufman's approach to this problem was discussed in the preceding module.

Clearance procedures are an especially valuable tool in establishing authority relationships within the organization. As we have mentioned before, a good deal of organizational activity involves decision making, and decision making almost inevitably involves the exercise of discretion. Individuals must decide how to use this discretion. In order to ensure equitable decisions, many written communications will require clearances before they are actually sent to their destination. Such a system of clearances will reflect the authority structure of the organization. Some organizations consider the system of clearances so important that they establish a documents control section, which must approve every document distributed. A documents control section may also be given responsibility for checking communications for clarity and style in presentation.

Disadvantages of Formal Communications Procedures

While formal communications may facilitate coordination of organizational activity, it may also inhibit organizational activity. For the time it takes to write each additional report, some employee is prevented from working on organizational goals. For each additional clearance that some document must receive, a decision is delayed. Also, the more individuals who must approve some decision, the greater likelihood that it will be vetoed by someone.

In their efforts to achieve coordination and adhere to proper protocol, public organizations often make communications proliferate. "Red Tape" is the common cry of citizens who seek to qualify for some program or achieve some government clearance and find that yet one more approval is needed.

Communications that result in "red tape" are a prime example of the costs of communications. While the need for communications is great, too much of a good thing can be counterproductive. Another way of stating this is that communications have their costs. While the organization is communicating, it cannot be doing other things. Formal communication networks may detract from the effectiveness of the public organization in achieving its goals.

Formal communications also may have distorting effects. As information passes through more and more channels, it tends to become misinterpreted and misread. One advantage of flat organizations over highly structured, hierarchical organizations is the minimization of communications passing through multiple layers of the bureaucracy. Such communications are subject to distortion and delay.

A potent argument against hierarchy and large organizations in general is the need to limit communications costs. As organizations increase in size and complexity, the costs of internal communications increase dramatically. For this reason, the creation of bureaucracy is a costly enterprise and should not be undertaken without some compelling need. It is not always easy to find the happy medium, where communication ensures coordination and eliminates unnecessary delay.

INTRODUCTION TO EXTERNAL COMMUNICATIONS

If effective communication within a public organization is critical, communication with the outside world is equally important. Public organizations exist to respond to the needs and demands of the outside world and they must be continually adapting to changes in these needs and demands. They also expect the outside world to abide by their decisions; therefore, they must communicate their findings and policies. The very operation of public organizations depends upon a constant flow of information to the outside world and back to the organization. For example, unless a school system knows what job openings exist, it cannot provide the proper training. Unless fire fighters know the condition of a burning building, they cannot do their job well. Unless legislators know what citizens think about abortion and drug use, they cannot formulate politically feasible solutions to these problems. The exchange of information is critical to the operation of any public organization.

But the need for information flow between public organizations and the outside world has other purposes, too. Since public organizations depend upon the support of clientele, elected leaders, appointed officials, and the general public, unless they provide information justifying support, they may find themselves out of business. Furthermore, many public organizations are involved in fields where knowledge is constantly changing. In these situations, the need for information about new developments is an important concern. Communication between public organizations and the outside world, then, is a mutual relationship that both seek and need.

Intergovernmental Communications

Since public organizations are part of a larger governmental structure, their day-to-day relationships are intertwined with other public organizations. They must be constantly in touch with parts of their own agency or department as well as other agencies and departments of their own and other levels of government. Because of the existence of national, state, and local governments, agencies often must be concerned not only with their own agency but with those that may have overlapping jurisdiction.

In order to obtain better communications among differing public organizations, interagency task forces are sometimes established, as well as intergovernmental coordinating groups. The Councils of Governments (COGS) are federally sanctioned mechanisms to obtain cooperation among local governmental units in metropolitan areas where the need for communication may be extremely compelling.

A large part of the work of elected executives and higher appointed bureaucrats is to achieve coordination among component organizations. The need for coordination, in response to the proliferation of governmental units, has led to increasing reliance upon enlarged staffs at the executive level of government. Presidents, governors, and mayors have developed elaborate staff mechanisms for achieving this coordination. Of special importance in coordinating communications is the budget office. The federal Office of Management and Budget, functioning within the executive office of the president of the United States, has made special efforts to achieve coordination among diverse governmental units. Their efforts relating to federal grant programs provide an interesting example of how a formal mechanism for communication develops in response to the need for coordinating government activity.

In the period since the end of the Second World War, government grant programs have increased dramatically. Most federal agencies administer some program that provides funds to local governmental units. Most local governmental units receive funds from diverse sources within the state and federal governments. This complex and overlapping reality means that grant programs may be working at cross purposes rather than toward common ends. For example, one federal agency may grant funds to a county for major highway expansion at the same time that another agency grants funds for a mass transportation project that seeks to reduce highway use. Another federal agency could grant monies for job training programs that are already being offered by local high schools. Another federal agency might grant urban renewal funds to the same area that is being designated for preservation by a local government agency.

To minimize the chances of government grant programs working at cross purposes, the federal Office of Management and Budget issued circular A – 95 on July 24, 1969, implementing sections of the Intergovernmental Cooperation Act. Circular A – 95 requires that state and local agencies applying for federal assistance notify state and regional clearinghouses of their action.

This governmental policy, mandated by the Office of Management and Budget, has its counterpart in many specific programs that require approval from state and federal agencies that may be specifically involved in similar programs. But the proliferation of the need for written clearances may lead to delay, undermining the purpose. Bureaucratic red tape at it again. In an effort to achieve greater coordination and ensure that government does not work against itself, programs may be delayed or never implemented because of failure or delay in obtaining approvals. Care must be taken that formal communications such as these clearance procedures do not end up subverting the goals of the public organization. Formal communication networks that are intended to further organizational goals can become, instead, one more impediment.

Organizations' Relationships with Elected Officials

Public organizations also have a special relationship to elected executives and legislators who approve top agency personnel, provide financial resources, and determine their basic organization. In seeking to develop and protect their support, public organizations go out of their way to respond to elected officials. This is the basis for the effectiveness of Congressmen and state legislators in dealing with administrative difficulties. An individual may have difficulty in getting an agency to respond. But if a legislator calls a situation to the attention of the agency, a response is more likely. The agency may at some juncture need that legislator's vote for an appropriation or some new legislation. Agencies know that it is best to cultivate and protect their support within the legislature. Of course, a similar relationship exists with elected executives. Since the agency officials may in fact depend upon the elected executives for their job in addition to their budget, they will be quite solicitous of their requests.

In addition to processing complaints from elected officials, the agency will go to considerable lengths to impress elected officials with their ability and need for support. Letters may go out to individual legislators soliciting their support, informal briefings will be held, and tours may be arranged. The efforts of the Pentagon to impress legislators with trips to installations around the world is well known and sometimes of questionable propriety.

Federal agencies are particularly solicitous of certain Congressional committee chairpersons who control legislation pertaining to their agencies, particularly appropriation legislation. Often strong informal relationships will develop between committee leaders and agency heads, bypassing ties between agencies and the elected executive. Such institutions as the Army Corps of Engineers are notorious for their ability to work directly with the legislature and to bypass the elected executive. Is such a development more or less democratic? Is legislative accountability preferable to executive accountability? What distinguishes relationships of accountability from those of mere mutual back-scratching?

While the tendency of bureaucratic organizations and their leaders is to formalize communications with elected officials through periodic written reports, almost inevitably informal communications develop. Elected officials often seek to influence the direction of agency activity and obtain special consideration for projects that may benefit individuals or groups to whom they are indebted. One form such informal communication takes is the "contract" by which elected leaders seek special consideration or a favor, usually in return for continued support of the agency.

An interesting development among American public organizations is the institution of a formal mechanism for communication between public organizations and elected officials through the establishment of lobbying offices. Such a practice is particularly evident at the state and national levels, where local governmental units will often hire full-time employees to represent their interests before Congress and the state legislatures. This representation may extend to the higher executive levels as well.

Communicating with Clientele Groups

The need for influencing decisions at higher levels of government, which gives rise to lobbying efforts on behalf of public organizations, is also directly linked to the concern for building clientele relationships. Perhaps the most constant flow of information is directed toward clientele groups, those individuals who are the recipients of agency action.

The Bureau of Motor Vehicles, for example, might need to inform drivers of a change in registration fees or a change in speeding regulations and penalties. When the clientele group is large, communication will often take place through the media: newspapers, television, and radio. Direct mailing may be used when the costs can be kept low, leaflets may be printed up and posted or distributed in public places.

Where agencies set formal policies and regulations, they will appear in an official publication. Federal regulations are printed in the *Federal Register.* Similarly, government requests for bids on equipment and services are printed in specified publications.

Often meetings, public hearings, or informal briefings will be called by agencies to inform clientele groups of new policy. Where clientele groups maintain continuing relationships with an agency, they may be brought in to help develop new policies. Informal contacts will also reinforce and facilitate these relationships.

Sometimes the consultation between agencies and clientele groups becomes more formal and institutions are created to accomplish this. Advisory groups often have the purpose of institutionalizing contact between agencies and clientele groups. Such groups, in addition to providing communication, are very valuable in providing support to the agencies. Particularly when the agency must compete with other agencies for funding before elected or appointed officials, the support of clientele groups will be a great help.

Communicating with the Public

Public organizations direct special attention to other agencies, elected officials, and clientele groups. But they are also concerned with their general impact on public opinion. Increasingly, government officials are conscious of the need to undertake systematic public relations efforts.

While it is clear how the environment of public organizations and their very rationale leads to public relations efforts, some basic questions remain unresolved. At what point do public relations efforts become self-serving and directed at the perpetuation of bureaucracy, rather than at serving the public interest? At what point is the use of public funds to mold the opinions of others, including high-level officials, an illegitimate enterprise? On the other hand, when public organizations must operate in an area where private organizations operate too, what rules should govern their efforts? For example, can a federal agency advertise its findings about smoking and lung cancer? Can it force cigarette companies to modify their advertising? What should the role of the government be in espousing a particular point of view about the nature of the energy crisis? Can private energy companies compete with federal resources?

Can the federal government compete with private resources? Should it?

Recently, a great deal of controversy centered on a decision by the City University of New York to spend a sum of money on a public relations campaign to improve its image. Was this a legitimate expenditure? Does it make a difference if the money was privately raised? How can the City University compete with other public sector and private sector institutions without a considerable public relations effort?

The extent to which public funds should be spent in attempts to influence public opinion is subject to dispute. But the need to project a suitable public image is recognized by most public officials.

A manager's ability to deal with problems of external communications is an important determinant of success in public organizations. As a way of developing your own abilities in this area, try the exercises below.

In-Basket Exercises*

In-basket exercises are a useful technique for improving management skills. They may be applied to almost any position in an organization and are particularly useful in today's world when paper flow is so pervasive an aspect of operating organizations. One of the ways of cutting bureaucratic red tape is by directing paper flow in more effective ways.

After you have completed the series of exercises, discuss the differing solutions. What makes for effective handling of written communications? What kind of written responses contribute to a resolution of problems? What kind just add to the bureaucratic red tape?

IN-BASKET INSTRUCTIONS

A. INSTRUCTIONS

Please place yourself in the position of LaMar G. Harris, Executive Director of the Hampshire Community Development Program. Respond to each of the ten items in your in-basket correspondingly.

Do not tell what you would do—do it. If you would choose to write a letter to Mr. Elwood Brown about his proposed ''Teenagers Trash Removal Project,'' actually write the letter and sign your name to it.

Do not write on the in-basket materials.

When you finish your response to an item, fasten it to the in-basket correspondence to which it refers and place it back in your envelope.

---

*Reprinted from J. William Pfeiffer and John E. Jones, eds., *A Handbook of Structured Experiences for Human Relations Training,* Vol. I (San Diego: University Associates Press, 1970). Used with permission.

B. Introduction to the Hampshire Community Development Program

Hampshire is a community of 150,000 and is located in the industrial section of the coal-rich state of Lincoln. Hampshire has doubled its population during the past twenty years due to the influx of industry following the war. Much of this population explosion has been Southern European immigrants, Mexican migrant farm workers looking for stable working conditions, and an increasingly large group of Southern Blacks who are drawn to industrial jobs in the North.

You were chosen Executive Director two years ago when the former Executive Director, a retired state legislator and native of Hampshire, was suddenly paralyzed by a stroke. He had been in the position only eleven months and had been the first Executive Director for CDP during its initial struggles. You are Black. You were raised in New York and come from a West Indian background, of genteel, if relatively poor, parents who believed strongly in education. You have a B.A. from Syracuse University in Psychology and an M.A. from CCNY in Urban Studies. You had planned to go on for a doctorate, but your wife became pregnant. Your adviser at CCNY heard about this opening in the CDP agency in Hampshire and suggested that you go for an interview. Although you were better qualified than other applicants, you were also the only Black interviewed, and you are well aware that your color was a deciding factor in their offering you the position. You accepted the position with some reluctance, but you decided that practical experience in your field would be valuable. You now plan to stay a third year before returning to school. Your wife has accepted a teaching positon and most of her salary will be saved to enable you to return to graduate school full-time. You spent four years in the Air Force between your B.A. and M.A., and you are now thirty-one years old.

Information about your personnel director and your director of research and planning are included in the following section. Other members of your staff include two social workers, four secretaries, and a general office staff of three. You also employ two nursery school supervisors, a thrift shop manager, three recreation directors, six assistant recreation directors, and the usual staffing for youth centers.

Today is Saturday. You have just returned from a CDP Directors' Conference in Washington and while stopping by for your mail, you decide to clean up your in-basket in preparation for what you know will be an exhausting week.

Your secretary, Minnie, is in the outer office, but no other staff member is about.

C. Key Personnel of HCDP

Secretary to the Executive Director: Minnie Brown

She is an inheritance from the former Executive Director and is extremely valuable to you because of her Hampshire background and her knowledge of CDP history. She is a fifty-seven-year-old widow with a wit as sharp as her secretarial skills, and has always made you very comfortable in dealing with her.

Personnel Director: William H. Stanley

He is forty-six, married, with two children in high school. His wife's maiden name was Hampshire, but all that remains of her formerly wealthy background is expensive tastes. Stanley came to Hampshire to join his uncle's law firm but neglected his practice to keep up with the social whirl he was rushed into as a promising young bachelor. Two disastrous campaigns for state legislature and the death of his uncle finally led him to working as a tax accountant until he was hired by CDP. Stanley is reasonably effective in his job, but has a great need for ego satisfaction. He was sure that he would be appointed Executive Director, and had, in fact, taken over on his own volition for the three month period between executive directors.

Planning and Research Director: Henry ''Hank'' Snowell

He is thirty-eight and unmarried. He has a B.A. in sociology from Union State College in Wheelwright, Lincoln. He also has sixteen hours of graduate credit in social work which was completed during summers and evenings. Before his present position, he had been the assistant manager of a shoe store, where he had worked during the summers of his undergraduate days. His real interest, however, was working for his church, the Pentecostal Tabernacle, and for the YMCA, as a volunteer youth group organizer. His satisfactions from this volunteer work came through the self-appointed social work which he performed with Black and Mexican teenagers. He was well-known in Hampshire for his success with molding street gangs into productive project clubs. He feels some frustration in that his position does not allow him to work closely with the people involved in CDP programs.

IN-BASKET ITEM NO. 1

July 18, 1970
Box 285
Lukesville

Dear Mr. Harris,

You'll probably think it's funny, getting a letter from a guy in prison but Rev. Phillips our chaplin said it was worth a try.

I have served three and a half years on a ten year sentence for armed robbery and am about to be put on parole. I was only in the car with the guys that done it but we all got busted and I guess it was my good luck as well as bad luck to go to prison. Rev. Phillips got a hold of me right after I got here and really showed me how to put myself together. I had really known I was headed the wrong way in high school when Hank Snowell who I heard works for you now was down at the Y all the time getting the guys together to do projects. He really knew what he was talking about, even the religion part, but I was too stubborn to let myself be talked into it. Anyway I have grown up a lot in the last three years and a half and I think I would now like to work with kids the way Hank did and maybe show them how to get more out of their lives than prison. I have been a trustee for two years and have been incharge of basketball, baseball and swimming here. I know all about handling equipment and how to run things for recreation.

I am asking you to consider me for a job with HCDP when I get out if you need any recreation people. I guess there is nothing I'd rather do and could do a better job at.

Yours truly,

Fred Kleyer

IN-BASKET ITEM NO. 2

STANDARD WHOLESALE FOODS INC.

1850 Central, Hampshire, Lincoln
Abe Strauss, Owner and Manager
"We Go Whole Hog for Our Customers"

July 20, 1970

LaMar G. Harris
Executive Director
Community Development Program
120 E. State Street
Hampshire, Lincoln 11543

Dear Mr. Harris:

As a man who has a vital interest in the progress of Hampshire, I wish to express my admiration for the fine work you and your staff are doing for that unfortunate segment of our population who suffer from the heavy load of poverty. Believe me, as a man who came to this country at age twelve with nothing in my pockets but one American dollar and my mother's picture, I can appreciate how much your program must mean to these people.

I have been proud to be a part of your Hot Lunch program by supplying you with the most nourishing food at as reasonable a wholesale price as you would find anywhere in this country. By me, I get the pleasure of contributing something worthwhile, while at the same time increasing my volume of sales. I would like the opportunity of expressing my thanks to you in the best way an old ''neighborhood grocer'' knows how. Please drop by my office and pick up a nice Virginia ham for you and your wife.

Sincerely yours,

Abe Strauss

AS/jbc

IN-BASKET ITEM NO. 3

HAMPSHIRE HOUSE MERCANTILE

Est. 1861 *"Hampshire's oldest and finest department store"*
Home Owned — Julius M. Ruggles, President

Credit Department
July 20, 1970

LaMar G. Harris
Executive Director
Community Development Program
120 E. State Street
Hampshire, Lincoln 11543

Dear Sir:

We understand you employ a Mr. William H. Stanley as your Personnel Director. We feel you should call Mr. Stanley's attention to the fact that his account with Hampshire House is severely in arrears. There have been no payments of any amount paid to us since May 12, 1970. At that time we informed Mr. Stanley that any further charges to his account would not be authorized. In the past two months Mrs. Stanley has made three unauthorized charge purchases totaling 473.00. This brings their account to 2,356.23, or 1,356.23 over their maximum authorization.

As the Stanleys and Mrs. Stanley's family have been steady customers since this store was established, we have hesitated to embarass them by taking the obvious steps; however, we now feel that we have gone beyond our capacity to accept further neglect of this financial responsibility. If substantial payment is not made by August 1, 1970, we will be forced to turn over the account to a collection agency.

Thank you for your co-operation.

Yours truly,

Monroe J. Ruggles

Monroe J. Ruggles
Credit Manager

MJR/tt

IN-BASKET ITEM NO. 4

1919 Bedlow Street
Hampshire, Lincoln
July 21, 1970

LaMar Harris
Supervisor
HCDP
120 E. State
Hampshire, Lincoln

Dear Sir:

I am writing as a concerned Catholic mother. My son Anthony and my daughter Anna attend your recreation center on 8th Avenue after school and the Saturday night dances. Many of my friends children from St. Francis Parish also attend and they are behind me writing this letter. We feel that the recreation center idea is fine because it gives our children a place to go without running in the streets which is important to parents of teenagers. But what we want to know is why your recreation director, Mr. Glassing and your assistant director, Miss Borden as well as two pin setters in the bowling alley and the girl who is the snack bar waitress all have to come from the Pentecostal Tabernacle church. We know for a fact that these people invite our children to their church groups and even Sunday school. Miss Borden asked my daugher if she was "saved". The parents of St. Francis parish call that religious bias and even though they aren't as many Catholics who go to the recreation center as protestants, we understand that CDP was trying to help minority groups, not to force them under the influence of holy rollers!

The Catholic parents of St. Francis parish are asking that our Civil rights of religious freedom be given to our children. Leave religion out of your recreation program and also who you hire to work there. Can't a Catholic girl serve hot dogs and cokes as well as a Pentecostal Tabernacle girl?

Sincerely yours,

Marge O'Neill

IN-BASKET ITEM NO. 5

Standard Form 63
November 1961
GSA FPMR (41 CFR) 101-11.6

MEMORANDUM OF CALL

Date: 7-21-70
Time: 1:PM

TO—
Mr. Harris

☒ YOU WERE CALLED BY— ☐ YOU WERE VISITED BY—

Dan Thompson
Chief of Police

TELEPHONE:	Number or code 546-7708	Extension 236

☐ PLEASE CALL
☐ WILL CALL AGAIN
☐ RETURNING YOUR CALL
☐ IS REFERRED TO YOU BY:
☐ WAITING TO SEE YOU
☐ WISHES AN APPOINTMENT

Left This Message: The old grafter wants to set a trap for some ''pot pushers'' he thinks are hanging around the McGeorge St. Rec. center. Wants to plant young detectives among the kids; also has a kid who's going to point them out.

Received by mb

63-107 ★ U.S. GOVERNMENT PRINTING OFFICE: 1967 OF—275-003

IN-BASKET ITEM NO. 6

7-19-70

LaMar--

Harold Turkman came in to see me today and offered us all his old exercise equipment from the Bavarian Spa and Gym that folded a few months ago. Naturally he wants to use it as a tax write-off. We could use the stuff for the basement gym we're setting up in the old PS 47 grade school. Marion Jackson would also like a couple of things for her Slim Gym classes. I don't know if you want to deal with Turkman, of course. Whatever you decide, I told him it would come officially from you.

Hank

IN-BASKET ITEM NO. 7A

Mr. Harris--

Mr. Glen Otis, our distinguished advisory board president, came by here yesterday with this ugly little piece from the evening paper and asked you to field it. He has received at least a dozen phone calls about it since yesterday morning and is more than a little disturbed about it.

This Jonquil character is a frustrated social climber and general ''bad mouth'' concerning any Republican administration, but he is also fairly well known and respected enough to make things uncomfortable for us with this letter.

Minnie

IN-BASKET ITEM NO. 7B

HAMPSHIRE CHRONICLE

To the Editor of the Hampshire Chronicle:

It is my unfortunate duty as a citizen of Hampshire, a city of unusual integrity, to alert the good people who make this their home that once again, we have been plundered by one of the devious, greedy organizations who ask our money in the name of Christian charity and then line their own pockets, neglecting those they are alleged to be helping. Such an organization is CDP, yet another attempt by the government to pacify the underprivileged and allow our consciences to rest while the true plight of the poverty stricken and alienated minority is muffled by the back-slapping of self-satisfied administrators of so-called "programs." True, it is a government supported organization and therefore gleans our money through taxes; however, we are still, in the end, being fleeced of our charitable contributions.

We are not so naive as to miss the fact that the federal government spends wastefully, particularly on such "worthwhile" schemes as CDP. What has CDP done with this bountiful gift of Hampshire taxpayers' hard earned money? Has it built teenage centers which would be the pride of this community with every possible piece of equipment and physical facility? Has it provided new classrooms for its Headstart Program and hired the finest, best qualified teachers? Has it even drawn from our local supply of qualified men to make its administrators; men who know and understand the problems to be faced in Hampshire? The answer is no, to all points. A brief visit to any of the recreation centers will reveal that they have been converted from older buildings, probably long since condemned, such as the old PS 47 grade school, and are supplied with makeshift equipment and questionable people as staff. Certainly the children in Headstart should get a better place of learning than the Creamery basement or the unused corners of Jefferson Junior High. And who are they hiring to assist these children in learning? Not my wife, for example, a college graduate with two years of elementary school experience. No, citizens, the assistant at the Creamery Headstart program is a woman who had an eighth grade education and had been on welfare before she was hired. Her lack of qualifications is certainly no fault of hers, but they do give CDP an opportunity to pay a much smaller salary to her than they would to my wife. All this is run, not by a local man, but an import from New York, with a fancy education, who they thought would look good in the job because of his race.

Surely he has no personal interest in Hampshire. True, the assistant directors are local men, or at least they've lived here for a few years. Of course one is too busy at cocktail parties to take time to understand those not in his social set. His wife, by the way, has never dressed better.

The usual method of milking our tax dollars is through kick-backs from local contractors and wholesale suppliers. I do not have the information at this time to indicate exactly how it is being done, but what we must conclude is that large amounts of Government money are not finding their way to the minority groups CDP is supposed to serve, but to the pockets of CDP administrators. Neighbors of Hampshire, are we again too apathetic to root out these spoilers of tax money? Wake up and write your Congressman!

Hector Jonquil, CPA

IN-BASKET ITEM NO. 8

OFFICE OF THE MAYOR
CITY OF HAMPSHIRE

July 19, 1970

LaMar G. Harris
Executive Director
Community Development Program
120 E. State Street
Hampshire, Lincoln

Dear LaMar:

Millie and I were so pleased that you and Clairissa could make it to our Fourth of July Gala this year. It has become a real tradition for us in the past seven years and we were so disappointed last summer when you had to be out of town.

Millie was terribly impressed with all you said about the workings of CDP. She's very big on "causes," you know, and has really taken CDP to her heart since the Fourth. I might add that you and Bill Stanley make quite a team!

Bill informs us that there will be an opening on the Advisory Board of CDP beginning in September. I needn't tell you that Millie sees that as an ideal way for her to help share in the projects that CDP is accomplishing so well. Of course, her associations with other leading civic groups, etc., could provide a terrific liaison among Hampshirites who take their civic duties seriously and make CDP all the more effective.

Bill may have already discussed this with you. I'm sure Sara has put the bug in his ear since she and Millie are inseparable bridge partners.

Let me know how you think that Advisory Board position is shaping up. You probably have a lot of well qualified people in mind, but it never hurts to put in a plug for the little woman. She has an awful lot of influence as I discovered during two successful Mayoral campaigns.

Sincerely,

John E. Jacobs

JEJ/pep

IN-BASKET ITEM NO. 9

BENEVOLENT ORDER OF BOHEMIANS
Chapter No. 14
Hampshire, Lincoln

July 21, 1970

LaMar G. Harris
Executive Director
Community Development Program
120 E. State Street
Hampshire, Lincoln

Dear Sir:

As a member of a minority group with the same struggles, hopes, and frustrations as any other minority group, I find it difficult not to resent the fact that Bohemians have been ignored by such organizations as yours. True, we are much fewer in number than the Negro minority or the Mexican minority, but nevertheless, we daily suffer indignities which the Community Development Program is, in theory, attempting to eradicate. Our neglect goes even deeper. Not one man or woman of Bohemian background has ever been employed by CDP even though many families in Chapter Fourteen of the B.O.B. are below the income level set by your organization as a criterion for hiring. Not a single Bohemian pre-schooler has been admitted to your Headstart Program nor has any real attempt been made to make our children feel welcome at your recreation centers.

To favor any one minority group over another is to fail in your purpose, as I see it. Your cooperation would be greatly appreciated in the next month when children are preparing to return to school. Bohemian children have often been the target of verbal ethnic slurs and vicious ethnic "jokes". We all know how cruel children can be. Perhaps CDP could influence the educators of Hampshire to shoulder their duty to see that this kind of discrimination be put to a stop. Bohemians are going to be a part of this "Community" for a long time, and we want some "Development" now.

Sincerely yours,

James E Kolachi

James E. Kolachi
President
B.O.B. #14

IN-BASKET ITEM NO. 10

326 Jackson Boulevard
Hampshire, Lincoln
July 19, 1970

Dear Mr. Harris,

I feel obliged to write to you concerning my niece, Miss Ameila Mae Dillon. One of your staff members at the McGeorge Street Recreation Center, Eddy Daniels, who is one of the big shot directors there, has taken liberties with Miss Dillon and now she finds herself going to have a baby. She has worked at the McGeorge Street Recreation Center for five months as table games assistant, and though she's in charge of those games she ain't much more than a teenager herself in fact the same age as some of them. Is this the kind of man you are trusting teenagers with who would take advantage of a young girl after the Center was closed? I realize that it takes two and Amelia is not all innocent, but she said she loved him and now him saying it was probably one of the boys who hang out there at the Saturday night dances. Amelia has turned nineteen and wouldn't be fooling around with those younger boys, even if some of them do look older.

Mr. Harris, you are a colored man too and know that things ain't always easy for us, even when you can get a job mostly. Well, Amelia's mother is sick and can't work and her husband is long since gone. If Amelia can't work with a baby coming, I don't know what they'll do as there are four other children younger in the family. Lord knows I can't take them all in with my husband only getting unemployment money. Her mother wouldn't write to you but I believe that something should be done, and right now about Eddie Daniels messing around with young girls. You make it clear to him that he has to support that child.

Yours truly,

Lucy Jackson

COMMENT ON IN-BASKET EXERCISES

As you look back on your response to the in-basket exercises, try to assess your ability to handle external communications. Can you provide illustrations of the peculiar nature of public organizations and their concerns? Were you able to use your knowledge of public organizations in responding to these situations?

In Item 1, how was your response affected by the fact that you were handling an inquiry to a public organization with a particular responsibility for community development?

In Item 2, how was your perspective affected by the ethics of public organizations?

In Item 3, how did you balance the competing concerns of your agency's reputation and your employee's privacy and rights under the civil service regulations?

In Item 4, how does the religious dimension and religious diversity affect your action?

In Item 5, what are the competing considerations of protecting your agency image and avoiding possible charges of interfering with a drug investigation?

In Item 6, do the tax write-offs pose a problem?

In Item 7, were you able to defend your agency against charges of favoritism, kickbacks, and patronage?

In Item 8, would you take the mayor's advice?

In Item 9, how do you deal with the assertive ethnic group?

In Item 10, how do you respond to sex in the office and how is your perspective affected by your agency's position?

NOTE ON GATHERING INFORMATION

Public organizations need to provide other organizations, agencies, elected officials, and the public with information about their operations. They also need to gather information about the operation of other organizations. In part, this is a function of the struggle for survival in a political environment. An agency must know what its competitors are doing, what elected officials think, and what the public believes.

Every member of a public organization is in part responsible for making it aware of the developments in the larger world. Certain individuals will be designated to undertake this responsibility as part of their official duties.

This need to gather information about the outside world extends beyond the immediate survival needs of a bureaucracy in a competitive and changing world. Many public organizations operate in fields in which the state of knowledge is changing rapidly. As part of the development and maintenance of their expertise, bureaucrats must stay in touch constantly with the burgeoning knowledge in their fields. If individuals operate within a hospital or school or a rapidly developing field like space, this obligation and necessity is obvious. Like experts in other fields, government bureaucrats must read scholarly and professional publications and attend meetings and conferences to keep up with their fields.

A large part of government activity involves policymaking or rule making, which will be described in the following modules. One of the important questions being discussed about the operation of public organizations is how to ensure that when making these determinations, bureaucrats have the most up-to-date and relevant information. The ability of public organizations to acquire and use new knowledge in the policymaking process is an important problem and one which needs considerably more attention.

In some cases, government bureaus may be set up especially to take part in the development of scientific knowledge. The National Science Foundation and the National Institute of Health are prime examples of public organizations set up to help develop knowledge. Other government agencies may set up mechanisms to disseminate knowledge.

Finally, some public organizations are created for the very purpose of gathering information. Often referred to as intelligence agencies, especially when concerned with the gathering of military and defense information relating to a military adversary, these public organizations are judged by their ability to gather information from diverse sources.

In *The Nerves of Government,* Karl Deutsch has described government as a steering mechanism dependent upon the flow of communications. Certainly communications is a basic component of effective government, and government officials need to be sensitive to the enormous importance of information transfer.

As the development of knowledge and the means for disseminating innovations accelerate, public organizations must respond. No public servant can be effective without a comprehensive understanding of communications and how it affects the context of organization activity.

SELECTED BIBLIOGRAPHY FOR MODULE 4

ARGYRIS, CHRIS. *Personality and Organization.* New York: Harper and Row, 1957.

BARNARD, CHESTER. *The Functions of the Executive.* Cambridge: Harvard University Press, 1938.

CATER, DOUGLAS. *The Fourth Branch of Government.* Boston: Houghton Mifflin, 1959.

DEUTSCH, KARL. *The Nerves of Government.* New York: Free Press, 1963.

DOWNS, ANTHONY. *Inside Bureaucracy.* Boston: Little, Brown, 1967.

GOLDHABER, GERALD. *Organizational Communications.* Dubuque, IA: William C. Brown, 1974

GOLEMBIEWSKI, ROBERT T. *Behavior and Organization: O+M and the Small Group.* Chicago: Rand McNally, 1962.

HUSEMAN, RICHARD; LAHIFF, JAMES; and HATFIELD, JOHN. *Interpersonal Communications in the Organization.* Boston: Halbrook, 1976.

LEATHERS, DALE. *Nonverbal Communication Systems.* Boston: Allyn and Bacon, 1976.

PFEIFFER, J. WILLIAM, and JONES, JOHN E. *A Handbook of Structured Experiences for Human Relations Training.* La Jolla, CA: University Associates Press, 1972.

REDFIELD, CHARLES. *Communication in Management.* Chicago: University of Chicago Press, 1953.

SECTION

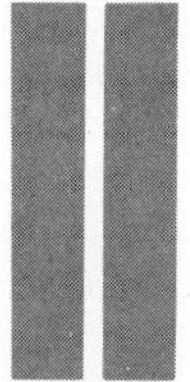

POLICY AND DECISION PROCESSES

Organization management is concerned with directing individual effort toward group goals. Certain events play a particularly important role in this process because of the generality of their impact. The terms *decision* and *policy* refer to important events in providing direction to organizational activity. Very often the most powerful individuals in an organization, who tend to be those with responsibilities at the top of the hierarchy, are referred to as decision makers or policymakers, because of their involvement in these key events. In a general way *decisions* and *policies* and *decision making* and *policymaking* are interchangeable terms. Our own preference for *policymaking* stems from its more limited use and its connection with events of greatest generality. Concern with decision making and policymaking, then, is concern with the generalized processes within and without the organization that provide direction to organizational activity.

Where do the goals of public organizations come from? As discussed above, one of the special features of public organizations is the extent to which they are accountable to elected officials. Therefore, they receive their general direction from legislatures and elected executives.

In order to coordinate the efforts of public organizations to accomplish the general good, a series of policy processes operate at federal, state, and local levels. Ordinarily the legislature is the highest policymaking authority, next comes the executive, the department heads, and so on down the hierarchy. Policies at the higher levels tend to be more general and also tend to be open to wider review and participation. But policies adopted at the lower levels may have surprisingly far-ranging consequences. Judicial decisions, too, while ordinarily specific and limited, may have broad impacts.

Government agencies spend a significant portion of their time in making rules governing the behavior of individuals and of groups. More rules and regulations, of course, do not necessarily lead to greater social good. Deregulation, the reduction of the scope and detail of rules, may at times be preferable.

Have you ever been stopped for speeding or for driving under the influence of intoxicating substances? If you have, you were accused of violating rules that were made by government. Do you know which organizations made these rules? Was it the state legislature, the state department of highways, the state police, the state courts, or some local agency? Chances are that several separate state and local agencies contributed to deciding whether or not you were speeding or intoxicated. While procedures vary from state to state and locality to locality, the state legislature ordinarily sets the broad guidelines regulating automobile drivers' conduct. State and local agencies are responsible for more specific regulations governing the interpretation of these standards and their enforcement. Do you think the existence of separate state systems of driving regulations is advantageous? Or would you favor greater uniformity throughout the country?

Federal regulations setting the maximum speed limit at fifty-five miles per hour encroach upon state prerogatives. They may eventually lead to more systematic national regulation of driving and of automobiles. Do you feel such an encroachment is justified? On what basis?

Antitrust regulations are government attempts to prevent corporations from becoming too powerful in a particular field of operation. Giant corporations such as General Motors and International Business Machines at various times have been forced to curtail certain activities because of government decisions that they have gained too much power in particular industries. Such controversies over monopolistic practices often involve millions of dollars in prolonged disputes. The Federal Trade Commission (FTC) and the Justice Department make many of these rules but must in the end defer to the judicial interpretation of often vague federal legislation.

The importance of the government's policymaking functions is so great and so pervasive that government is sometimes viewed as synonymous with policymaking. Introductory courses in American government invariably describe the main institutions of the national government in terms of their policymaking powers: Congress makes the laws, the president and the agencies enforce the laws, the Supreme Court and the federal judiciary interpret the laws. Nowadays the tendency is to move away from this simplistic view of American government (and government in general). Instead, policymaking is recognized as a governmental function at all levels. Driving rules may derive from general state law, but the highway department and the state police promulgate more detailed regulations. Similarly, after Congress enacts general antitrust laws, the federal judiciary and the FTC set more specific standards. Then it is up to the Department of Justice's Antitrust Division and the FTC to decide when to enforce these standards by taking action against specific companies.

Most government agencies are engaged in policymaking as an integral and important part of their operation. In large part the conduct of government may be understood as the creation and revision of policies and regulations.

The terms *policy* and *policymaking* are receiving increasing attention because of their usefulness as organizing principles for the study of government and governmental activity. They stress the importance of general principles and decisions. They also stress the similarities in decision making by different governmental groups and bodies. While recognizing that legislative, executive, judicial, and other forms of governmental institutions have distinctive patterns of making policy, the policymaking orientation stresses their commonalities.

It also allows for a more flexible understanding of the ways in which government acts, and recognizes that often more than one governmental structure is involved in the formulation of specific policies. Rather than concentrating solely on the legislature, the executive, or the judiciary, the policy perspective allows for the delineation of policy systems that may include a variety of governmental actors who interact in different ways. Nonetheless, policymaking is often focused within a particular institution, and in such cases an institutional context can be identified. Courts, legislatures, commissions, executives, and their subdivisions often serve as institutional contexts for the making of policy.

Policymaking occurs in response to the definition of some problem or issue that needs attention. Thus civil rights policy or defense policy may command public attention at different times. For example, during 1976, one of the most talked-about issues was unemployment, and so unemployment policy became an important focus of attention.

In order to gain a greater understanding of the policy process, here are some exercises and games that will enable you to gain direct experience in generating agenda items, formalizing an agenda, formulating a policy statement, and planning policy execution. These exercises require that the class focus on some particular area of substantive policy.

Before proceeding with these exercises, the class must choose a particular issue area and develop some substantive knowledge about that area. Some suggestions follow for selecting such an issue area and developing basic knowledge by writing a policy memorandum about it.

SELECTING AN ISSUE AREA

Part A

Divide the class into work groups of approximately six persons. Each group has five minutes to decide which issue it considers most important for current government action. An additional five minutes are allotted for developing a strategy to force the government to address this problem. Then each group will have the opportunity to explain its strategy to the class.

Among the questions that should be asked are: What determines the needs that individuals perceive for governmental action? What determines the ability of individuals to command the attention and respect of government officials? What aspects of the social and political system determine the impact of individuals on government officials?

Part B

Before going on, the entire group must decide upon a method for the initial definition of the specific issue area. Make up your own procedure or try one of these: (1) The group leader designates a topic. (2) Suggestions are solicited and several votes are taken among class members until one topic receives a majority of votes.

EXERCISE: *WRITING A POLICY MEMORANDUM*

In order to familiarize yourself with the particular policy area you have chosen, prepare a suggested policy to cope with an important problem agreed to by the entire class. Your work should take the form of a policy memorandum outlining the needs to which the policy responds, the individuals who are most concerned about the need or lack of need for such a policy, and how your suggested policy is related to the identified needs. This memorandum should be no more than three typewritten pages long.

Where would you find information for such a memorandum? Are you familiar with some issue from your job or from some recent television show or newspaper or magazine article? Have you seen a recent book on the topic? How would you develop a brief list of no more than ten sources of background information? Such a list, or bibliography, is the beginning of systematic research.

Some research hints: College and municipal libraries have many sources that can be used in policy research. The subject listing in the library catalogue is a good place to start in any library. Also look for indices, which list available material related to a particular subject. The Public Affairs Information Service, Public Administration Abstracts, and the Social Sciences Index are particularly useful. In case you need further assistance, ask the research librarian or consult research manuals on public administration and political science.

Many government processes are routine ones. Agents for the Internal Revenue Service check tax returns to make sure that claims are justified. Firefighters respond to calls for assistance. Driving licenses are processed. Schools are open and functioning. Although the routine tasks of government provide interesting material for the analysis of the operation of bureaucracy, some decision-making processes are particularly important. The policymaking focus emphasizes the nonroutine decisions that have special importance in determining what government will do and how it will do it.

Philip Selznick, a noted sociologist, refers to the "critical decision" that affects government operations. Raymond Bauer and Kenneth Gergen refer to the "leverage points" of the policy process. Both are attempting to differentiate the important from the routine areas of government decision making. While the routine should not be dismissed, the critical events assume particular importance in helping to understand what government is and how it affects us.

The Policy Process

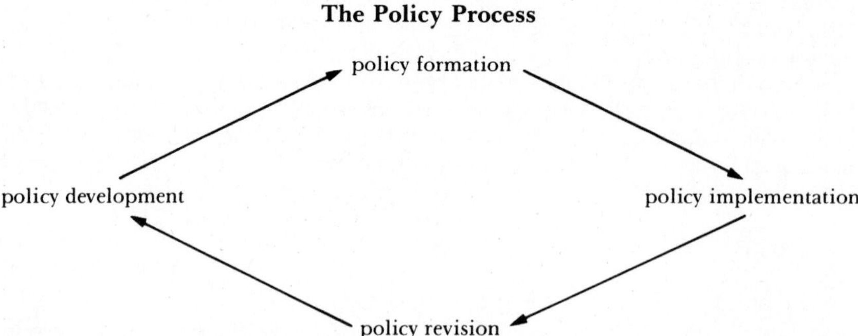

Policymaking may be thought of as a process beginning with the generation of policy initiatives by political leaders, followed by the formulation of policy in some institutional setting, the implementation of policy by public organizations, and finally the evaluation, revision, and development of new policy. This cycle is depicted in the accompanying figure on page 106.

In this set of modules three of these processes will be explored in depth: policy development, policy formation, and policy implementation. Policy revision will be discussed in the next section. In each case you will be asked not only to become familiar with some descriptive material, but also to participate in games aimed at providing an experiential base for understanding the operation of the policymaking process.

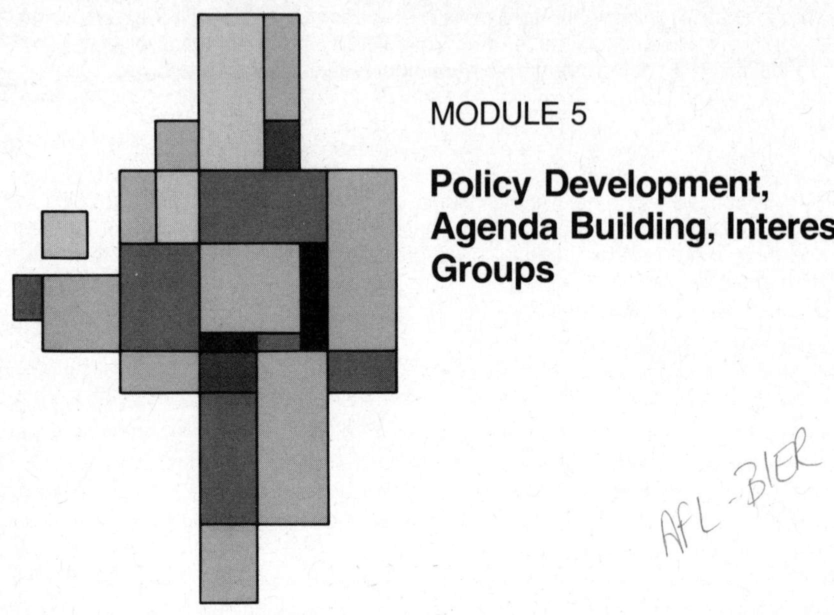

MODULE 5

Policy Development, Agenda Building, Interest Groups

INTRODUCTION

What makes government act? Or, what makes the policy process begin? From time to time issues emerge that grasp the imagination of the general public and the time and energy of government bureaucracies. How are these issues determined? Why was civil rights the consuming issue of the early 1960s? Why was the Vietnam war so important in the late 1960s? Why was the environment the concern of the early 1970s, and jobs and the economy the preoccupation of the mid-1970s? How are government priorities determined? How do issues capture the attention of Congress and the state legislatures, the president, governors, and mayors?

POLICY DEVELOPMENT

Policy development is the first phase of the process that leads to policy formation, policy implementation, and policy revision. An understanding of policy development must proceed from a more general understanding of the nature of government and its place within society. After all, government does not operate in a vacuum. According to the social contract theory, government derives from the decision of a group of people to pursue certain common purposes. While this theory, particularly in its literal form of an explicit contract among individuals, is no longer accepted as an adequate justification for government, the U.S. Constitution and the state constitutions are often viewed as contracts to create a government of limited powers for carrying out specific tasks.

A more contemporary view of government emphasizes the actual investigation of what it does, why it acts, and what the impacts of its activities are. David Easton, in his classic book, *The Political System,* espouses a general systems view of government as part of the political system imbedded in a larger social system. Using this perspective, the notion of policy development becomes one of attempting to understand how issues move from the general social system to become prominent in the political system, and then how issues come before specific institutional contexts, such as Congress, the state legislatures, the courts, agencies, and commissions. The diagram below is a representation of the systems view.

A Systems View of Policy Development

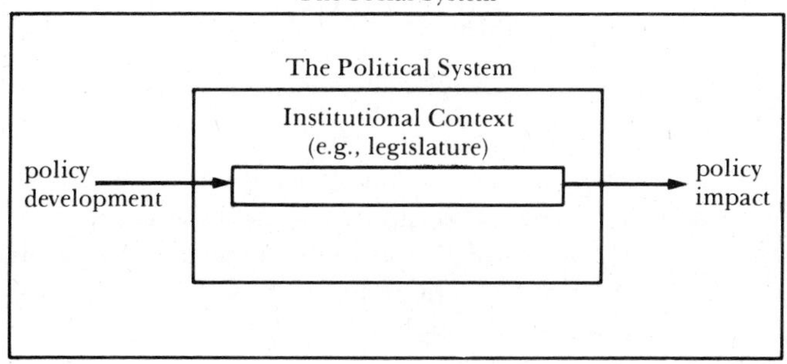

As the diagram indicates, once the policy development process reaches the institutional context for decision, and after policy is made or formulated, that policy will have an impact on the larger political and social system. The policy process emerges from society and focuses on institutional contexts. Government action, in turn, affects the larger political system and society as a whole.

To illustrate this, consider the civil rights controversies of the early 1960s. As pressures began building within the larger society, congressional action resulted in the passage of the Civil Rights Act of 1964 and the Voting Rights Act of 1965. These government policies had impacts on society in terms of discouraging segregated facilities and encouraging blacks to vote.

Opposition to the Vietnam war during the 1960s and the early 1970s resulted in executive action to curb American intervention. Some observers attribute Lyndon Johnson's withdrawal from the presidential race in 1968, Hubert Humphrey's loss in 1968, and Richard Nixon's emergence as expressions of societal demands to curtail American participation in the war. Finally, during the 1970s, American participation did cease.

Using the conceptual framework above, you can see that societal demands for action resulted in governmental response. You may have noticed that the original societal demands in this particular case arose from specific governmental policies and their impacts on the American people, such as the increase of military draft quotas. Such a relationship is not uncommon. This continuous and cyclical nature of the policy process will be explored throughout the next modules.

AGENDA BUILDING

The process of policy development is sometimes referred to as *agenda building* because it establishes an agenda for political leaders and governmental decision makers. Agenda building may be viewed as a two-stage process. First, the political system as a whole becomes sensitized to the need for a political response, and second, individual institutions are driven to action.

The political system becomes activated as social needs are transformed into political demands. Formal procedures like elections and referenda are one way in which this can be accomplished. The recent adoption by the California voters of Proposition 13 is one example. Heavy tax burdens and surplus state revenues led California voters to limit government taxing authority through the referendum process, a special procedure whereby the voters decide upon policy. Ordinarily policymaking authority is restricted to public institutions like legislatures and executives. Individuals also can express their views about social problems through communication with their political representatives and participation in interest groups and political parties.

The media play a critical role in transforming social needs into issues to which policymakers must respond. In the final analysis, however, it is political leaders themselves, whether elected legislators and executives, opinion leaders who head powerful institutions, or appointed officials, who have a large part in shaping the political agenda as it develops. It is these leaders, of course, who exercise preponderant influence in the articulation of specific institutional agendas

Each political institution has certain individuals or processes whose function it is to set the institution's agenda. For example, the Supreme Court has a formal process for setting its agenda. Those who wish to have cases reviewed by the court notify it, and then the whole court acts as a gatekeeper by voting on the cases it chooses to hear.

Within legislatures the gatekeepers are the party leadership and committee heads, who decide what matters will come before the larger body. They are, of course, deeply influenced by other political and community leaders. Often the elected executive performs an important agenda-setting function by proposing specific legislation.

The systems approach emphasizes movements across the barriers between the social system and the political system and those within the political system that separate the institutional decision-making subsystems. Agenda building involves moving issues across the barriers toward institutional reaction. Policy development, since it defines what the policy process will be and who will influence it, has a critical impact on the shape of final decisions.

INTEREST GROUPS

It is a truism of American politics that not all individuals and groups have equal power in formulating public policy. Clearly, within the agenda-building process, too, resources are unequally distributed. Those with superior wealth, social status, or political position have greater influence.

Sometimes the individuals who have the most power and influence in a society are referred to as the *elite*. This group has a preponderant influence on policy development. One of the questions about which political scientists disagree is whether elected officials and bureaucrats actually affect policy development or whether they are merely responding to the demands of the social elite, consisting of wealthy and prominent citizens.

Those who emphasize the cohesion and power of a social elite will stress their importance in setting the political agenda. They argue that once political decision makers begin their process of decision making, the definition of issues has already taken place, limiting the choices of the political leaders and resulting in greater control by the social elite. Peter Bachrach and Morton Baratz, in *Power and Poverty*, emphasize the importance of agenda building by focusing attention on nondecisions. They argue that the issues that never come before institutional decision makers, the nondecisions, by limiting the scope of decision making, greatly affect the exercise of power by socially prominent and economically powerful individuals.

A central dilemma of democratic theory has been how individuals acting by themselves can affect governmental policy. Agenda setting is in some ways the most important and the most elusive stage of the policy process. How does an individual who wants to change American foreign policy have his or her views acted upon? How can a citizen who is out of work and seeks to move government toward job creation strategies influence policy? How does the naturalist who seeks preservation of our land and natural resources make government act? How does a conscientious police officer who witnesses departmental corruption act to make a difference?

A number of political scientists, known as group theorists, have pointed out that although individuals by themselves have little influence over public policy, they can join with other individuals to form groups with greater influence. Arthur Bentley, in his early work, *The Process of Government,* and David Truman, in his more recent work, *The Governmental Process,* have argued that group activity pervades governmental operations. These groups are the key to understanding how modern-day democracies work. Group theorists have been particularly concerned with the operation of nongovernmental interest groups.

Can you name any interest groups that influenced the development of civil rights, environmental policy, or Vietnam policy? Indeed, if you are familiar with any of these areas you will realize that interest groups played critical roles in developing the agenda that preceded public action. For example, the National Association for the Advancement of Colored People (NAACP) was critical in the definition of the civil rights problem and in mobilizing support, as was its legal arm, the NAACP Legal Defense Fund. The Student Nonviolent Coordinating Committee (SNCC), Martin Luther King's Southern Christian Leadership Conference (SCLC), and the Congress of Racial Equality (CORE) were also active. Such national groups as the Sierra Club and the Wilderness Society help stimulate interest in environmental issues.

Interest groups that exist for only a short period of time, for a specific and limited purpose, are sometimes referred to as *ad hoc groups.* Often they perform a vital role in mobilizing political support for issues that are new on the political agenda, and their development is a clue to a rising interest in particular issues. After an initial period these groups will often disappear, either through collapse or merger with similar groups. Many ad hoc civil rights, antiwar, and environmental groups are no longer in existence.

While the operation of interest groups in the development of public policy is great, as is their influence at later stages, it should be clear that not all individuals belong to interest groups, are equally influential in them, or have the same ability to initiate new groups. The fact that some individuals make their voices heard through interest groups is no guarantee that all individuals can be heard in this way. Interest group participation requires time, energy, money, and motivation, which are not equally distributed among the population. Yet these groups do provide an important avenue for influencing public policy.

Other channels exist for influencing government policy. The media can be important in raising issues to public awareness and then stimulating government action. The media are particularly important in helping to transform social needs into political demands. By focusing on and therefore defining newsworthy individuals and causes, the media have a strong impact on agenda building. For example, participants in the civil rights and antiwar movements found that often their influence depended on their treatment by the media. Commentators and reporters have the opportunity to influence public policy while performing their everyday jobs.

Another influence channel can be public office itself. Elected representatives and elected executives, presidents, governors, mayors, and appointed officials may affect public policy through direct decision making. Often even more potent a weapon is the ability of officeholders to influence the decisions of other officeholders, through persuasion, the mobilization of public opinion, or the exchange of favors. As the government of the United States has become increasingly complicated and as the involvement of government in new areas has continued, the government officeholder gains more and more power over policymaking, either directly or through the ability to influence others.

If the difficulties of individuals in affecting the agenda-building process in legislatures and commissions are great, the difficulties of affecting executive action, particularly that taken at lower levels of agencies, may be even greater. At higher levels agency visibility is greater and independent citizen surveillance is more likely. Government officials at the lowest levels have a special responsibility to undertake agenda building in an open and responsible way. They have a great deal of control over agenda building at lower government levels, and because of their official positions, may be able to influence agenda building at higher levels. These officials can sometimes wield considerable policymaking power. It may be truer than you think that the way to influence government policy is to become a policymaker yourself.

AGENDA BUILDING IN THE POLICY PROCESS

Approaches that emphasize the incremental nature of decision making also focus upon the importance of agenda building. Charles Lindblom and Herbert Simon emphasize that policymaking does not take place in the abstract, but in the real world, affected by the present and the past. Only occasionally, they assert, can policy be developed rationally apart from the solutions of yesterday and the possibilities for tomorrow. Policymaking is limited by the number of solutions that can be considered and the power realities of the moment which usually will not stand for abrupt modification. As a result of these limitations, Simon claims we must settle for less than optimal or "satisficing" decisions. Similarly, Lindblom and Braybrooke describe a process of disjointed incrementalism which bases policymaking upon successive approximation. It makes small steps, with a constant progression from policy development to policy formation, implementation, and revision. Agenda building thus is a continuous process and interdependent with prior and future stages of the policy process.

Agenda building is the process by which government responds to the needs of the society. Agendas are the basis of all policy. Since policies ordinarily can be written down, agendas, which are really preliminary statements of policy, also can be written. But an agenda is not a definitive statement of policy. It may be conceived of as a list of items that center around central concerns that might form a policy statement. An agenda represents a broadly cast group of suggestions for proposed action that becomes recognized by policymakers, those who formulate policy, as the basis for a policy statement.

Agenda Building Exercise

PHASE 1—GENERATING AGENDA ITEMS

Using the policy area that was agreed to in the discussion in Section II, each work group should generate a list of approximately twenty-five items, which could form the basis of an agenda. The items should be as specific as possible, so that at a later stage in the process they can form the basis of adopted policy. One member of each group will be the recorder and will write down items suggested by other members. In order to facilitate the flow of ideas a technique known as nonjudgmental brainstorming will be used. Group members are expected to encourage one another to make suggestions and not censor or react negatively to the suggestions of others. The object of this group process is to maximize the number of items generated in a short, five- to ten-minute period.

What are the strengths and weaknesses of brainstorming as a technique for generating agenda items? To what extent does it reflect societal pressures?

Having generated a list of twenty-five proposed policy initiatives in a particular area, the small groups should reduce the number of items to the ten that reflect most exactly the group perspectives. This reduction process should take no more than ten or fifteen minutes. The groups may want to adopt special rules to facilitate this process.

Which items tended to remain? To be eliminated? What rules were adopted to facilitate the process?

PHASE 2—FORMALIZING AN AGENDA

During the process of agenda building the undefined and vague demands of individuals and groups begin to crystallize, placing specific demands before institutional decision makers and within policy subsystems. Think of the ways in which civil rights demands began to take shape, or how environmental issues assumed greater definition. This phase of the process is concerned with constructing an agenda consisting of a number of items to be placed before the institutional decision makers.

Agenda building is a process by which demands of individuals and groups became publicized and exposed to the competing demands of others. In order for demands to reach policymakers they need to have a certain level of support and recognition among the individuals and groups who are defining a particular area of public policy.

To begin this phase, each group publicizes its proposed agenda items, either by presenting other groups with Xeroxed lists or writing the items on the board. Then each group will be given the opportunity to select ten items from the lists of others which most nearly meet their requirements. Any item that receives the support of two groups in addition to the proposing group will be placed on the formal agenda. (This presupposes at least five groups. Reduce the requirement of two additional supporters to one for less than five groups.)

COMMENTS ON THE AGENDA BUILDING EXERCISE

Three aspects of agenda building have been highlighted: the selection of an issue area, the agreement upon a preliminary agenda, and the formalization of an agenda through interaction among groups. Can you explain how each of these phases operated in some particular substantive policy area with which you are familiar?

What are the determinants of issue area selection? Under what conditions does an issue generate governmental response? Another way to phrase this question is: Under what circumstances does a sufficiently broad spectrum of politically influential individuals consider an issue important enough that government must respond? Three crucial elements are: Who is affected? How are these effects perceived? Is sufficient public concern mobilized to convince policymakers that action is warranted?

NOTE ON INFLUENCING AGENDA BUILDING

Civil rights was not a new issue in terms of needs in the early 1960s, nor was it new in terms of perceptions, although perceptions did change. The critical element was the mobilization of political influence. Increased government activity, including the landmark Supreme Court case of *Brown* v. *Board of Education,* individual initiative through dramatic actions such as sit-ins, and a general mobilization among the black community and some portions of the white community, all combined to raise the issue to the attention of political decision makers. The Vietnam war inspired an overwhelming amount of political mobilization efforts against it, and meant tremendous inconvenience for young men who would otherwise pursue private careers. Environmental issues developed as a result of increasing industrial pollution, recognition of the limitations of resources such as fossil fuels, and the formation and activation of environmental action groups. Dramatic events often mobilize political forces. But government action requires continued political mobilization efforts by individuals and groups who attempt to move public policy onto the action agenda. Often the formation of new groups precedes such changes, and in fact, can be a reliable indicator of change.

Once an issue assumes importance in the public sector and moves onto the agenda of the political system, it becomes further refined by the efforts of individuals and groups who influence the way others perceive it. Influential groups, including interest groups, perform a particularly important function within the political system. As such groups define their own positions, they articulate the issues. The most influential groups and individuals compete among themselves to agree upon the basic outlines of a desirable governmental response.

The development of an agenda involves the elimination of items unacceptable to veto groups, those holding predominant political power. At this stage a majority of support is not necessary, but substantial support is ordinarily a prerequisite for inclusion on the agenda that will form the basis of institutional policymaking.

A critical difference between the previous exercises and agenda building in the real world is the distinction between the policymakers and the influencers. In these exercises the agenda was developed from items proposed by individuals and groups, as if everyone had an equal opportunity to propose items for incorporation on the agenda. While the early stages of agenda building may be comparatively open, as the process progresses toward policy formation, policymakers begin playing a more important role. Some policymakers function as "gatekeepers," deciding which agenda items are admissible for general consideration and which items will not be considered. In order to influence the determination of policy, even at a fairly early stage, it is often necessary to have a good knowledge of the policymaking process and access to the gatekeepers. Within a legislature, this final stage of agenda building, which merges with policy formation, may be controlled by all members of the legislature, but more usually by a smaller number of members influential in a particular area, usually committee heads and party leaders. Without access to the gatekeepers an individual's impact on legislative policymaking may be foreclosed even before decisions have been made. Access to executive and agency policymaking, too, is controlled by gatekeepers who determine the agenda prior to policy formulation. Be sure to remember the distinction between the policymakers and those attempting to influence policy. It is closely related to the concepts of mass and elite, which are used in sociological and political theory to distinguish those having the predominant power, or the elite, from those remaining, the masses. Sometimes policymakers are labeled the political elite, while influencers having especially good access to policymakers are termed social elite or influentials.

Often the focus for the analysis of agenda building is at the highest levels: the legislature and the elected chief executive. This occurs because the broadest and most dramatic examples of policy development are at these levels. Yet this bias introduces an element of distortion into an overview of policy development.

One of the consequences of the growth of public organizations has been the increasing complexity of policymaking. A particularly prominent example of this movement of policymaking into the agencies below the legislature and the chief executive is the growth of the power of regulatory agencies. The Food and Drug Administration issues regulations about safety in the use of food substances, and may decide to ban certain food substances. The Federal Communications Commission regulates radio and television and so sets standards for broadcasting.

The process of policy development in these areas may be different from that in legislatures and elected executives. While the general activation of policy issues is similar, the development of the institutional agenda is different. In independent regulatory commissions the small number of individual commissioners may be important in setting the agenda.

The individuals or corporations being regulated may themselves be prominent in raising issues for decision, or for that matter, in limiting the agenda of the commission. The legislature and chief executive also may be prominent in individual issues and in setting the institutional agenda by actual definition of the statutory authority of the agency or by the selection and confirmation of individuals having a particular viewpoint about the commission's role.

During the 1970s consumer groups have become more prominent in pressuring the commissions to take particular stands on issues. For example, groups at the state levels have pressured for greater recognition of consumer interests in the setting of utility prices. Another area in which consumer groups have been prominent is the attempt to have the Federal Communications Commission limit certain types of programming on television.

Individuals and groups often find it more difficult to influence commissions than legislatures or elected executives. They tend to be less open to the public and less in the public eye. Since their membership is not elected they are not responsive in the same way to local constituents. But commissions, with their national and state orientations, requirements for public hearings, and wide policy implications, are still subject to considerable public pressure.

As the process of policy development moves down to the lower levels of the bureaucracy, however, the policy development process can be more and more shielded from the public. What determines when police officials decide to adopt new policies on prostitution or speeding violations or traffic regulations? What determines when school officials decide to change policies regarding promotion of students or treatment of student suspensions? What determines when local welfare officials decide to enforce rules against cohabitation or allow minimum levels of income for individuals on welfare?

Lower-level officials, of course, are subject to the constraints of higher-level policies. Changes in traffic regulations, state laws involving suspensions of students, and federal welfare regulations may force lower-level bureaucrats to react. Yet there are still large areas of discretion where bureaucrats have to innovate and develop new policies. Often these policies can have large-scale implications for the everyday lives of citizens.

To be sure, in some areas strong clientele groups will provide a stimulus to the policy development process. But ultimately policy development at the lowest levels is dependent on the quality of individuals serving and the nature of incentives within the organization to change and reward innovation. To some extent the creation of a strong civil service with capable, motivated individuals is the best insurance. But more attention is being directed nowadays to creating incentives within public organizations to stimulate and reward policy innovation at the lowest levels.

SELECTED BIBLIOGRAPHY FOR MODULE 5

BACHRACH, PETER, and BARATZ, MORTON S. *Power and Poverty.* New York: Oxford University Press, 1970.

BAUER, RAYMOND, and GERGEN, KENNETH, eds. *The Study of Policy Formation.* New York: Free Press, 1968.

BENTLEY, ARTHUR. *The Process of Government.* Chicago: University of Chicago Press, 1908.

COBB, ROGER W., and ELDER, CHARLES D. *Participation in American Politics: The Dynamics of Agenda-Building.* Boston: Allyn and Bacon, 1972.

DYE, THOMAS R. *Understanding Public Policy.* Englewood Cliffs, NJ: Prentice-Hall, 1972.

EASTON, DAVID. *A Framework for Political Analysis.* Englewood Cliffs, NJ: Prentice-Hall, 1965.

JONES, CHARLES. *An Introduction to the Study of Public Policy.* North Scituate, MA: Duxbury, 1979.

LINDBLOM, CHARLES, and BRAYBROOKE, DAVID. *A Strategy of Decision.* New York: Free Press, 1963.

LOWI, THEODORE, and STONE, ALAN. *Nationalized Government: Public Policies in America.* Beverly Hills, CA: Sage Publications, 1978.

SELZNICK, PHILIP. *Leadership in Administration. A Sociological Interpretation.* New York: Harper & Row, 1957.

TRUMAN, DAVID B. *The Governmental Process.* New York: Alfred A. Knopf, 1962.

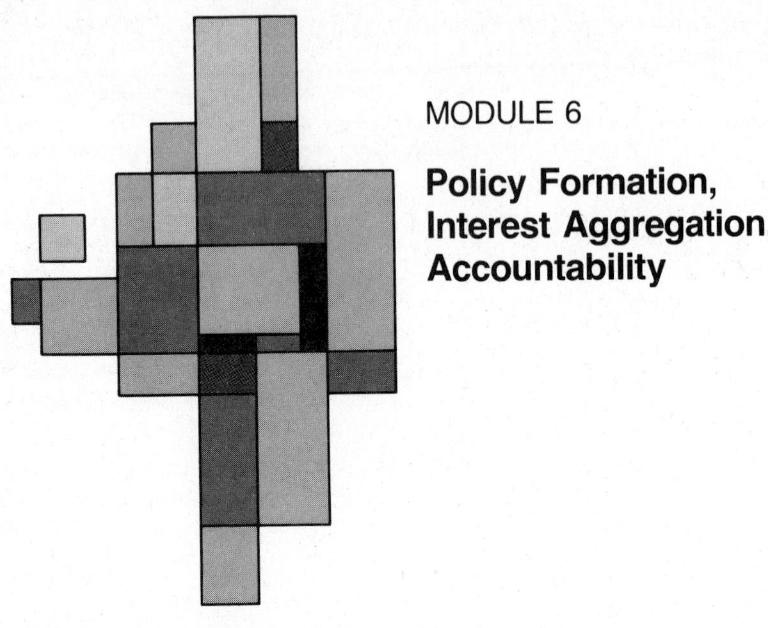

MODULE 6

Policy Formation, Interest Aggregation, Accountability

INTRODUCTION

In the words of a prominent political scientist, Harold Lasswell, "Politics is the study of who gets, what, when, and how." Another political scientist, David Easton, has called politics the study of the authoritative allocation of values. A large part of government activity involves the formulation of policies to decide who gets what. Most people, most of the time, abide by the decisions government makes. It is government that decides who pays how much taxes, how taxes are spent, and what rules individuals and groups must observe in carrying out many aspects of their daily business. Rules governing individual and group behavior can come from other sources, too. Personal habits may be regulated by religious or corporate organizations to which one belongs. Trade associations and even criminal networks may regulate corporate and group behavior. But the most pervasive and comprehensive set of rules governing individual and group behavior in the United States derives from government. The impact of governmental activity is not only large, but is increasing in the United States and in most parts of the world. That is one reason why the study of public policy is becoming increasingly important.

Government is made up of individuals. So when government formulates policy, it is because individuals have acted. Very often government decisions are made by groups of individuals, although sometimes individuals act alone. This occurs particularly in situations that are less concerned with broad policy than with a specific response to a particular situation.

Policy formation can be accomplished through formal or informal mechanisms. The easiest to study is that which occurs in formal situations, such as laws passed by a legislature, regulations promulgated by an executive or agency, or decisions rendered by a court. Often informal mechanisms develop for decision making and rule making, which may become formal over time. And formal institutions may often have informal structures for making decisions.

The study of policymaking not only explains how government works, but also enables students to gain a greater understanding of how to influence the policies that will affect them. Understanding the public policy process means being able to affect that policy.

While the formal and informal mechanisms for making public policy are numerous, certain types of institutions figure most prominently. These deserve special consideration.

Laws

Lawmaking often is viewed as the most important example of policymaking. Interpretations of the separation of powers doctrine in the Constitution usually emphasize the law-making or policymaking function of Congress. Congressional legislation and the process by which it is adopted has a particular importance because of its impact. Scholars have noted, however, the increasing tendency for broad general rules to be promulgated by the president, department secretaries, and lesser officials. In fact, since administration of governmental services requires adherence to consistent policies even at the lowest levels, most administrators make policy. Similarly, courts must formulate general principles of case law for the purpose of making decisions. The development of the English common law, which arose from decisions by individual judges, is a clear example of judicial policymaking over a prolonged period of time.

A legislature is a group of representatives of a community that is given the authority to make rules of general applicability for that community. Usually the representatives are selected from specific geographic areas. The legislature makes policies, commonly referred to as laws, according to an explicit procedure, often requiring a majority vote of those representatives, or legislators, who are present. Legislators often serve part-time, assuming other jobs when the legislature is not in session. This is particularly true at the state and local levels in the United States.

Legislatures are often quite large — the House of Representatives has 435 members — and for this reason usually develop both formal and informal structures that assign certain individuals to specialized responsibilities. Most American legislatures have a number of elected leaders and committee chairpersons, who often exercise considerable influence.

While the focus of legislative policymaking is the formal vote, which determines whether a particular bill will become a law, the informal processes are often more important. These processes are dependent upon the influence structure of the legislature. Often elected party leaders assume formal responsibilities, as for example the speaker in the House of Representatives or the majority leader in the Senate. In full-time bodies like Congress, a committee system operates that provides focus for the policymaking process. Many observers of Congress have focused on these committees as the center of Congressional influence.

Commissions and Boards

Somewhat similar to legislative institutions are commissions and boards, which function at all levels of government. Of the commissions, regulatory commissions such as the Federal Power Commission (now part of the Department of Energy) and the Federal Communications Commission are the most well known; of the boards, boards of education, which administer local school districts, are perhaps the most well known. Boards and commissions are often appointed, although boards of education are most often elected. Boards tend to have a more limited scope as opposed to the more general orientation of a legislature. They also tend to be smaller in membership. Often their membership is part-time and unpaid. The smaller membership of boards and commissions tends to reduce the development of internal power structures, and members tend to be more equal in their exercise of authority.

Commissions and boards increase the channels for influencing government policy. In this respect they contribute to what is sometimes called American pluralism, the proliferation of decision-making agencies to decentralize political authority and allow for multiple points of access by nongovernmental actors.

Executives

While the U.S. Constitution speaks of the executive's responsibility for executing the law as opposed to making the law, the complexity of twentieth-century government has led to an increasing lawmaking orientation on the part of executives. The president issues executive orders, which are very similar to laws, in setting general policies that individuals both within and outside of government must obey. In addition, most agencies are engaged in rule making on a continuing basis.

Executive rule making differs from legislative rule making in that it rarely occurs during a formal session, when a large number of individuals vote. A reflection of this difference is the tendency to refer to executive rule making as decision making, and legislative rule making as policymaking. Both processes often involve discussions and compromises in much the same way. While the formal structure of bureaucratic power tends to be more hierarchical, as explained in Module 3, and to depend more on individual decision, policy formation often involves a whole range of individuals and groups. For example, requirements for prepublication of proposed executive or agency regulations and public hearings on proposed actions are not uncommon. Even when executives or agencies would like to minimize the involvement of individuals or groups, they often find that such attempts backfire. Agencies find that in order to develop support for policies and to be able to enforce them, adequate consultation with those who will be affected by the policies, including formal involvement, is often helpful.

Aside from the efforts of individuals outside administrative agencies to influence agency decisions, the internal operation of agencies encourages group as opposed to individual decision. As Herbert Simon, in his classic treatise, *Administrative Behavior*, points out, individual decisions by an administrative employee planning and executing his or her own work certainly occur. But to an enormous degree administrative activity is group activity, requiring the coordination of several individuals. Coordination requires group decision and procedures for arriving at and accepting those decisions.

Chester Barnard, in *The Functions of the Executive,* argues that executives spend a good deal of their time avoiding making formal decisions on their own. In fact, he cites with pride his tenure as head of the New York Telephone Company, when he only infrequently was forced to make decisions:

> . . . I tried to recall an important general decision made by me on my initiative as a telephone executive within two years. I could recall none, although on reviewing the record I found several. On the other hand, I can still recall without any record many major decisions made by me "out of hand" when I was a Relief Administrator. I probably averaged at least five a day for eighteen months. In the latter case I worked with a very noble group but a very poor informal organization under emergency conditions . . . . [p. 226]

Although Barnard is pointing out the advantages of establishing informal executive organizations to reduce the necessity for active intervention by managers, this also illustrates a larger point: that managers, especially public managers, try to avoid disputes. Most laws, executive orders, and decisions are in effect formal notice that all is well. Where there is agreement, authority is not questioned.

Leonard Sayles strikes a similar note, deemphasizing the importance of decision making. He is quick to criticize the standard view of management, which conceives of the manager as decision maker with a certain amount of authority to make certain types of decisions that must be carried out by subordinates who have the responsibility of following orders. Instead, he prefers a view of planning and decision making that places these activities within the total interaction pattern known as management.

With striking poignance, Sayles quotes outgoing Secretary of State Dean Acheson's criticism of new Secretary of State John Foster Dulles's job expectations:

> He told me that he was not going to work as I had done, but would free himself from involvement with what he referred to as personnel and administrative problems, in order to have more time to think.
>
> I did not comment, but was much struck by the conjunction of ideas. I wondered how it would turn out. For it had been my experience that thought was not of much use without knowledge and guidance, and that who should give me both and how competent they would be must depend on how they chose, dealt with, assigned and promoted these people and established the forms of organization within which they worked . . . .*
>
> This absorption with the Executive as Emerson's "Man Thinking," surrounded by a Cabinet of Rodin statues, bound in an oblivion of thought . . . seemed to me unnatural. Surely thinking is not so difficult, so hard to come by, so solemn as all this.†

On the whole it can be asserted that executive policymaking tends to be less formal and more centralized than legislative policymaking.

Court Decisions

In contrast, judicial policymaking is distinctive in at least two ways. First, almost all decisions are made on the basis of some concrete case before a court. Second, most decisions, except those by some appeals courts and higher courts, such as the Supreme Court, are made by a single individual in an atmosphere in which political considerations are minimized. In spite of the constraints imposed by these conditions, judicial policymaking manages to set rules of wide applicability that very

---

*Leonard Sayles, *Managerial Behavior* (New York: McGraw-Hill, 1964), p. 208.

†Dean Acheson, "Thoughts about Thoughts in High Places," *The New York Times Magazine,* 11 October 1959, pp. 20, 21.

often have far-ranging consequences. If you are tempted to question the extent of judicial impact, consider the court decisions that declared segregated schools in violation of the Fourteenth Amendment of the Constitution, made available to Congress President Nixon's tape recordings, and established new rules regarding the rights of criminal defendants to procedural protections. Judicial policymaking based upon decisions in individual cases is a pervasive aspect of the American judicial system. It derives both from the Anglo-American tradition of common law and the prerogatives assumed by the Supreme Court in interpreting the Constitution.

You will now have the opportunity to experience the process of policy formation by participating in POLFORM, an original game. POLFORM is an abstraction of the policymaking process that is modeled on the operation of a legislature, but approximates other collective decision-making processes.

As you attempt to investigate the dynamics of policymaking, recall some of the issues that have been discussed. How are collective decisions made? How does the influence structure of the policymaking body affect the outcome? How do those outside the decision-making process gain access to the policymakers? What are the procedures for arriving at policy? What criteria would you use in evaluating the quality of the policy?

POLFORM

To help you understand the process of collective policymaking, you will be placed in a simulated institutional context referred to as a *Collpol.* A Collpol is a group of approximately six individuals charged with the task of arriving at a policy statement for some previously selected area of public policy. You will immediately see differences between the Collpol in which you serve and specific Collpols (policymaking bodies) operating in the real world.

You may find that you have little expertise in the policy area selected. Don't be discouraged. Many members of Collpols around the country find themselves in similar situations. Direct your attention to the clash of diverse opinions that become modified and compromised as the Collpol moves to a collective decision.

PHASE I

Developing a Policy Position

In order to prepare for your role in the Collpol it is first necessary to develop a specific position. To accomplish this, you will be handed an agenda, preferably the agenda that was developed in the previous module.

Your first task is to transform this vague and diffuse agenda into a coherent statement of public policy reflecting your own particular perspective. In arriving at this statement it is perhaps easiest to reflect your own personal beliefs. Alternatively, you might want to assume the position of a legislator, attempting to reflect the views of residents of a particular legislative district.

Now revise the written agenda, indicating for each item whether you would eliminate, retain, or revise it. Please indicate these revisions on the written agenda with care. Be sure to carry out the revisions in triplicate. These revisions should reflect a position you can readily advocate in future discussion. They should reflect your best judgment of a sensible, effective policy in the area chosen for action.

Simple Interest Aggregation

After each participant, or Tor, has committed his or her position to writing, Collpols will be formed. A Chief Tor will be selected for each Collpol. Each Tor retains one copy of the proposed policy and gives the other two copies to the Chief Tor and the instructor. For the next ten minutes the Chief Tor will study the proposed policies submitted by the members of the Collpol. At the close of the ten-minute period the Chief Tor will read a policy statement that not only represents his or her own perspective, but is calculated to gain the support of as many of the Tors in the group as possible. A poll of all the Tors will then be taken, indicating whether or not they support the entire proposed policy. The votes for and against the policy as a whole will be reported to the whole class. A successful Chief Tor will win the support of at least a majority of the Tors.

Meanwhile, Tors are meeting with one another within their Collpol to form coalitions of two or three individuals. At the end of the ten-minute period each Tor must become part of a coalition, whose formation is indicated by agreement upon a new, revised coalition policy, representing an amalgam of the interests of those joining the coalition. Three copies of this coalition policy should be prepared.

PHASE II — COMPLEX BARGAINING

For this phase two new Chief and Assistant Chief Tors will be designated from the Chief Tors in Phase I. The class will be consolidated into two Collpols. (Usually, combining the earlier Collpols is most efficient and also allows for the preservation of coalitions.) Copies of coalition policies will be provided to the instructor. The Chief Tors and assistants will have twenty minutes to review coalition policies and discuss the positions of the newly formed coalitions with the Tors. They will bargain for the support of these coalitions by agreeing to revise their policy statements to include items suggested by the Tors. At the end of the period, record the number of supporting, opposing, and abstaining votes. The Chief Tor and assistants are rated on the percentage of affirmative votes for their proposed policy. The remaining Tors are rated by multiplying each of the coalition items that appear in the final policy by 50 and dividing by the number of members of the coalition.

PHASE III — BARGAINING INVOLVING INTEREST GROUPS

If time permits, try this revised version of POLFORM. In each of the two Collpols formed during Phase II, two or more Tors are asked to assume new roles as Mobes. A Mobe will not take part in the final vote to adopt policy, but will attempt to influence the final policy by bargaining with the Chief Tors and other Tors for changes in the policy in exchange for payoffs. Each Mobe will refer back to his or her original proposed policy statement, generated in Phase I.

Mobes are given a total of 100 points to award to individual Tors for supporting designated revisions. A contract is made by a Mobe and a Tor (including the Chief Tor), committing to writing an agreement specifying the number of points to be awarded and the changes in the policy statement that the Tor must support. The instructor receives a copy of the contract.

This revised version of POLFORM runs exactly like the preceding version, except that the Mobes will attempt to influence the Tors through the development of contracts, and the Tors will attempt to enter into contracts with Mobes that result in influence points. Scoring in this revised version is slightly different. The Chief Tor and assistants will calculate their scores by adding the percentage of Tors supporting them to the number of influence points they have won from the Mobes. Coalitions of Tors calculate their scores by adding 50 points for each of their coalition items on the final policy directive and then adding the number of influence points they receive from Mobes. Mobes calculate their scores by multiplying by 30 the number of their proposed items that appear on the final policy, as specified in a contract.

COMMENT ON POLFORM

In Phase I, was it easy for you to assume a preliminary position? To what extent did your lack of familiarity with the issues under consideration hinder your ability to assume the stance of policymaker?

During Phase I, how effective was the Chief Tor in arriving at a consensus position to which all the members of the Collpol were willing to subscribe? What kinds of skills make a Chief Tor effective? How did the incentives for supporting the Chief Tor differ from incentives Chief Tors can ordinarily count upon?

How easy was it to form coalitions as a prelude to Phase II? What were the major determinants of successful coalition formation? What aspects of real-life policymaking, which were not present in this simulated environment, facilitate coalition formation?

Why was the task of the Chief Tor in Phase II more difficult than that of the Chief Tor in Phase I? To what extent was persuasion effective on the part of the Chief Tor? The other Tors? What was the basis of influence of the Chief Tor over the final policy statement? What strategic moves were successful on the part of the Tors? To what extent could a skillful Tor influence the policy outcome? How? To what extent is the concept of leadership described in Module 3, above, applicable here?

What was the major difference between Phase II and Phase III? Can you relate the distinction between Tors and Mobes to a distinction made earlier in the text in Module 2? What are the determinants of success for Mobes? For Tors? Do policymakers always exercise more influence than Mobes? Under what conditions are Mobes most successful? Do Mobes have counterparts in agenda building? How would their roles differ from those of Mobes in POLFORM? Can you think of analogies to contracts between Mobes and Tors that occur in the real world?

In the scoring of Phase II, is it more advantageous to be a Chief Tor or a Tor? How does the scoring affect the play of the game? In Phase III, is it easier for the Chief Tor, individual Tors, or the Mobes to accumulate higher scores? Can you develop a rationale for the particular scoring system used? Could you suggest a better system?

NOTE ON POLICYMAKING ROLES, ACCOUNTABILITY, AND RULEMAKING

At the beginning of POLFORM each Tor was asked to indicate a policy position by revising the list of agenda items into a coherent policy. Did you base your initial policy position on your own predilections or did you attempt to reflect the views of your constituents?

Policy positions are reflections of the individuals taking those positions. Conflict among individuals drives the process of policy formation. Policymakers are constantly attempting to arrive at formulations of policy that will be acceptable to a diverse group of individuals.

Delegate and Trustee

One of the ways of analyzing the differences among policymakers is through an understanding of their role orientations. In a sense, what you were asked to do was to choose a role orientation for the purposes of playing POLFORM. If you chose to reflect the wishes of some constituency, you were assuming a *delegate* role orientation. If you chose to reflect your own beliefs, you were assuming a *trustee* orientation. The dilemma that policymakers face in choosing between these differing orientations is very real. To what extent should a policymaker follow the dictates of his or her own conscience or the wishes of the individuals he or she represents? This dilemma, which was first pointed out by Edmund Burke in the 18th century, remains important to this day. It is particularly poignant for elected officials, who stand to lose their offices if they choose the trustee orientation too often.

Sometimes a policymaker may voluntarily violate his or her constituency's wishes for the sake of what can be considered higher principles. During the early part of the 1970s, when abortion reform legislation was being considered in many state legislatures, a New York state legislator cast the deciding vote in favor of abortion reform. He made a brief speech from the floor of the Assembly in which he stated that he was following his conscience even though he knew he would be defeated for reelection, since his constituency was heavily Catholic and opposed to laws permitting abortions. Sure enough, during the next election he was defeated. Is this an example of the frustration or success of democracy? Should an elected representative be a *delegate* or a *trustee*? Burke certainly would have recognized the right of a legislator to act for the greater good even while violating the wishes of his or her constituency.

Accountability

While elected policymakers who take unpopular stands may sometimes receive retribution at the polls, in many cases such retribution is not forthcoming. A policymaker must decide many issues and the voters often must balance a stance on one issue with a stance on another. Furthermore, voters often may not be aware of the specific stances that policymakers take. In addition to the difficulties of finding out how a representative votes on all issues is the added burden of learning about positions on issues that don't come to a vote. Often action taken in committee or away from public view may be critical to the formation or frustration of new policy. Yet individual voters may have little knowledge of a representative's informal actions.

The citizen's difficulties in influencing policy is further complicated by the extent to which policies are now made by appointed employees or those in the civil service. These individuals are only indirectly accountable to the public. Since the 1950s American political scientists have been pointing up the dangers inherent in the proliferation of government bureaucracy and its attendant policymaking authority, which is insulated from public view and review.

Although the growth of government bureaucracy in the post-World War II period has been particularly rapid, trying to achieve popular control over administration is much older. Democratic theory suggests that responsible bureaucracy results from the fact that top appointed officials, who exercise control over governmental bureaucracies, are appointed by elected executives or legislatures. While such reassurances may be theoretically satisfying, the difficulties of establishing an effective system of accountability are much greater.

An important tool in controlling administration in the United States has arisen from judicial willingness to review decisions by administrative agencies. Reinforced by provisions of the Administrative Procedure Act of 1946, which extended and clarified the rights of individuals to judicial review of administrative determination, the federal and state courts have evolved an extensive body of administrative law, which seeks to minimize the abuse of administrative discretion and guarantee minimum procedural safeguards to individuals affected by such decisions.

Alternative approaches to control of bureaucracy have gained considerable attention recently. Decentralization of large cities is one suggestion for reasserting popular control over bureaucracy. Another is the development of legislative control mechanisms. Particularly at the national level, the committee system has resulted in considerable ability to review administrative procedures. Legislators elected directly by popular vote are thus reasserting popular control over administration. Centralized complaint mechanisms, include legislative ombudsmen following the Swedish example, also have been tried in some states and cities, although the ombudsman institution has been more successfully introduced in several of the British Commonwealth countries. An ombudsman or other centralized complaint mechanism allows individuals who feel that they have been treated unfairly by administrators to seek help. The effectiveness of such mechanisms depends upon the stature of those heading the offices, the investigative techniques, and the enforcement tools available.

To a large extent, however, the responsiveness of government bureaucracy may depend upon the extent to which career civil servants accept their responsibility to serve the American people. Strengthening procedures for the recruitment, selection, and training of civil servants is an important part of insuring responsive government. Some approaches are discussed above in Module 2.

Rules Governing Policy Formation and Development

Policy formation is considerably more constrained than policy development. In policy development rules are less well defined and the ways in which individuals interact are less structured. For example, in Module 5, after the groups generated twenty-five items, they found different ways of reducing that number to the ten items submitted to the larger group.

Some groups went down the list and decided by consensus of all the members which ten items to select, perhaps agreeing first on a smaller number, then slowly agreeing to other items. Others might have taken a vote on each item, setting aside those that received more than a certain number of votes and voting once again on the remaining items. What technique did your group use?

By contrast, in Phase I of POLFORM, a policy consisting of a number of specific items was adopted only if a majority of the group voted for it. This rule was specified in advance and constitutes part of the definition of POLFORM. In Phase II of POLFORM, additional rules were added for coalition formation and interaction between the Chief Tor and individual Tors to allow for persuasion and political bargaining. In Phase III, rules were added to govern the interaction of Mobes with Tors and to provide for a more complicated scoring system. Indeed, this progression from simpler to greater differentiation of roles and to more complicated rules marks the transition of policy development to policy formation.

The rules governing policy development and formation in the real world are obviously much more complicated than the rules used above. Each institutional setting for the policy process ordinarily will be governed by its own rules, yet certain similarities may be observed. Sometimes, in deference to the gamelike quality of the policy process, particularly during policy development and policy formation, these are called "rules of the game."

"Rules of the game" is a broad classification including at least three different types of rules: (1) procedures, (2) amenities, and (3) coalition principles. *Procedures* are rules that indicate how individuals participating in the game must proceed. During the final phase of POLFORM, Mobes and Tors were required to enter contracts by writing down a particular agreement. Rules governing the introduction of legislation up to a certain date, the requirement that executive orders be published in a certain place at a certain time, and filing dates for legal actions are all procedural rules, which must be adhered to in order to participate in the policy process. Procedural rules are ordinarily written and formally adopted by the policy body itself or set down in the document creating the institution. Often procedural rules are subject to change periodically, as at the beginning of a legislative session. The so-called cloture rule in the United States Senate, which used to require a two-thirds vote to cut off debate and force a vote on legislation, is an example of a procedural rule that is subject to revision each time the Senate convenes.

The policy process also includes customary, unwritten rules, or *amenities,* which are followed for reasons of tradition. The members who have served for a longer period of time and have accumulated greater seniority are often treated with greater deference. In the United States Senate, for example, these legislators are given their choice of committees to chair in addition to such considerations as choice of office space. In hierarchical organizations, advice-seeking and deference often follows traditionally defined informal channels as well as hierarchically defined paths indicated by formal organization structure. The United States Supreme Court uses customary rules in honoring a code of silence about the deliberations of the body and deciding who should be responsible for writing particular decisions.

Finally, rules exist governing the processes of bargaining and negotiation among individuals. These rules, or *coalition principles,* make use of compromise and side payments. Compromise is a process in which two or more individuals each decide to give in a little on their positions. For example, if the legislative leaders want to pass a budget of $2 billion and the governor wants a budget of $2.5 billion, a compromise would be reached if both support a budget of $2.25 billion. When each side gives up an equal amount, such as in the case cited, the compromise may be labeled "splitting the difference." It is a common technique that is used at all levels of society.

A more complicated principle of bargaining involves side payments. If the governor insisted on a budget of $2.5 billion and could promise the speaker of the assembly his or her support in a run for the governorship at a later date, the technique of bargaining becomes a side payment. One party supports the other in this instance in return for the other's support in another situation. Where side payments are directed toward the personal benefit of the individual, rather than directed toward program considerations, the individual is open to charges of bribery. Some types of side payment may be illegal, for example, if a legislator accepts a sum of money in return for support of a particular bill. Other gray areas may cause public officials and private citizens greater difficulty in deciding upon the legality or morality of the side payment. Legislators may support legislation in return for promises of votes, campaign support, and campaign contributions. Exactly when such bargaining, which is central to the group decision process, becomes bribery needs to be defined more precisely. It is one of the central concerns when attention is focused on ethics and conflicts of interest.

The existence of extensive rules governing the process of policy formation should not be surprising to students of public organizations and policy, for a striking characteristic of public organizations is the importance of rules. That is why the process of policy formation, and indeed the entire policy process, must be understood as a process of interaction among individuals occupying certain organizational positions and abiding by certain rules. This approach to understanding the public policy process may be categorized as the bureaucratic model.

Graham Allison has described the Cuban missile crisis in a classic analysis of executive policymaking, focusing on a narrow issue but having broad implications for international relations. After reading this case, prepare an analysis differentiating the major roles, describing their interactions, and pointing out the impact of specific rules on the outcome.

CONCEPTUAL MODELS AND THE CUBAN MISSILE CRISIS*

THE U.S. BLOCKADE OF CUBA: A THIRD CUT

The Politics of Discovery

A series of overlapping bargaining games determined both the *date* of the discovery of the Soviet missiles and the *impact* of this discovery on the Administration. An explanation of the politics of the discovery is consequently a considerable piece of the explanation of the U.S. blockade.

Cuba was the Kennedy Administration's "political Achilles' heel."[85] The months preceding the crisis were also months before the Congressional elections, and the Republican Senatorial and Congressional Campaign Committee had announced that Cuba would be "the dominant issue of the 1962 campaign."[86] What the administration billed as a "more positive and indirect approach of isolating Castro from developing, democratic Latin America," Senators Keating, Goldwater, Capehart, Thurmond, and others attacked as a "do-nothing" policy.[87] In statements on the floor of the House and Senate, campaign speeches across the country, and interviews and articles carried by national news media, Cuba — particularly the Soviet program of increased arms aid — served as a stick for stirring the domestic political scene.[88]

These attacks drew blood. Prudence demanded a vigorous reaction. The President decided to meet the issue head-on. The Administration mounted a forceful campaign of denial designed to discredit critics' claims. The President himself manned the front line of this offensive, though almost all Administration officials participated. In his news conference on August 19, President Kennedy attacked as "irresponsible" calls for an invasion of Cuba, stressing rather "the totality of our obligations" and promising to "watch what happens in Cuba with the closest attention."[89] On September 4, he issued a strong statement denying any provocative Soviet action in Cuba.[90] On September 13 he lashed out at "loose talk" calling for an invasion of Cuba.[91] The day before the flight of the U-2 which discovered the missiles, he campaigned in Capehart's Indiana against those "self-appointed generals and admirals who want to send someone else's sons to war."[92]

On Sunday, October 14, just as a U-2 was taking the first pictures of Soviet missiles, McGeorge Bundy was asserting:

> I *know* that there is no present evidence, and I think that there is no present likelihood that the Cuban government and the Soviet government would, in combination, attempt to install a major offensive capability.[93]

In this campaign to puncture the critics' charges, the Administration discovered that the public needed positive slogans. Thus, Kennedy fell into a tenuous semantic distinction between "offensive" and "defensive" weapons. This distinction originated in his September 4 statement that there was no evidence of "offensive ground to ground missiles" and warned "were it to be otherwise, the gravest issues would arise."[94] His September 13 statement turned on this distinction between "defensive" and "offensive" weapons and announced a firm commitment to action if the Soviet Union attempted to introduce the latter into Cuba.[95] Congressional committees elicited from administration officials testimony which read this distinction and the President's commitment into the *Congressional Record*.[96]

---

*Graham T. Allison, "Conceptual Models and the Cuban Missile Crisis," *American Political Science Review,* 1969, Vol. 63, pp. 712–715.

What the President least wanted to hear, the CIA was most hesitant to say plainly. On August 22 John McCone met privately with the President and voiced suspicions that the Soviets were preparing to introduce offensive missiles into Cuba.[97] Kennedy heard this as what it was: the suspicion of a hawk. McCone left Washington for a month's honeymoon on the Riviera. Fretting at Cap Ferrat, he bombarded his deputy, General Marshall Carter, with telegrams, but Carter, knowing that McCone had informed the President of his suspicions and received a cold reception, was reluctant to distribute these telegrams outside the CIA.[98] On September 9 a U-2 "on loan" to the Chinese Nationalists was downed over mainland China.[99] The Committee on Overhead Reconnaissance (COMOR) convened on September 10 with a sense of urgency.[100] Loss of another U-2 might incite world opinion to demand cancellation of U-2 flights. The President's campaign against those who asserted that the Soviets were acting provocatively in Cuba had begun. To risk downing a U-2 over Cuba was to risk chopping off the limb on which the President was sitting. That meeting decided to shy away from the western end of Cuba (where SAMs were becoming operational) and modify the flight pattern of the U-2s in order to reduce the probability that a U-2 would be lost.[101] USIB's unanimous approval of the September estimate reflects similar sensitivities. On September 13 the President had asserted that there were no Soviet offensive missiles in Cuba and committed his Administration to act if offensive missiles were discovered. Before Congressional committees, Administration officials were denying that there was any evidence whatever of offensive missiles in Cuba. The implications of a National Intelligence estimate which concluded that the Soviets were introducing offensive missiles into Cuba were not lost on the men who constituted America's highest intelligence assembly.

The October 4 COMOR decision to direct a flight over the western end of Cuba in effect "overturned" the September estimate, but without officially raising that issue. The decision represented McCone's victory for which he had lobbied with the President before the September 10 decision, in telegrams before the September 19 estimate, and in person after his return to Washington. Though the politics of the intelligence community is closely guarded, several pieces of the story can be told.[102] By September 27, Colonel Wright and others in DIA believed that the Soviet Union was placing missiles in the San Cristobal area.[103] This area was marked suspicious by the CIA on September 29 and certified top priority on October 3. By October 4 McCone had the evidence required to raise the issue officially. The members of COMOR heard McCone's argument, but were reluctant to make the hard decision he demanded. The significant probability that a U-2 would be downed made overflight of western Cuba a matter of real concern.[104]

The Politics of Issues

The U-2 photographs presented incontrovertible evidence of Soviet offensive missiles in Cuba. This revelation fell upon politicized players in a complex context. As one high official recalled, Khrushchev had caught us "with our pants down." What each of the central participants saw, and what each did to cover both his own and the Administration's nakedness, created the spectrum of issues and answers.

At approximately 9:00 A.M., Tuesday morning, October 16, McGeorge Bundy went to the President's living quarters with the message: "Mr. President, there is now hard photographic evidence that the Russians have offensive missiles in Cuba."[105] Much has been made of Kennedy's "expression of surprise,"[106] but "surprise" fails to capture the character of his initial reaction. Rather, it was one of startled anger, most adequately conveyed by the exclamation: "He can't do that to *me!*"[107] In terms of the President's attention and priorities at that moment, Khrushchev had chosen the most unhelpful act of all. Kennedy had staked his full Presidential authority on the assertion that the Soviets would not place offensive weapons in Cuba. Moreover, Khrushchev had assured the President through the most direct and personal channels that he was aware of the President's domestic political problem and that nothing would be done to exacerbate this problem. The Chairman had *lied* to the President. Kennedy's initial reaction entailed action. The missiles must be removed.[108] The alternatives of "doing nothing" or "taking a diplomatic approach" could not have been less relevant to *his* problem.

These two tracks—doing nothing and taking a diplomatic approach—were the solutions advocated by two of his principal advisors. For Secretary of Defense McNamara, the missiles raised the spectre of nuclear war. He first framed the issue as a straightforward strategic problem. To understand the issue, one had to grasp two obvious but difficult points. First, the missiles represented an inevitable occurrence: narrowing of the missile gap. It simply happened sooner rather than later. Second, the United States could accept this occurrence since its consequences were minor: "seven-to-one missile 'superiority,' one-to-one missile 'equality,' one-to-seven missile 'inferiority'—the three postures are identical." McNamara's statement of this argument at the first meeting of the ExCom was summed up in the phrase, "a missile is a missile."[109] "It makes no great difference," he maintained, "whether you are killed by a missile from the Soviet Union or Cuba."[110] The implication was clear. The United States should not initiate a crisis with the Soviet Union, risking a significant probability of nuclear war over an occurrence which had such small strategic implications.

The perceptions of McGeorge Bundy, the President's Assistant for National Security Affairs, are the most difficult of all to reconstruct. There is no question that he initially argued for a diplomatic track.[111] But was Bundy laboring under his acknowledged burden of responsibility in Cuba I? Or was he playing the role of devil's advocate in order to make the President probe his own initial reaction and consider other options?

The President's brother, Robert Kennedy, saw most clearly the political wall against which Khrushchev had backed the President. But he, like McNamara, saw the prospect of nuclear doom. Was Khrushchev going to force the President to an insane act? At the first meeting of the ExCom, he scribbled a note, "Now I know how Tojo felt when he was planning Pearl Harbor."[112] From the outset he searched for an alternative that would prevent the air strike.

The initial reaction of Theodore Sorensen, the President's Special Counsel and "alter ego," fell somewhere between that of the President and his brother. Like the President, Sorensen felt the poignancy of betrayal. If the President had been the architect of the policy which the missiles punctured, Sorensen was the draftsman. Khrushchev's deceitful move demanded a strong counter-move. But like Robert Kennedy, Sorensen feared lest the shock and disgrace lead to disaster.

To the Joint Chiefs of Staff the issue was clear. *Now* was the time to do the job for which they had prepared contingency plans. Cuba I had been badly done; Cuba II would not be. The missiles provided the *occasion* to deal with the issue: cleansing the Western Hemisphere of Castro's Communism. As the President recalled on the day the crisis ended, "An invasion would have been a mistake—a wrong use of our power. But the military are mad. They wanted to do this. It's lucky for us that we have McNamara over there."[113]

McCone's perceptions flowed from his confirmed prediction. As the Cassandra of the incident, he argued forcefully that the Soviets had installed the missiles in a daring political probe which the United States must meet with force. The time for an air strike was now.[114]

The Politics of Choice

The process by which the blockade emerged is a story of the most subtle and intricate probing, pulling, and hauling: leading, guiding, and spurring. Reconstruction of this process can only be tentative. Initially the President and most of his advisers wanted the clean, surgical air strike. On the first day of the crisis, when informing Stevenson of the missiles, the President mentioned only two alternatives: "I suppose the alternatives are to go in by air and wipe them out, or to take other steps to render them inoperable."[115] At the end of the week a sizeable minority still favored an air strike. As Robert Kennedy recalled: "The fourteen people involved were very significant . . . . If six of them had been President of the U.S., I think that the world might have been blown up."[116] What prevented the air strike was a fortuitous coincidence of a number of factors — the absense of any one of which might have permitted that option to prevail.

First, McNamara's vision of holocaust set him firmly against the air strike. His initial attempt to frame the issue in strategic terms struck Kennedy as particularly inappropriate. Once McNamara realized that the name of the game was a strong response, however, he and his deputy Gilpatric chose the blockade as a fallback. When the Secretary of Defense — whose department had the action, whose reputation in the Cabinet was unequaled, in whom the President demonstrated full confidence — marshalled the arguments for the blockade and refused to be moved, the blockade became a formidable alternative.

Second, Robert Kennedy — the President's closest confidant — was unwilling to see his brother become a "Tojo." His arguments against the air strike on moral grounds struck a chord in the President. Moreover, once his brother had stated these arguments so forcefully, the President could not have chosen his initially preferred course without, in effect, agreeing to become what RFK had condemned.

The President learned of the missiles on Tuesday morning. On Wednesday morning, in order to mask our discovery from the Russians, the President flew to Connecticut to keep a campaign commitment, leaving RFK as the unofficial chairman of the group. By the time the President returned on Wednesday evening, a critical third piece had been added to the picture. McNamara had presented his argument for the blockade. Robert Kennedy and Sorensen had joined McNamara. A powerful coalition of the advisers in whom the President had the greatest confidence, and with whom his style was most compatible, had emerged.

Fourth, the coalition that had formed behind the President's initial preference gave him reason to pause. *Who* supported the air strike — the Chiefs, McCone, Rusk, Nitze, and Acheson — as much as *how* they supported it, counted. Fifth, a piece of inaccurate information, which no one probed, permitted the blockade advocates to fuel (potential) uncertainties in the President's mind. When the President returned to Washington Wednesday evening, RFK and Sorensen met him at the airport. Sorensen gave the President a four-page memorandum outlining the areas of agreement and disagreement. The strongest argument was that the air strike simply could not be surgical.[117] After a day of prodding and questioning, the Air Force had asserted that it could not guarantee the success of a surgical air strike limited to the missiles alone.

Thursday evening, the President convened the ExCom at the White House. He declared his tentative choice of the blockade and directed that preparations be made to put it into effect by Monday morning.[118] Though he raised a question about the possibility of a surgical air strike subsequently, he seems to have accepted the experts' opinion that this was no live option.[119] (Acceptance of this estimate suggests that he may have learned the lesson of the Bay of Pigs — "Never rely on experts" — less well than he supposed.)[120] But this information was incorrect. That no one probed this estimate during the first week of the crisis poses an interesting question for further investigation.

A coalition, including the President, thus emerged from the President's initial decision that something had to be done; McNamara, Robert Kennedy, and Sorensen's resistance to the air strike; incompatibility between the President and the air strike advocates; and an inaccurate piece of information.[121]

---

85. Sorensen, *Kennedy,* p. 670.
86. *Ibid.*
87. *Ibid.,* pp. 670ff.
88. *New York Times,* August, September, 1962.
89. *New York Times,* August 20, 1962.
90. *New York Times,* September 5, 1962.
91. *New York Times,* September 14, 1962.
92. *New York Times,* October 14, 1962.
93. Cited by Abel, *op. cit.,* p. 13.
94. *New York Times,* September 5, 1962.
95. *New York Times,* September 14, 1962.
96. Senate Foreign Relations Committee; Senate Armed Services Committee; House Committee on Appropriation; House Select Committee on Export Control.
97. Abel, *op. cit.,* pp. 17–18. According to McCone, he told Kennedy, "The only construction I can put on the material going into Cuba is that the Russians are preparing to introduce offensive missiles." See also Weintal and Bartlett, *op. cit.,* pp. 60–61.
98. Abel, *op. cit.,* p. 23.
99. *New York Times,* September 10, 1962.
100. See Abel, *op. cit.,* pp. 25–26; and Hilsman, *op. cit.,* p. 174.
101. Department of Defense Appropriation, *Hearings,* 69.
102. A basic, but somewhat contradictory, account of parts of this story emerges in the Department of Defense Appropriations, *Hearings,* 1–70.
103. Department of Defense Appropriations, *Hearings,* 71.
104. The details of the 10 days between the October 4 decision and the October 14 flight must be held in abeyance.
105. Abel, *op. cit.,* p. 44.
106. *Ibid.,* pp. 44ff.
107. See Richard Neustadt, "Afterword," *Presidential Power* (New York, 1964).
108. Sorensen, *Kennedy,* p. 676; Schlesinger, *op. cit.,* p. 801.
109. Hilsman, *op. cit.,* p. 195.
110. *Ibid.*
111. Weintal and Bartlett, *op. cit.,* p. 67; Abel, *op. cit.,* p. 53.
112. Schlesinger, *op. cit.,* p. 803.
113. *Ibid.,* p. 831.
114. Abel, *op cit.,* p. 186.
115. *Ibid.,* p. 49.
116. Interview, quoted by Ronald Steel, *New York Review of Books,* March 13, 1969, p. 22.
117. Sorensen, *Kennedy,* p. 686.

118. *Ibid.*, p. 691.
119. *Ibid.*, pp. 691 – 692.
120. Schlesinger, *op. cit.*, p. 296.
121. Space will not permit an account of the path from this coalition to the formal government decision on Saturday and action on Monday.

SELECTED BIBLIOGRAPHY FOR MODULE 6

ALLISON, GRAHAM. *Essence of Decision: Explaining the Cuban Missile Crisis.* Boston: Little, Brown, 1971.

———. "Conceptual Models and the Cuban Missile Crisis." *APSR* 63 (1969): 712.

ANDERSON, JAMES E. *Public Policy-Making.* New York: Praeger, 1975.

BARNARD, CHESTER. *The Functions of the Executive.* Cambridge: Harvard University Press, 1938.

BAUER, RAYMOND A., and GERGEN, KENNETH J., eds. *The Study of Policy Formation,* New York: Free Press, 1968.

BURKE, EDMUND. "Speech to the Electors of Bristol," in *Collected Works,* vol. II. (1774).

EASTON, DAVID. *The Political System.* New York: Alfred Knopf, 1964.

GRODNOW, FRANK. *Politics and Administration.* New York: Russell and Russell, 1900.

LASSWELL, HAROLD. *Politics: Who Gets What, When, How.* New York: McGraw-Hill, 1938.

LINDBLOM, CHARLES. *The Policy-Making Process.* Englewood Cliffs, NJ: Prentice-Hall, 1968.

LINDBLOM, CHARLES, and BRAYBROOKE, DAVID. *A Strategy of Decision.* New York: Free Press, 1963.

SHARKANSKY, IRA. *Public Administration, Policy-Making in Government Agencies.* Chicago: Markham, 1970.

SIMON, HERBERT. *Administrative Behavior.* New York: Free Press, 1945.

WAHLKE, JOHN, et al. *The Legislative System.* New York: John Wiley and Sons, 1962.

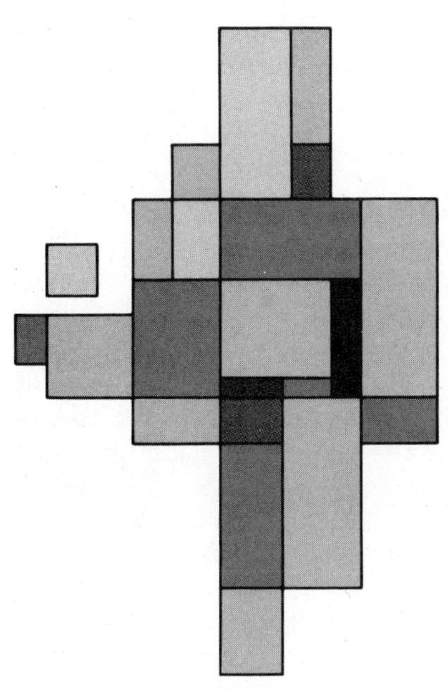

MODULE 7

Policy Implementation, Planning, Intergovernmental Relations

INTRODUCTION

Policy formation, the fashioning of laws, executive orders, judicial decisions, and other rules, is relatively open to the influence of nondecision makers. A previous module stressed the importance of policy development in limiting the range of alternatives before the formal or informal agreement on how to proceed, or policy formation. Lost opportunities during the policy development phase may foreclose many options. And unfortunately the opportunities for influencing policy development often are limited by specific knowledge about its dynamics. Similarly, policy implementation may be critical and yet often overlooked by observers of the policy process.

DISENCHANTMENT WITH THE GREAT SOCIETY

During the middle and late 1960s, under the leadership of President Lyndon Johnson, an extraordinary volume of legislation was passed, much of it associated with the well-publicized War on Poverty. The Civil Rights Act of 1964, and the Voting Rights Act of 1965 were passed. The Office of Economic Opportunity was created, along with community action agencies. New subsidy programs were enacted in the areas of education, manpower, housing, urban renewal, and medical care. Yet by the early 1970s dissatisfaction with Johnson's War on Poverty was rampant.

This disenchantment was often greatest among those groups that had looked upon Johnson as a friend and ally. Increasingly, questions were being asked about the effectiveness of the War on Poverty.

Johnson succeeded in winning legislative victories. Trading on public sentiment after the death of John Kennedy and on his own skill in dealing with Congress, he succeeded where other presidents, including John Kennedy, had failed. But passing laws does not by itself solve social problems. Did the War on Poverty reduce the number of the poor? Did it increase the political power of the poor and the nonwhite? Did it provide better access to jobs for the disadvantaged? Did it improve the educational opportunities of the poor? While the answers to these questions require considerable analysis and discussion, in general most observers would agree that the Great Society programs enacted by President Lyndon Johnson fell far short of the ambitious goals they proclaimed.

Many of the Great Society policies that were articulated and enacted into law were never successfully implemented. The gap between hope and reality, between policy and their realization, is indeed formidable. The lack of success of the Great Society programs has emphasized that point. A book entitled *Implementation,* by Aaron Wildavsky and Jeffrey Pressman, highlights this point and is an example of the redirected attention to implementation of public policy.

Implementation

The administration of public policy is basically the chore of the line agencies reporting directly to the elected executives. They provide the everyday services of government, like supplying water, police and fire protection, collecting taxes, and issuing driver's licenses. In theory, government proceeds from the implementation of broad statements of policy. But the broad statement of policy contained in legislation, an executive order, or a decision by an elected executive rarely provides detailed instructions. Most policy is not effective until it is translated into concrete government activity by the responsible agency.

As discussed above, the major day-to-day activities of government are carried out by the departments and agencies functioning directly under the elected executive. Implementation of policy thus becomes translated into activity by the individuals working in these public organizations. Since much of this implementation effort requires the refinement of the general policy established by legislatures and elected executives, or in some cases, the judiciary, these subordinate departments and agencies themselves become involved in policymaking at a lower level.

Implementation may require the creation of new agencies, changes in existing ones, or merely changes in the current rules. For example, when many states and localities became conscious of the need to protect the environment, new agencies were set up to administer new regulations, whose broad outlines were contained in legislation. A new agency is not bound by the practices of the past. New staff members committed to the new tasks can be selected. Sometimes changing existing agencies is easier and less costly than creating new ones; the danger is that the existing agency will be hampered in carrying out its new function because of existing demands on the organization. When new policy involves merely drawing up new rules, existing agencies often are charged with their implementation.

All government agency activity is directed toward fulfilling goals and purposes enunciated in a policy statement. In this sense policy implementation and execution is part of the larger operation of public organizations. But policy implementation and execution that occur after the initial enunciation of new policy deserve special attention. Often they require changes in work schedules and organizational structures. It is this aspect of policy implementation which will be the subject of this module.

A classic example of policy implementation is the administrative activity that follows the passage of legislation marking a major departure from the past. While administrative officials may influence the legislative process and shape the character of the legislation, they must follow the policies enunciated by the legislature. Legislation may be unclear, may require apparently irreconcilable alternatives, and generally may create a whole range of difficulties for the actual implementation of the stated purposes. This process may involve, in David Truman's words, "turning the controversial into the routine," for often major legislative departures involve strong conflicts and disagreements among the affected parties.

Yet in the case of major legislation, the administrative staff must implement the broad policies enunciated by the legislature. This process involves continuing interaction with the groups to be served and those to be affected as well as with the bureaucrats who must administer the programs. It involves many layers of activity, including the formulation of policy, as the administrators fill in the policy gaps that the legislation has created.

Intergovernmental Programs

The process of implementing federal legislation often involves interaction between the federal government and state and local governments. Especially since the end of the Second World War, federal legislation has tended to involve programs reaching down to state and local governments. In part this reflects the growing reliance of government programs on federal tax sources. These programs have made understanding fiscal federalism and intergovernmental relations critical for public managers. Table 7 – 1 shows the growth of intergovernment transfers during the course of the twentieth century. In 1978, 22 percent of state and local funds came from the federal government in a variety of ways.

TABLE 7 – 1 State and Local Government Revenues
(in millions)

Fiscal Year	Total General Revenue	From Federal Government	Percentage of Total from Federal Government
1978	$315,960	$69,592	22.0
1976	256,176	55,589	21.7
1974	207,670	41,820	20.1
1972	166,363	31,253	18.8
1970	130,756	21,857	16.7
1960	50,505	6,974	13.8
1950	20,911	2,486	11.9
1940	9,609	945	9.8

SOURCE: U.S. Bureau of the Census, *Governmental Finances in 1977 – 78* and other selected years

The most common distinctions among grant programs concern the specificity of the program and the funding mechanism. Programs that focus on specific areas, like Title I of the Elementary and Secondary Education Act or vocational education are known as categorical programs, because they focus on specific categories. Grant programs, like those operating in the areas of law enforcement and community development, cover a wide range and are known as bloc-grant programs. The latter may often be used for a variety of purposes. Revenue sharing is an extremely broad bloc-grant program since its use covers a broad field.

The other major dimension in differentiating grant programs is whether they are funded on a project basis, based on specific submission and competition with similar programs, or whether they are funded on the basis of an objective formula that determines how much a particular locality or other unit will receive. The ability to select particular projects means that federal agencies can limit the use of funds to specific purposes and priorities. Formula grants, on the other hand, increase the discretion of local agencies in using funds, and decrease their accountability to federal or state agencies.

Now consider Title I of the Elementary and Secondary Education Act of 1965, a categorical, formula grant program, and the problems of implementation that followed passage of its legislation. The following excerpt is from a book by Stephen Bailey and Edith Mosher, *ESEA: The Office of Education Administers a Law.* The passage describes the implementation efforts surrounding Title I of the Elementary and Secondary Education Act of 1965. Title I was the main provision of the first major national program of federal aid to education, outside of vocational education. With minor exceptions, up until that time education had been funded exclusively by state and local governments. Title I provided monies to local school districts for developing special programs for children from poverty-level families. These special programs are called compensatory programs, since they are intended to make up for the deprivations of a poor family environment by providing extra school services. The implementation of Title I involved major changes in the United States Office of Education, which was given responsibility for administering the program. The next case study illustrates the implementation problems in a federal grant program that depends upon the activities of state and local officials.

ESEA: The Office of Education Administers a Law*

IMPLEMENTING TITLE I: THE SETTING

The scope of the task of administering Title I of ESEA was unprecedented. Subject to qualifying conditions for approvable projects, nearly 25,000 school districts in 54 States and territories were entitled to spend more than a billion dollars within 15 months, on a specifically targeted group: the educationally disadvantaged. For the initiation of the program to be smoothly integrated with preparations for the school year beginning in September, 1965, the tool-up period for school officials would have been, theoretically, the last three months of FY'65 (April – June) and the first quarter of FY'66 (July – September 1965). But monies for the Act were not even appropriated until September 23, 1965. To launch such an enormous undertaking would take at the very least a number of months. As a result, those responsible were beset not only by the inherent size and difficulties of tasks of implementation but also by mounting pressures to overcome a serious time-lag in putting the funds to work before the statutory deadlines for their expiration. The months spent in gearing up would bring the calendar closer and closer to the end of the fiscal year in which the money was to be spent.

---

*Stephen K. Bailey and Edith K. Mosher, *ESEA: The Office of Education Administers a Law* (Syracuse: Syracuse University Press, 1968), pp. 100 – 109.

These tight realities were further complicated by the fact that the enactment of Title I found educators, including those in USOE, in a poor state of readiness to move rapidly in carrying out its unfamiliar demands. To begin with, Title I was targeted to the very group of students for which traditional local school services had been least satisfactory. Although a few districts had had special programs to meet the needs of educationally disadvantaged children, these efforts had provided little certainty as to what activities were really effective. Furthermore, there was a widespread shortage of personnel qualified to plan and operate such projects. In fact, many districts entitled to Title I funds had no previous experience in carrying out federally-connected projects of any kind.

These general handicaps were substantial in themselves. However, as knowledge of the provisions of Title I became more widespread, it was apparent to local school administrators that other headaches were involved. The requirements that Title I projects be designed to meet the needs of educationally disadvantaged children, and be of appropriate size, scope, and quality, clearly implied that the services provided would have to be additional to, but not isolated from, the regular school offerings for such children. And the statutory emphasis on measuring the educational achievement of the beneficiaries of Title I projects appeared to lead in the direction of a national assessment of a school's effectiveness — a development long feared and resisted by school administrators throughout the country.

Hope, anxiety, uncertainty, inexperience, and fear at the local level comprised the intellectual and emotional setting within which USOE and SEA's had to implement much of the new experiment in national educational policy represented by Title I of ESEA.

ESEA TASK FORCE ACTIVITIES, APRIL TO JUNE, 1965

Even though the reorganization of USOE was not to be completed before June 15, structural arrangements were made in mid-April to handle the initial tasks of implementing ESEA. The Executive Group set up a special Planning Group under the chairmanship of Russell Wood, then in the Office of Administration, later Acting Director of the Office of Program Planning and Evaluation. Task forces were organized for each of the ESEA titles, with staffs of 10 to 12 persons selected from throughout the agency for their competency in the various areas relevant to each title. In addition, three specialized subgroups were designated to work on services common to the implementation of all the titles: i.e., data sources and needs, form design, and fiscal requirements. The Executive Group assigned the highest priority to the preparations to launch Titles I and V — Title I because of its size and complexity; Title V because of the patent necessity of strengthening the administrative capacity of State educational agencies for their role in implementing new Federal programs including Titles I and II of ESEA.

The specific mission of the Title I Task Force was to develop regulations, guidelines, and the official forms required to administer the largest of the ESEA programs.

Other immediate USOE responsibilities for Title I were handled outside the task forces. For example, the National Center for Educational Statistics was made responsible for working with the Bureau of the Census and the Welfare Administration of HEW in bringing together the data required by the Title I formula. The appointment of the National Advisory Council, required by Section 212 of the Act, received top level attention in the Office of the Commissioner. During May, Associate Commissioner Reed, the former Deputy Commissioner, planned a series of regional meetings of leading school administrators, state and local, at which various high ranking officials of USOE explained the new legislation. As coordinator of the ESEA task forces, Wood periodically reported their problems and progress to the Executive Group, transmitted clarifications of policy decisions to the task forces, and saw to it that they held to specified deadlines.

TITLE I: A SUMMARY OF SEQUENCE

The tasks of the Office of Education in implementing Title I may be grouped under the following classifications: (1) the development of standards and procedures for the funding and control of authorizations; (2) the construction of ground rules and guidelines for educational programming and project design; and (3) the preparation and analysis of reports and other informational and administrative data. These activities are logically sequential in the sense that funding-authorizations and program regulations are essential for subsequent official action, and reports must be based on some period of program execution. However, in the shaping of Title I, anticipatory and unofficial actions became important preludes to official decisions and rule-making. To illustrate, USOE officials held the first round of a series of regional meetings in May, 1965, to provide advance information to, and seek advice from, the educational community at a time when the preparation of official guidelines was just getting started. During the summer of 1965, official guidelines were actually drafted. In November, 1965, a number of USOE officials attended the annual conference of the Council of Chief State School Officers in Honolulu. This participation led shortly thereafter to some official changes in the Title I guidelines. The entire cycle of pre-clearance, official drafts, and post-clearance was reactivated on a small scale when Title I was amended in October, 1965, to include handicapped children in state-supported institutions. Since the activities described under (1), (2), and (3) above were to some extent all going on concurrently, Table 6 [Table 7 – 2] has been provided as an aid in clarifying the chronological sequence of implementation in the 15-month period between April, 1965 and July, 1966.

TITLE I: AUTHORIZATION FUNDING AND CONTROLS

The first major task to confront those charged with implementing Title I was the development of standards and procedures for the funding and control of authorizations to the States and through the States to the local educational agencies.

The funding of authorizations involved two separate tasks for the implementation architects: first, determination of grant entitlements (i.e., how much money could be allotted to each school district); and second, development of criteria for the design and approval of the local programs. The analytic separation of these interrelated procedures reflected an important policy assumption: that whereas grants were to be made to school districts in accordance with measures of economic need, children were to participate in the program's benefits solely on the basis of relative "educational disadvantage." The result of this policy distinction was to separate the tasks of fiscal and program administration and to create a source of confusion for LEA's. A number of school districts assumed that if they qualified under the Title I formula they could spend federal money on programs benefiting *all* children. That is, they viewed ESEA as *general aid* distributed on a basis of a "poverty" formula, rather than as *aid to the educationally disadvantaged* distributed according to a "poverty" formula.

TABLE 7–2. Chronological Sequence of Major Implementation Activities for Title I
April, 1965 – July, 1966

Activities	April to June, 1965	July to September, 1965	October to December, 1965	January to July, 1966
Funding — Authorizations and Controls	USOE consulted with Census Bureau and Welfare Department of HEW on basic data requirements (May).	USOE sent SEA's suggested form for providing assurances of compliance and Census data for minor governmental subdivisions (July 30). USOE computed maximum grant entitlements to county level and notified SEA's (Aug. 26). Thirty SEA's submitted assurances and received authority to commit FY'66 funds (Sept. 23).	Remaining SEA's submitted assurances and received funding authorizations; all SEA's computed sub-county entitlements and notified LEA's (Nov.). USOE requested SEA's to supply basic data for computing grant entitlements under Public Law 89-313 (Nov.). Project design and approval activities got underway in nearly all States (Nov. – Dec.).	USOE sent SEA's instructions for grant applications under Public Law 89 – 313 (Feb.); sent notifications of their grant entitlements (April). USOE sent cut-off dates for SEA approval of new projects to be funded in FY'66 (April); deadline for all FY'66 project approval was June 30. HEW staff prepared draft *Audit Instructions* (July).
Preparation of Regulations, Guidelines, and Project Application Forms	USOE Title I Task Force appointed (April). CSSO reviewed draft *Regulations* (June 24 – 25).	Representatives of church groups reviewed the draft *Regulations* (July and August). USOE urged SEA's to prepare for project approval workload and provided draft of *Project Application Form* (July 30). USOE sent final version of *Regulations* to SEA's (August 26) and published them in *Federal Register* (Sept.). USOE compiled draft *Guidelines* (Aug. – Sept.).	USOE provided SEA's with supply of printed *Project Application Form* and requested copies of SEA approved applications (Sept. – Oct.). USOE draft *Guidelines* discussed at regional meetings (Oct. 14 – 29), CCSSO conference, and meeting of CCSSO representatives (Nov.). Targeting provisions modified, and final version sent to SEA's (Dec.).	USOE sent SEA's revised instructions for FY'66 *Project Application Form* (Jan.) and a revised *Form* and instructions for FY'67 (June). Revised version of *Regulations*, with Public Law 89 – 313 amendments published in *Federal Register* (March). USOE asked SEA's to submit complete descriptions of organization and staffing arrangements (July).

Reports			USOE sent SEA's instructions for interim annual report (Dec.).	SEA's submitted interim reports which USOE summarized; USOE also compiled *Report on 484 Title Projects* (Feb.). National Advisory Council completed first report (March) and contracted for consultants to review summer projects (June). USOE published *Chance for a Change* and *Report on the National Conference for Education of the Disadvantaged* (July). USOE sent SEA's instructions for first annual report, due Dec., 1966 (April).
Administrative and Informational Services	USOE and State officials discussed ESEA implementation at regional meetings (May).	DPO collected informational materials on educationally disadvantaged children; began year-long program of dissemination to SEA's (Sept.). USOE reorganized; DPO made responsible for Title I (July). Congress passed FY'66 appropriations for ESEA (Sept. 23).	DPO officials conducted regional "roadshows" on Title I implementation (See *Guidelines* item above).	DPO conducted field program reviews and held regional conferences on evaluation (March – May). National Conference on Title I (July).
Related Events	Ink Committee appointed (April); completed survey of USOE (June).		Congress passed Title I amendments in Public Law 89 – 313 (Oct.).	Congressional Education subcommittees held hearings on amendments to ESEA (March – April).

The task of developing funding-authorizations and controls was fairly familiar, technical, and relatively non-controversial.

Several sections of the statute dealt almost exclusively with fiscal administration. Section 203 gave the Commissioner of Education the authority to determine both the eligibility of school districts for grants and, if satisfactory data for the purpose were available, the amount of their maximum basic grants.

Since the collection and analysis of precise demographic data for the purpose of determining a school district's eligibility under the Title I formula was bound in some cases to be an attenuated process, pragmatic bench-marks had to be substituted for refined calibration — at least for FY'66. Otherwise, time taken in establishing eligibility would have denied most LEA's any funds at all. In consequence, a division of labor was worked out between Federal and State officials. In all but 11 States, USOE determined eligibility and aggregate maximum grants only to the county level—using data from the decennial census of 1960 along with records of the payment of aid-to-dependent-children grants during calendar year 1962. The states whose school districts were not coterminous with census-tabulated units were authorized to compute allocations to school districts at the sub-county level.

Congress had settled temporarily on the use of out-of-date national demographic and economic measures on the grounds that they were the best available. However, it soon became apparent that the task of applying uniform criteria for the purpose of making sub-county allocations was complicated (1) by the difficulties of adjusting census-tract data to school district populations; (2) by the inconsistency or incompleteness of other data sources; and (3) by geographical variations in the jurisdiction of different kinds of school districts (e.g., elementary vs. K – 12 districts). These were among the first problems explored jointly in conferences of USOE and groups of state officials, and a pilot survey was conducted to test the feasibility of alternate methods of procedure. The final decision was that the States could enjoy flexibility in choosing among several bases for computing sub-county allocations, but that the same basis had to be applied throughout the State. Detailed rules were drafted to guide the states in treating uniformly a variety of school district boundary conditions.[2]

The Census Bureau and the Welfare Administration of HEW provided USOE with the requisite statistics, and in July, USOE supplied the State education agencies with the census tract data for their minor governmental subdivisions, alerting the SEA's to their forthcoming task of computing sub-county allocations. The State agencies were also sent instructions on the method of submitting assurances of intent to participate in Title I grants. Such assurances were dictated by Section 206 of ESEA. On August 26, the States were notified of the maximum county-level allocations, and immediately following the approval of the First FY'66 Supplemental Appropriation Act on September 23, the 30 states which had already filed satisfactory assurances were authorized to commit Title I funds upon approval of LEA project proposals. By late October, practically all of the States had submitted assurances, and had notified the LEA's of their entitlements. By that same date, a number of States had actually launched the process of reviewing local project applications.

As to the adoption of grant payment procedures and subsequent fiscal requirements, two factors eased the workload of the implementation period. The

---

2. *Code of Federal Regulations,* Title 45, Sections 116.4 – 116.7

first was that "obligation accounting" and "letter of credit" systems for requesting, expending, and reporting on federal grant funds had already become familiar to a number of state and local school administrators under previous legislation and could readily be incorporated into the Title I Regulations and Guidelines.[3] The other factor was related to levels of funding for FY'66. Section 208 provided for "ratable reductions" of total amounts for which LEA's were eligible under the Title I formula in case appropriations were insufficient to pay the full entitlements. As noted in Chapter II, the initial FY'66 appropriations were substantially lower than the Administration's estimate of requirements; but they were also open-ended. That is, USOE did not need to revise the basic entitlements downward. Instead, in March, 1966, USOE simply requested supplemental appropriations to cover revised estimates of the amounts to be obligated by the LEA's during the remainder of FY'66.[4]

When it appeared that substantial amounts could not be used for projects during the regular school term, Commissioner Howe joined OEO officials in an urgent appeal to school administrators to develop Title I programs for the summer of 1966. The SEA's had a special interest in making it possible for the LEA's to claim full entitlement, since the amount of funds available for state administrative purposes was computed on the basis of funds obligated for approved projects.

USOE officials were not only concerned about under-expending FY'66 appropriations; they also feared that a last-minute rush to obligate funds would lower the standards for planning and approving Title I funds. In what school administrators protested as a precipitate and arbitrary move, Commissioner Howe issued instructions on April 2, 1966, setting deadlines for project submission and approval. The State agencies were instructed not to approve proposals involving construction, related equipment, or major capital outlay after April 6, and not to approve proposals submitted after May 2.[5]

In spite of (perhaps because of) such strictures, USOE reported that 89 per cent of available funds, or $826 million, was obligated prior to the close of the fiscal year. About $250 million of the $959 million appropriated was approved for projects to be undertaken during the summer of 1966.[6]

With regard to fiscal accountability for the Title I projects, the official Federal issuances became progressively tighter. The earliest regulations referred in general terms only to provision of "proper fiscal controls" at the State and local levels.[7] Six months later, the revised regulations amplified this requirement in a new section on fiscal audits.[8] Further detailed Federal restrictions were issued to

---

3. The relevant instructions are to be found in the USOE publication *Financial Management of Federal-State Education Programs,* OE-10019, 1962. There have been some persistent problems in meshing Federal, State, and local accounting and auditing requirements and procedures. See the response to questions on this matter made by Associate Commissioner Harris in *Hearings Before the Special Subcommittee on Education, on the U.S. Office of Education,* 89th Cong., 2d sess., House, 311–12.

4. Title I funding for FY'67 turned out to be much more complicated. *Hearings Before Subcommittees of the Committee on Appropriations,* Supplemental Appropriation Bill, 1967, 89th Cong., 2d sess., House, Part I, 450–463.

5. Memoranda from the U.S. Commissioner of Education to Chief State School Officers, April 2 and April 6, 1966; Memorandum of John F. Hughes, Director, Division of Program Operations, to Title I Coordinators, April 14, 1966.

6. *Education USA,* National Education Association, September 8, 1966, 12; December 8, 1966, 90.

7. *Code of Federal Regulations,* Title 45, Section 116.31(d).

8. *Ibid.,* Section 116.48.

ensure SEA uniformity with regard to disbursing and accounting procedures, forms, and impending audits. The SEA's had overall supervision of LEA fiscal operations, but Federal surveillance was also to be provided both in the form of program reviews by USOE personnel at unspecified intervals, and annual fiscal audits by the HEW staff. Both activities would normally be concerned only with the State level of operation but could be extended to the LEA's if Federal officials found State controls inadequate.

On July 1, 1966 the HEW Audit Agency issued very detailed *Interim Audit Instruction C–10* to apply to the initial review of Title I operations. Auditors were to be concerned primarily with fiscal records and procedures, but they were also to mesh their activities with those of the USOE officials responsible for administrative and program reviews.

During the first year of Title I implementation, Federal officials were seeking to develop systematic compliance by SEA's and LEA's in matters of fiscal accountability and, at the same time, to encourage them to exert initiative in designing their educational programs for disadvantaged children so as to fit local needs and circumstances. These objectives, however, called for different kinds of competency and orientation on the part of school administrators. The FY'66 experience indicated that achieving the first objective may be easier than the second. The SEA's and LEA's protested the paperwork imposed by the fiscal accounting, but the requirements were more definite and less troublesome for them than those connected with project design. Students of the administrative process have pointed out that zealous attention to accounting and auditing considerations can subvert flexible and innovative programming.[9] The effects of the Federal fiscal procedures on the educational policy outcomes of Title I were not evident during the early months of the program, but, at an evaluation session in the winter of 1966, urban school officials reported particular difficulty in assimilating Title I projects into their regular programs because of the Federal requirements of entirely separate accounting systems.[10] One of the continuing problems in all systems of public accountability is what Professor Wallace Sayre of Columbia University has called the danger of "the triumph of technique over purpose."

COMMENT ON IMPLEMENTING TITLE I

Having read about the implementation efforts following the adoption of Title I, do you understand why implementation of this program might have been difficult? What did the effort involve besides setting up new rules? Who was given responsibility for planning? What were the major tasks of implementation? How much time was available? In overseeing the fiscal dimension, why might federal officials be concerned with school districts that sought to use Title I as general aid? Why was accurate demographic data important? How accurate was the data used in making the first year allocations? Why did fiscal issues take precedence over program issues during the first year?

---

9. See Frederick C. Mosher, *Program Budgeting: Theory and Practice* (Chicago: Public Administration Service, 1954), 226.

10. See *Education USA,* National Education Association, December 29, 1966, 108,

NOTE ON IMPLEMENTATION PLANNING

An important part of the implementation of new policy is the process of planning. Sometimes agencies have policy planning staffs for this purpose. Policy planning is nothing more than coordinated forethought to decide what new policies are needed and what should be done to implement them. Often policy planning involves the establishment of a new program. This is especially true when it aims at the utilization of grant monies provided by another level of government or some private agency. A program is a general term to refer to a focused governmental activity designed to bring about certain outcomes.

Program or policy planning aimed at implementing new policy begins with a review of the formal statement of policy and derives specific objectives and an organizational framework to meet those objectives. The steps in the planning process, while varying according to the policy and the existing organizational structure, will usually include the following:

1. assignment of planning responsibility
2. review of policy goals
3. development of specific objectives
4. generation of alternative approaches
5. assessment of alternative approaches
6. selection and approval of approach
7. designation of implementation personnel
8. assessment and review

These steps in the policy planning process must be adapted to the specific policy under consideration. Let's look at each of these steps in greater detail.

Assignment of Planning Responsibility

In the most straightforward example of policy implementation the legislation or executive order promulgated will designate the department secretary or a bureau chief as the individual responsible for carrying out policy. In some cases the head of the unit responsible for carrying out the policy will be designated to plan for its implementation. However, in many cases the identity of that individual will not be immediately known and the responsible executive may in fact want to consider various options. In this case an ad hoc or temporary group may be assigned to undertake implementation planning. The individuals may be selected from within or without the organization or combine insiders with outsiders. Another alternative is the designation of a permanent planning staff within the organization.

Review of Policy Goals

Once a planning group has been chosen, the first task is to review the broad mandates incorporated in the policy statement to provide a general orientation. Where implementation of a specific law or executive order is involved the document itself may contain an explicit statement of goals. However, such an explicit statement may be ambiguous. Further investigation of the circumstances of policy formulation may be necessary, including discussions with policymakers or backup staff. Where policy directives are vague or even nonexistent, communications between the policymakers and the policy implementers may be the only way of orienting the new planning group in the right direction. Unless a consensus among the planners on the goals of the policy is reached, even where there may be conflicting goals, further planning efforts will be frustrating and nonproductive.

Development of Specific Objectives

Once the basic goals of a policy have been understood, they must be translated into the specific setting in which policy is being made. Policy planners must focus on how the goals can be implemented in the environment in which they operate. Since these objectives are going to form the basis for the development of implementation plans it is critical that they be both realistic and acceptable to those responsible for carrying out plans. The planning group should be integrated with the work groups that will be responsible for carrying out the policy. Policy planning should be at the lowest level possible and involve those who will actually be executing the policy. If the operational groups are involved in the planning effort, an important step to building commitment to the objectives and goals will have been taken and implementation will be that much closer.

Generation of Alternative Means

Once specific objectives have been set, a plan of action for carrying them out must be arranged. Where possible several different options should be explored. Such a process helps build group understanding of the problems of implementation and ensures that the most obvious approach to a particular problem will not be adopted at the cost of omitting a more effective or imaginative one. While large bureaucratic organizations often are limited in the approaches they may take, this constraint argues even more strongly for the consideration of alternative plans of action. Unless special efforts are made, the tendency to choose the most obvious plan can result in a striking lack of imagination.

Assessment of Alternative Approaches

Having examined several possible alternative plans of action for implementing policy objectives, the planning group must compare them. Sometimes the group will be required to choose among them; in other instances they will be asked to submit their evaluations and recommendations to others for a final decision. The assessment of various alternatives may be a difficult and imprecise task. It is also a task that may require special expertise. The techniques for assessing alternative approaches depend upon the specific situation. They often involve forecasting techniques that allow the projection of future consequences. Some of these techniques will be described in the next series of modules. They are often referred to as techniques of policy analysis, since they compare competing approaches and their consequences.

Selection and Approval of Approach

Depending upon the particular situation, the policy analysis process may lead to more or less conclusive results. The importance of the decision to the overall organization, the opinion of the planning group's expertise by higher officials, and the specific circumstances all will affect the likelihood that the planning group's suggestions will be followed. If the planning group is going to be involved in implementation efforts or if it is an ongoing organizational structure, the extent to which its suggestions are utilized will have a future impact on the effectiveness of the implementation and on further planning activities. It is not wise to create planning groups whose recommendations are not going to be respected. It is important that the relationship between the planning groups and the individual or groups creating them be based on mutually understood expectations.

Designation of Implementation Personnel

An important part of planning for a new program is the careful consideration of who is actually to do it. Where possible, it may be preferable to designate an existing structure within the organization. However, often no single structure or individual is suitable, because of either background or current responsibilities. Sometimes a conflict between existing responsibilities and new responsibilities suggests the need for a new organizational unit. The creation of a new unit also has symbolic value, as it highlights new departures, and may be preferred for that reason. New organizational structures, however, involve high organization costs. If a new structure is created to carry out a new policy, an ad hoc arrangement may be created rather than a new permanent organizational unit. Ad hoc approaches have been increasingly popular, particularly when a policy cuts across the responsibilities of several existing units. An interdepartmental coordinating task force or project management team consisting of members of several departments may be set up for implementing such new policy.

Assessment and Review

Increasingly attention in public policymaking is being paid to the evaluation phase. Since the policymaking process is continuous, as has been outlined above, review and revision of policies are constantly undertaken. For review and revision to be most effective, information about the success of the policy planning is needed. Policy evaluation provides such information if properly included in the planning process.

These basic steps in the policy planning process will vary, depending on the particular type of implementation situation.

Planning occurs at all organizational levels. An increasing recognition of the difficulties of implementing public policy has led to greater emphasis on planning for implementation even at the policy formation phase. Legislative subcommittees and the staffs of elected executives will attempt to anticipate problems of implementation prior to setting forth policy statements.

But once a policy has been articulated and must be carried out, the heart of implementation occurs. Where a policy involves merely the application of a new rule, such as a change in the speed limits for automobiles, implementation may be inconsequential. But if, for example, a new law did away with radar enforcement of speeding limits, the implications might be substantial, requiring a new system for apprehending speeders.

Planning for implementation refers to action taken by responsible officials to carry out the directives included in a new or changed policy. In the federal government the department secretary, who often has a policy planning staff or some equivalent unit, ordinarily takes primary responsibility for policy implementation. But implementation planning occurs at all organizational levels. At lower levels it tends to merge with operational functions and be performed on an ad hoc basis by specifically designated individuals. In state government, policy-planning units are also emerging at the highest executive level as part of the governor's office and at the department level. Similarly, city governments, particularly the larger ones, are creating policy-planning units. Implementation planning, carried out by both permanent and ad hoc groups, permeates the policy process and is a central element of policy implementation.

Whether new policy involves changes in regulations, trimming expenditures, or broadening services, implementation must proceed according to some plan and the explicit preparation of such plans is a first step toward the realization of goals and objectives. In order to give you a better understanding of what implementation and implementation planning involves, you will be asked either on an individual basis or in a group situation to prepare plans for the implementation of several different types of policies. As you confront each situation, try to compare it to the others. What general principles can you discern to characterize the planning process?

Please consider each of the scenarios presented below. Your instructor may ask you to prepare an individual or group response to each. The term *scenario* has become an important part of the language of planning, particularly associated with the study of the future. A scenario is the presentation of a hypothetical situation to elicit a response. Scenarios allow us to use our imaginations by responding to situations that are not necessarily taken from the real world, although hypothetical situations may be based upon a real situation. They can be used in individual or group exercises to expand the imagination and provide practical experience in planning. You will most probably never have to respond to situations exactly like the ones you will consider here, but if you understand these examples thoroughly, you will be able to see their similarity to situations you will encounter as a practicing bureaucrat.

Planning can be executed by individuals acting singly or by a group. For purposes of this exercise, it is suggested that the class be divided into groups. At appropriate intervals debriefing should occur to allow for the benefit of interaction among the groups. If desired, a group leader or planning chief may be selected to facilitate and structure group input.

Scenario I — New Services

New policies often involve the development of services that previously have not been provided by government. Implementation, in this instance, requires decisions about who is to perform these services. Should a new organizational unit be created or should an existing unit be given new responsibilities? Almost always new public services involve some existing governmental activities that must be coordinated. Sometimes the easiest approach is to give the new responsibilities to those already exercising related responsibilities. On the other hand, the performance of new responsibilities may be hindered by the experience of existing organizations in dealing with a different set of problems.

You are working on the policy planning staff of a hypothetical large city of approximately 1,000,000 in population. The mayor informs you that the city council has just passed the following resolution: That the city shall henceforth provide emergency services for its citizens, including emergency medical treatment, transportation to hospital facilities on an emergency basis, and rescue from imminent danger. Prepare a plan of action, including a time schedule, following the steps in policy planning outlined above. Some suggested issues for concern are listed below:

1. How would you organize a planning group to deal with this problem? Whom would you choose to participate in such a group? What background skills and information need to be at the disposal of the group?
2. Formulate specific objectives appropriate to the city.
3. Which existing governmental agencies do you suppose would be providing some of these services already? Are any nongovernmental agencies currently performing any of these services?
4. What alternative approaches for accomplishing these goals exist? Should the city provide services itself, contract out with private associations, or subsidize existing agencies?
5. If the city wants to provide services directly, should it expand the responsibilities of existing agencies, create a new agency, or establish a coordinating mechanism to orchestrate the efforts of existing agencies?
6. What types of assessment and review would you use to evaluate the policy that is finally chosen?

Scenario II — Cutting Back Services

If the creation of new government services was the theme of the late 1960s, cutting back government services was the theme of the 1970s. During the middle of the decade many large cities, particularly the older cities of the East and Midwest, found that their revenues could not meet the continuing press of new services, higher salaries, and inflation. The national recession undermined the taxing ability of local governments and the pinch resulted in severe financial difficulties. While deficit spending was possible as an interim measure, its continued use threatened to undermine the financial integrity of large cities, which depend upon the investing public for municipal bond financing.

You are an aide to a big-city mayor faced with a 5 percent shortfall in revenues for the fiscal year. The mayor seeks to adjust expenditures during the second half of the fiscal year to achieve a balanced budget. Develop a plan for making the necessary cuts, following the steps outlined above.

In developing your plan consider some of these questions. In order to implement the cuts for the second half of the year, would you cut across the board or selectively? What criteria might you use in making the selective cuts? Present two or three alternative approaches to cutting expenditures. What would be your recommendation as the best approach to making cuts in a specific city? How would you judge the success of your policy?

To what extent would political considerations enter into budget-cutting strategies? Why do those responsible prefer to cut expenditures of equipment and supplies before cutting expenditures for personnel? When faced with the prospects of cutting welfare or police services, which would create the most difficult political reverberations?

How do problems of budget cutting at state and national levels differ from those at the municipal level? Is deficit financing easier or more difficult at the national level? What are the competing interests at the state and national level and how do they differ with those at the local level? Sometimes these competing demands on government are referred to as tradeoffs. A cut in one area may alleviate the necessity for a cut in another. Can you trade off deeper cuts in some areas to save other areas? On what bases can tradeoffs be made?

Scenario III — Program Planning

Program planning has become an increasingly important activity of government, stimulated in part by the growth in intergovernmental grants. These are monies made available by one level of government to another. ESEA, Title I (discussed above), is an example of such a grant program. Often these grants require the development of a formal program proposal to explain how the grant will be used. A program is a specific approach to the solution of some problem through the organization of human and fiscal resources. Often a program is planned in response to a request by an outside agency for the submission of proposals. This approach allows the granting agency to set certain guidelines, while requiring the submitting agency to suggest how it will carry out its proposed program.

Since World War II the federal government has adopted major grant programs in the areas of highways, education, manpower, community development, and law enforcement. Intergovernmental grants are an important source of state and local funds.

In designing programs to the specifications of a particular government agency, it is important to understand the goals of the overall program and how they are interpreted by those who administer them. The ability to develop good program proposals is critical for taking advantage of intergovernmental grants.

Skills in developing, running, and evaluating programs are in great demand today in the public sector. To help develop your own skills, formulate responses to one or more of the scenarios below.

1. You are on the policy-planning staff of a large city police department, which has been allocated $100,000 for improvements in criminal justice. Prepare an outline of the policy-planning process.
    a. In setting specific objectives, choose ones that can be evaluated at a later stage. What types of objectives are most desirable, those focusing on the incidence of crime, or those focusing on the nature of police services?
    b. Suppose your specific objectives were: to decrease the number of muggings and assaults; to maintain more accurate information about their occurrence; and to develop staff capacity for recording muggings and assaults. What are some possible alternative approaches for reaching these objectives?
    c. Can you think of appropriate changes in the relationship of the police department to the judicial and probation systems?
2. You are on the policy-planning staff of a new superintendent of a large city school system attempting to qualify for a grant of $150,000 to help poverty-level youngsters. Develop a process for spending the money, including specific objectives and a prepared course of action.
3. You work for a county executive who has just received an allocation of general revenue sharing monies for 1984, the current fiscal year. The

executive feels there is a surplus of $200,000. Recommend a program for county government. Do you know what kinds of programs are not permitted under the provisions of general revenue sharing?

NOTE ON OBSTACLES TO IMPLEMENTATION

The American governmental tradition has been both visionary and skeptical. We demand much of government, yet we do not really believe that government is capable of doing very much. We enunciate the goal of equal opportunity, but are unwilling to spend enough money for the education of the poor. We believe that government officials should be beyond reproach, yet we pay them low salaries, force them to retain second jobs that may induce conflicts of interest, and discourage our best students from public service by poor compensation and dire pictures of stultifying bureaucracy. We enact prohibitions on liquor and drugs, but hesitate to provide resources to law enforcement agencies to counteract black market activity. And we seem to be immobilized when it comes to dealing with organized crime. We believe in a government of great performance and a government of minimal effort. The dream and the reality do not jibe.

In general the gap is great between the goals of governmental policy and actual accomplishments. Implementation is the rub. How does government bring about those states of affairs to which it is committed? Or, stated in another way, how can government ensure implementation of its policies?

Government, it should be recalled, is a cooperative effort among individuals for the attainment of common goals. Implementation of public policy is therefore the use of human and material resources to achieve certain goals. As you have read the materials above and participated in the exercises, you should sense that achieving goals is not always easy, nor is the enunciation of common goals.

It is one thing to legislate compensatory education for children from poverty backgrounds; it is another to actually accomplish it. It is one thing to decide to provide new emergency services; it is much more difficult to actually establish an effective mechanism. It is one thing to decide to cut back services to achieve a balanced budget; it is another to decide which services should be cut, and then to cut them. It is one thing to plan a program within guidelines established by the federal government; it is another to make that program accomplish its objectives. The obstacles to implementation may be summarized as follows:

1. Lack of agreement about goals. Often the policy process does not reach a true consensus, even though a law is passed or a formal statement is issued. If the individuals responsible for implementation do not believe in a common set of goals, or cannot convince those affected by the policy to abide by these common goals, the chances of implementation are minimal.

2. ***Policy inadequacy.*** The policy enacted may not provide a means to the stated goals. Sometimes this may involve insufficient funds or resources. The authority to do what needs to be done may not be granted. Ideals cannot be attained without the wherewithal to achieve them.

3. ***Insufficient implementation planning.*** Even if a policy is designed to enable the attainment of its stated objectives, that is no guarantee of its success. A policy must be carried out by competent individuals who do not come into conflict with other government officials working in allied fields. It makes no sense to catch criminals if the mechanism for detaining and punishing them is not working; it makes no sense to require those receiving welfare to work, if no jobs are available. Success requires proper planning and coordination with existing government programs.

4. ***Inadequate staffing.*** Government policies are carried out by individuals. Unless these individuals have the proper training and dedication and feel they are part of a carefully designed organization, they will not be successful. Never forget that people carry out policy. Unless these people have the ability to execute the policy, it cannot be put into effect.

5. ***Resistance of those affected.*** Government policies, especially those adversely affecting individuals and corporations, need some cooperation from those affected. The federal income tax system would break down unless most of the people, most of the time complied reasonably well with the regulations. The government could not possibly force each individual to pay his or her fair share of taxes. Depending upon the severity of the impact on individuals and groups and their relative power in the society, the resistance to a policy may spell its death. For example, prohibition was never effective because too many people were not willing to comply and the costs of enforcement would have been too great.

Regulatory agencies, those responsible for ensuring that large industries such as utilities, airlines, and drug companies act in the public interest, are constantly confronted by a dilemma. In order to be successful they need to curry the favor and compliance of those regulated, but they thereby risk becoming the captives of those they attempt to regulate.

6. ***Inadequate analysis.*** The processes of analysis may not truly reflect reality. The means selected may be inadequate. Projections may be faulty. It may be that penalties planned as deterrents will not work as envisioned.

*7. **Faulty review process.*** Implementation is not a process that begins today and ends tomorrow; it takes place over a sustained period of time. Unless a review process is built in so that an approach can be changed as feedback from its impact is obtained, implementation is unlikely. Ongoing evaluation may make the difference between good intentions and good effects.

Overall, it is important to remember that governmental activities and programs are ways of affecting people. Particularly where government programs seek to change behavior or reallocate resources, resistance can be expected. The enunciation of policy by itself is ineffective against resistance. Much more is required, including sustained effort and the resources to implement the policy. Unfortunately, too often political leaders find that it is convenient to concentrate on the enunciation of policy and deemphasize the implementation aspects. That way resistance does not have to be overcome.

In the series of scenarios above you were asked to propose a new program in response to the requirements of a higher level of government. In recent years such requests have become frequent, as a result of the increasing tendency of government to assume part of the costs of many programs. The basic impetus for this development has been the strong position of individual and corporate income taxes, which are the main sources of federal taxes. In an era when property, sales, and other state and local taxes have not expanded at the same rate as corporate and individual taxes, the demands have been great for shifting to federal support for many programs.

Federal support, however, runs against the grain of American governmental institutions, which have tended to mount service programs at the state and local levels. A partial answer to this dilemma has been the use of intergovernmental transfers through a variety of grant programs. Federal grant programs have remade the relationships between the federal government and state and local governments by greatly increasing federal involvement in such areas as highways, education, welfare, and even law enforcement, areas at one time believed to be within the purview only of state and local governments.

Federal grant programs pose two major problems for policymakers: How should the money be distributed? What controls should the federal government retain over the use of the monies? These are both aspects of the larger problem of ensuring that the federal government gets what it wants out of the program. Since the federal government in most of these programs relates to the state and local governments, the question must be: How can the federal government ensure that the state and local governments carry out the goals of the program? Implementation is a difficult enough problem when discussing the relationship between legislation and executive action; how much more complicated when another layer of government is introduced.

Studies of federal grant programs often find that the goals of the programs may not be clearly stated or may be contradictory. If you think back to the policy formation process, you may remember that the processes of bargaining and negotiation may easily lead to policies that mean different things to different participants. But even where a clear agreement may exist about policy, the goals may be so broad as to invite ambiguity. Furthermore, even where agreement as to the goals of policy may be reached, the policy may not be a logical means to that end. And finally, even if the policy is basically designed to bring about the goals it seeks, the process may subvert effective implementation.

The discussion above about the implementation of the Elementary and Secondary Education Act of 1965 raised many of these problems. To some it was merely a way of providing general aid to education. To others it was a means for helping needy school systems. And for others it was meant as a program to aid youngsters from poverty backgrounds.

Another example of the conflict between competing interpretations of policy goals is the Youth Employment Program that has employed large numbers of young people during the summer. To some it was a program to provide income for poor children; to others it was an attempt to increase the likelihood of future employment. And to others it was a program to provide needed services while helping disadvantaged youth.

The grants administered by the Law Enforcement Assistance Administration (LEAA) is another example of a major federal program designed to improve services basically under the control of local governments. Grants were provided for local police departments to help bolster law enforcement services. At first the grants went largely for equipment, and many police forces stocked up on questionable weapons. Later the grants went for personnel, and provided assistance to local governments that were finding their revenues insufficient to cover ordinary operating expenses. Improvement in the actual delivery of services has been disappointing, but goals not originally enunciated in the legislation were accomplished.

In many areas of policy, the process of implementation may be as simple as shifting to one consolidated waiting line instead of four separate lines at an unemployment office, or as complex as establishing a national system for rationing gasoline. In its broadest sense, implementation is the basic activity of public organizations. Most public organizations spend their time implementing policies that have been decided upon in some public forum. Yet the study of implementation that focuses on major policy departures is particularly critical to the effective functioning of public organizations. The ability of government to meet the challenges of the day depends upon its ability to formulate wise policies and see that they are implemented. The formulation of policy leads to goals and expectations. Without proper implementation, government is nothing more than pipe dreams and bureaucratic incompetence. Today's skepticism about the ability of government to perform well makes effective implementation more important than ever.

SELECTED BIBLIOGRAPHY FOR MODULE 7

BAILEY, STEPHEN, and MOSHER, EDITH. *ESEA: The Office of Education Administers a Law.* Syracuse: Syracuse University Press, 1968.

BARDACH, EUGENE. *The Implementation Game.* Cambridge: MIT Press, 1977.

DERTHICK, MARTHA. *New Towns In-Town.* Washington, D.C.: Urban Institute, 1972.

MCLAUGHLIN, MILBREY W. *Evaluation and Reforms: The Elementary and Secondary Education Act of 1965/Title I.* Cambridge: Ballinger, 1975.

PRESSMAN, JEFFREY L. and WILDAVSKY, AARON B. *Implementation.* Berkeley, Los Angeles, London: University of California Press, 1973.

RADIN, BERYL. *Implementation, Change and the Federal Bureaucracy: School Desegregation in HEW, 1964 – 1968.* New York: Teachers College Press, Teachers College, Columbia University, 1977.

TRUMAN, DAVID. *The Governmental Process.* New York: Alfred Knopf, 1962.

WILLIAMS, WALTER. *The Implementation Perspective.* Berkeley, Los Angeles, London: University of California Press, 1980.

WILLIAMS, WALTER, and ELMORE, RICHARD F., eds. *Social Program Implementation.* New York: Academic Press, 1976.

SECTION

TECHNIQUES OF POLICY ANALYSIS

Section II used a bureaucratic process model to explain how the public policy process operates. The interplay of individual and group interests through the development, formulation, and implementation of public policy was explained in terms of negotiation, compromise, and bargaining processes.

One of the questions that may have occurred to you is whether this process of bargaining and negotiation results in the best possible policy. Just such a question has concerned policymakers for a long time. Is there such a thing as *the* public interest? Is it ever possible to say that a particular course of action is best for the country or the community, or must each public policy be viewed merely from the perspective of individual and group interests? The French philosopher Jean Jacques Rousseau framed this question in terms of whether there is a general will, that is, an imperative for the total political community.

The quest for the public interest is outlined in contemporary form in a well-known article by Glendon Schubert, "Is There a Public Interest Theory?"* This quest for the specific course of action, one preferable for the entire community as opposed to a policy in the interest of a specific group, underlies the controversy between incremental and rationalist approaches to understanding the public policy process. Incrementalists emphasize the constraints on the public policy process imposed by the politics of decision making. Since change from year to year is constrained by the conflict of interest among individuals and groups affected by policy change, emphasis should be placed on adjusting individual and group interests, rather than finding some best possible policy. Rationalists stress the necessity of looking anew at public

---

*In Carl Friedrich, ed., *The Public Interest* (New York: Atherton Press, 1966), pp. 162–176.

policy at regular intervals and trying to determine the best or optimal policy. They stress the importance of applying analytic techniques to the assessment of alternative policy options.

The tension between incremental and rational approaches to understanding public policy is also reflected in competing theories of decision making. Attempts to understand decision making have sought to reconcile the desire to optimize or seek the best possible solution with the difficulties of real-world decision making. Herbert Simon introduced the term "satisficing" for describing decisions that are not the best possible ones, but are still very good decisions. He argued that because of the constraints on the decision-making process, particularly the lack of knowledge that sometimes characterizes decision making, those in authority were forced to settle for a good decision rather than the best possible solution.

Lindblom's incremental approach to decision making emphasizes not only informational and time constraints, but the political setting in which departures from the past are often difficult. In an effort to capture the true character of public decision making, Lindblom and Braybrooke have coined the term "disjointed incrementalism" to capture the desire to optimize amid existing constraints.

As you will note, the terms *decision making* and *policymaking* in some ways are very similar. Decision making is ordinarily used when referring to managers functioning at lower levels and policymaking when referring to legislatures, political executives, and higher level administrators. Policymaking tends to emphasize major decisions that are often subject to group processes and the participation of numbers of individuals.

As you were formulating your own position in POLFORM, and as you attempted to argue or to convince others that your position should be adopted, you may have realized that the justification of a particular position may be a very complicated affair. Depending upon the area of public policy that was the focus of POLFORM, very basic questions probably arose about the effects of that policy and its impact on society. Often during the bargaining process, competing views of the effects of particular policies form the basis of efforts to persuade individuals and groups to change their attitudes. Whether a particular individual or group advocates a policy depends in part upon their assessment of its consequences for them. It is largely because of this desire to anticipate the consequences of policy that knowledge is of central importance in the public policy process.

The policy process is a continuous one. Once policy is implemented, it is always subject to revision and adjustment. But how do policymakers decide to change policy? Often changes come about because the effects of the policies are different from those anticipated by their makers. For example, when Congress first passed legislation requiring pollution controls on automobiles, few legislators understood the implications for the automobile industry. When the Supreme Court first ordered integration of dual school systems in the South, the implications for Northern cities were not generally understood.

The difficulties of anticipating the consequences of public policy reinforce the cyclical movement from policy development through policy formation, policy implementation, policy revision, and back to policy development. The fact that policy formation and implementation do not last forever is a built-in corrective. Sometimes this process of movement through subsequent revisions is referred to as successive approximation. Even though initially the policy was not doing exactly what it was intended to do, after the policymaking cycle has occurred several times, the policy effects may be much closer to the original desires of the policymakers.

This gap between the objectives of the policymakers and the actual impacts of public policy is a central dilemma of the policymaking process. It results in great losses of resources that are expended in useless, even counterproductive ways. But it is an area, fortunately, in which policymakers and a new breed of public servant, the policy analyst, are developing techniques of increasing utility. To the extent that the impacts of public policy may be anticipated, the choice of policies is improved. Better choices result in better utilization of resources.

Yehezkel Dror, one of the foremost proponents of the need for greater use of policy analysis, points out that while the importance of governmental decisions and the knowledge base for making policy is increasing, the utilization of knowledge is not keeping pace. According to Dror, the quality of public policymaking improves much more slowly than it might, given the actual increases in knowledge. He calls for greater use of knowledge in the design of the policymaking apparatus and in the choice of competing policies.

It is in the last area that Section III will concentrate: using knowledge to ensure that the best possible public policies are formulated and implemented. As you consider the relationship of knowledge to policymaking, try to answer some of the following questions:

1. Can you substantiate or disprove Yehezkel Dror's general contention that the available knowledge has increased substantially within the last decade, with respect to a particular policy area?
2. Are there areas that are more likely to involve extensive knowledge requirements and other areas that are less likely to involve knowledge requirements?
3. How is knowledge relevant in making national policy relating to the welfare system? What sort of knowledge might help you to determine whether or not a negative income tax would be a sensible policy for the United States? What knowledge would you require to set pollution standards for automobiles? What knowledge would you require to determine whether the financing of education should be changed to a statewide system or to a national system?
4. In your judgment, is legislative policymaking or executive policymaking better adapted to utilize knowledge?
5. Can you think of an example where knowledge itself becomes a source of power? Give an example of an individual or an institution you know that exercises political influence because of its peculiar access to knowledge.
6. What is an example of some specific change in public policymaking machinery during the last decade that has improved knowledge utilization?

According to Dror, policy assessment is in essence finding the answers to two questions: What are the outputs, results, or benefits of a particular policy? What are the inputs or costs of implementing that policy? Then, inputs subtracted from outputs provides a measure of the quality of that public policy, the net output.

Substantial difficulties may arise, however, in calculating net output in specific situations. This is especially true where the goals and objectives of policy are ambiguous, ill defined, contradictory, or contested. In order to calculate net output, the policy must be well defined and its objectives clear. Could you calculate the net output of a public high school during a particular one-year period? How would you define output: employed graduates, happy graduates, smart graduates, creative graduates, wealthy graduates? Could you calculate the net output of a shoe factory? What about the space program? The military? A public transportation system? A private bus company? Or a regulatory policy aimed at protecting health or safety?

Recognizing that net output may be difficult to compute, Dror suggests that secondary measures of public policy be computed and used as substitutes for net output. These secondary measures, according to Dror, are useful insofar as they approximate the net output measures. Even though Dror focuses on real output, that is, the effects of public policy on social situations, the quality of the public policy statement itself may be used as a secondary measure. Statements that are clear, internally consistent, compatible with other policies, comprehensive, and concrete lead to a greater likelihood of successful policy impact. Feasibility of output also may be considered and probable real output may be used as a secondary measure.

Another set of useful secondary measures are those associated with the quality of the policymaking process itself. Examples are the degree to which the policy process is updated and revised, the extent to which feedback from the policy process is used to revise policy, and the extent to which the development of policy strategies is an integral part of the policy process. The existence and quality of structural units to evaluate and redesign the policymaking process, to explicitly carry out long-range policymaking and research and development, and to carry out the various phases and aspects of the policymaking process are other secondary measures of net output. Other secondary measures using input include qualifications and motivation of personnel, availability of knowledge and information, and equipment.

Dror himself agrees with others like Lindblom and Simon, that optimal solutions are not always possible and that measuring net output may be quite difficult. Nonetheless, he argues that policymakers and policy analysts have not set their sights high enough. Too often the difficulties of adopting optimal solutions and even measuring net output have discouraged them from using knowledge at their disposal.

Whatever your own view of the need for greater use of analytic techniques in the public policy process, the trend today is in that direction. While analytic techniques are directly related to the evaluation and revision of policy, they are also relevant in the other phases of the public policy process. More and more, policymakers try to anticipate possible consequences and measure real effects by systematic consideration at every stage of the policy process.

This next series of modules will explain the use of several analytic techniques for improving the quality of policymaking. The first module describes systems analysis, a comprehensive approach to analyzing public policy alternatives. The second module will illustrate a particular technique that can be used within a systems analysis for calculating the impact of a public policy: benefit/cost analysis. The final module in this section will consider two techniques for predicting future policy impacts, when more precise techniques are unavailable: the Delphi technique solicits expert opinion, and cross-impact analysis allows for the visual display and group analysis of the probable impacts of a number of interrelated factors.

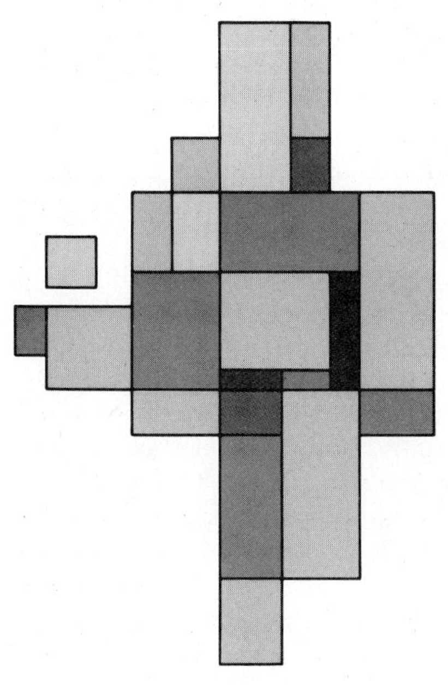

MODULE 8

Systems Analysis of Public Policy, Program and Performance Evaluation

INTRODUCTION

Systems is one of the most overworked terms in the language of social science. Political science students may be familiar with the concept of the political system developed by David Easton. This concept was explained in Module 5 in the discussion of agenda building. Systems analysis in this module has a different focus and orientation. It is much closer in meaning to the word *systematic* for it refers to a systematic approach to the analysis of public policy. One of the foremost proponents of systems analysis, E.S. Quade, says the term *systems analysis* may be used to refer to any orderly analytic study designed to help a decision maker identify a preferred course of action from among possible alternatives.

Systems analysis as described in this module is an explicit, very general procedure that can be used to assess alternative public policy options. It is a sequence of activities that can be undertaken with respect to any problem or policy that public decision makers may confront. In some ways, systematic approaches to the analysis of public policy are as old as government itself. Amid the bargaining and negotiation that characterize government action, some individuals have always set about to systematically consider possible alternative policies and their likely outcomes. In this sense, systematic consideration is nothing more than orderly, rational consideration of possible public policy.

SYSTEMS ANALYSIS AND OPERATIONS RESEARCH

The current interest and attention, even excitement, that systems analysis has engendered in the public sector stems from its coupling with mathematical techniques, often referred to as operations research, which have been greatly facilitated by the development and general availability of large-scale data processing capabilities.

During the Second World War, operations research, first referred to as operational analysis by the British, became a valued and respected tool in the development of weapons systems. In fact, explicit use of the term *systems analysis* derives from its application as an extension of operations research in the field of weapons systems development. Groups of scientists, including physicists, biologists, statisticians, and mathematicians, were organized in operations analysis teams to solve critical problems. Operations research was especially useful in guiding the development of weapons systems, choosing the most effective approaches, and avoiding excessively costly ones.

After the Second World War, some analysts, who had been using operations research in weapons development, sought to extend their analysis into broader questions of national security policy. Could the techniques of operations research be used in a more open-ended situation to decide among alternative weapons systems or to weigh competing national security objectives? Despite the skepticism of more traditional military policy experts, those seeking to expand operations research techniques were successful. Since the early 1960s, systems analysis has been an increasingly important tool in the development of national security policy.

Perhaps the most important difference between the first applications of operations research and the development of systems analysis is that systems analysis openly questions policy objectives, vigorously explores possible alternative solutions, and questions criteria for assessing these alternatives. By adding these features, operations research became transformed into a more broadbased tool for policymaking.

Operations research has also been used for many years within the civilian sector. *Queuing theory* has been used to develop schedules to meet varying service demands. *Linear programming* has been used to choose the optimal mix of resources given certain desired levels of production. Such problems are characterized by well-defined goals and objectives. The application of mathematical models in these situations can provide additional knowledge with great precision.

But what of problems in which objectives are not so clearly specified and criteria for evaluating alternatives may not be so obvious? Many social problems that government handles involve ambiguous goals and objectives. Furthermore, decisions must often be made swiftly without the complete information required by many mathematical models. While the application of systems analysis to public policy may have seemed inevitable, its actual use has developed slowly.

Credit for transforming systems analysis into a more generally useful tool must in large measure be given to Robert McNamara, the secretary of defense appointed by President John Kennedy, who served also under President Lyndon Johnson. McNamara was a civilian put in charge of a large and specialized bureaucracy, dominated by military men, in the technical area of arms development. How could he, when presented with a controversy between the Army and the Navy or the Air Force, decide which weapons system should be favored? Policy decisions involving one weapons systems over another can involve billions of dollars.

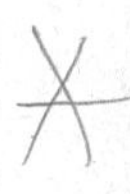

By the time McNamara took over as secretary of defense in the early 1960s, operations research techniques were spilling over into national security matters and systems analysis had already been recognized as an important new technique. McNamara, with the assistance of two members of his staff, economists Charles Hitch and Roland McKean, set the basis and theory for creating systems analysis as a broadbased tool for analyzing public policy. In their book, *The Economics of Defense in a Nuclear Age,* Hitch and McKean argued that national security and, by implication, governmental policy in general, may be conceptualized as one large economic problem. The resources of the nation can be used to satisfy any combination of goals, one of which is national security. Once the nation decides how much it is willing to devote to national security, it can then decide how to spend those resources most efficiently. McNamara went on to develop an approach to compare the usefulness of different weapons in achieving certain objectives. Which system, he asked, provides the biggest bang for the buck — the most military power for a given level of resources?

McNamara's approach, which seemed so successful in the Department of Defense, was soon recommended for other federal departments. President Lyndon Johnson's attempt to develop a federal Planning, Programming, and Budgeting System (PPBS) drew upon McNamara's approach. But as PPBS was applied to the areas of welfare, education, the environment, and antitrust policy, difficulties arose in specifying goals and objectives. The comprehensive rationality implicit in PPBS could not be applied to the federal system as a whole.

A formal inquiry into such matters as weapons development, force posture design, or the determination of strategic objectives came to be referred to as a systems analysis. A typical analysis might investigate whether a nuclear-powered aircraft carrier should be developed;

whether tactical nuclear weapons could be substituted for greater numbers of troops in Western Europe; and whether a cruise missile should be included in a disarmament agreement. Systems analysis is an explicit way of looking at choices that have to be made under uncertain conditions and choosing the best course of action. It differs from operations research in attempting to answer more basic questions, and often achieves less reliable answers. While often utilizing operations research techniques, systems analysis, even when applied to weapons systems, requires the exercise of personal judgment, not merely the application of some mathematical principle.

In the next several pages, each of the steps in a systems analysis — specifying objectives, defining alternatives, calculating impacts, and assessing alternatives — will be considered in turn.

OUTLINE OF A SYSTEMS ANALYSIS

As indicated above, systems analysis is a general term of reference for an explicit, rational procedure for assessing alternative policies or programs. The conduct of a systems analysis will differ according to the individual who conducts it, but the basic steps will generally be the same.

A systems analysis consists of series of procedures undertaken in sequential form. The number of steps and the separation of one step from another will differ depending upon the source that is consulted. Our approach involves the following four basic steps: (1) specifying objectives, (2) defining alternatives, (3) calculating impacts, and (4) assessing alternatives. Each of these steps will be considered in turn.

Specifying Objectives

Every systems analysis begins with a specification of objectives of the particular policy under consideration. In some cases, this task is relatively straightforward; in others, it represents a substantial portion of the analysis. Policy objectives may be stated in the task description, or the analyst may have to develop the objectives from available sources.

The most obvious source for policy objectives is the statement of the policy itself. Often a statement of policy, especially when in the form of legislation, will itself set forth general goals if not specific objectives. Otherwise, it may be necessary to investigate the process of policymaking by referring to written records of the deliberations of policymaking bodies, such as boards, legislatures, or committees within the legislature. In some cases, interviewing the chief participants may be necessary. In other cases, more extended analysis of the policy may be required.

While the existence of explicit and easily ascertainable objectives simplifies systems analysis, these objectives may require further analysis. Since policy is often the result of political compromise, the objectives may be stated in ambiguous or even contradictory fashion. The unraveling of these objectives, their refinement, and sometimes the open acknowledgement of their inadequacy should be clearly indicated in a systems analysis.

Sometimes it may be necessary to conduct a hypothetical analysis, choosing a single objective or a group of objectives as the basis for the analysis, even though they may not represent the objectives of the policymakers. In many analyses, the clarification of the objectives, noting ambiguities and contradictions, may constitute a major portion of the analytic task.

To the extent that a small, clear, noncontradictory group of objectives can be specified, the systems analysis will be greatly facilitated. As the number of objectives increases, as their clarity diminishes, as their relative importance varies and their contradictory nature emerges, the analysis becomes more difficult and open to question.

As a first exercise, the class may want to consider a policy discussed in previous modules. Each class member might try to develop a set of policy objectives. After setting objectives on the basis of your own understanding of the policy, compare your views with those of other class members. How can you account for disparities in defining the objectives of the same policy?

Read the excerpts below from the Manpower Development and Training Act of 1962. Specify the objectives based upon the excerpt.

Statement of Findings and Purpose, "Manpower Development and Training Act of 1962" (Public Law 87 – 415)

Sec. 101. The Congress finds that there is critical need for more and better trained personnel in many vital occupational categories, including professional, scientific, technical, and apprenticeable categories; that even in periods of high unemployment, many employment opportunities remain unfilled because of the shortages of qualified personnel; and that it is in the national interest that current and prospective manpower shortages be identified and that persons who can be qualified for these positions through education and training be sought out and trained, in order that the Nation may meet the staffing requirements of the struggle for freedom. The Congress further finds that the skills of many persons have been rendered obsolete by dislocations in the economy arising from automation or other technological developments, foreign competition, relocation of industry, shifts in market demands, and other changes in the structure of the economy; that Government leadership is necessary to insure that the benefits of automation do not become burdens of widespread unemployment; that the problem of assuring sufficient employment opportunities will be compounded by the extraordinarily rapid growth of the labor force in the next decade, particularly by the entrance of young people into the labor force, that improved planning and expanded efforts will be required to assure that men, women, and young people will be trained and available to meet shifting employment needs; that many persons now unemployed or underemployed, in order to become qualified for reemployment or full employment must be assisted in providing themselves with skills which are or will be in demand in the labor market; that the skills of many persons now employed are inadequate to enable them to make their maximum contribution to the Nation's economy; and that it is in the national interest that the opportunity to acquire new skills be afforded to these people in order to alleviate the hardships of unemployment, reduce the costs of unemployment compensation and public assistance, and to increase the Nation's productivity and its capacity to meet the requirements of the space age. It is therefore the purpose of this Act to require the Federal Government to appraise the manpower requirements and resources of the Nation, and to develop and apply the information and methods needed to deal with the problems of unemployment resulting from automation and technological changes and other types of persistent unemployment.

Next, consider the successor to the Manpower Development and Training Act (MDTA), the Comprehensive Employment and Training Act (CETA). Specify its objectives.

Title I — Comprehensive Employment and Training Act

Description of Program. Sec. 101. It is the purpose of this title to establish a program to provide comprehensive manpower services throughout the Nation. Such program shall include the development and creation of job opportunities and the training, education, and other services needed to enable individuals to secure and retain employment at their maximum capacity. Comprehensive manpower services may include, but shall not be limited to, programs and activities designed to carry out the purpose of this title, such as —

(1) outreach to make persons aware of the availability of manpower services and persuade them to use such services,
(2) assessment of the individual's needs, interests, and potential in the labor market and referral to appropriate employment, training, or other opportunities,
(3) orientation, counseling, education, and institutional skill training to prepare the individual to enter the labor market or to qualify for more productive job opportunities,

(4) training on the job,
(5) payments or other inducements to public or private employers to expand job opportunities, but payments to employers organized for profit shall not exceed the difference between the costs of recruiting, training, and providing supportive services for low-income persons and those regularly employed,
(6) services to individuals to enable them to retain employment,
(7) payment of allowances to persons in training for which they receive no remuneration and payment of such allowances for transportation, subsistence, or other expenses incurred in participating in manpower services or employment as are necessary to enable the individual to participate therein,
(8) supportive services to enable individuals to take advantage of employment opportunities, including necessary health care and medical services, child care, residential support, assistance in securing bonds, or any other necessary assistance incident to employment, and any other service needed to participate in employment or manpower services,
(9) development of information concerning the labor market and activities, such as job restructuring, to make it more responsive to objectives of the manpower services program,
(10) manpower training, employment opportunities, and related services conducted by community-based organizations,
(11) transitional public service employment programs, and
(12) any programs authorized by part A of title III and by title IV of this Act.

December 28, 1973; Public Law 93 – 203.

Now, compare the objectives of MDTA with those of CETA. How can you account for differences in the objectives? Why do policy objectives change over time? Which aspects of the CETA objectives are most likely to change in the future? What is the basis for your projections?

Now, look back at the policies and the objectives you considered. Did your own value preferences affect your choice of objectives? This phase in a systems analysis is probably more subject to the analyst's own values than any other, for it is the objectives of a policy that express the values inherent in the policy.

How successful were you in making objectives as specific as possible? Were your objectives specific enough so that you would be able to tell whether or not the policy was successful? Unless objectives are chosen that are relatively concrete and susceptible to measurement, it will be difficult to evaluate the effects of the policy. The specification of objectives often involves two conflicting considerations. On one hand, the specifications of objectives that are concrete and easily measured is dictated by their importance in carrying out the subsequent steps in the analysis. On the other hand, the quest for concrete, measurable objectives may deemphasize certain aspects of the policy that are more important, even if more ambiguous and difficult to measure.

Next, choose a policy recently adopted by your local government. Can you specify the objectives of the policy? What are your sources? Try to specify objectives for a policy recently adopted by your state government, or the federal government.

Defining Alternatives

Once objectives for some policy have been agreed on, at least for purposes of the analysis, alternative courses of action can be developed. Remember, the purpose of a systems analysis is to decide among alternative courses of action. Indeed, sometimes the alternatives will be developed prior to a rigorous definition of objectives. In assessing the relative strengths of two weapons systems, for example, a significant part of the analysis may consist of defining the objectives these respective systems are expected to accomplish. In assessing whether a private or public system of garbage collection should be adopted, an initial agreement on objectives is required. Are unit costs the only consideration? What about the effects of disposal on environmental conditions? Should a public executive consider issues such as loss of jobs for public employees and possible involvement of criminal elements?

In some instances, objectives can be stated quite precisely. A system of response to emergency requests for assistance might seek the objective of a response within five minutes. Alternative deployments of emergency vehicles might be specified precisely through the use of formal mathematics. Where the objectives are clear and limited and mathematical techniques are available, operations research techniques can be used to specify and test various alternatives.

In less rigidly circumscribed situations, however, generating alternatives may be a wide-ranging creative enterprise. When alternatives are chosen whose effects are difficult to calculate, systems analysis becomes more difficult and more tenuous. At some point the selection of alternatives may make it so difficult to calculate effects that a systems analysis will not be very helpful. Creativity in the definition of alternatives may limit the applicability of systems techniques.

Even creative alternatives, though, must be feasible. The constraints on policymakers may operate to eliminate large numbers of alternatives. A systems analysis that introduces unlikely alternatives runs the risk of summary rejection. Policymakers and those who attempt to influence policymaking can use such obviously infeasible alternatives to undermine confidence in the systems analysis itself. Whenever such options are considered, it is wise to clear them with the policymakers who have requested the analysis.

Now, try your hand at developing alternative courses of action, given a set of objectives. Your ability to develop realistic and effective alternatives will in part depend on your knowledge of the field. Particularly if you are working with objectives unfamiliar to you, it might be more fruitful to work in groups rather than individually on this project.

Developing Alternative Policy Options

Starting either from the objectives you developed in the previous exercise or objectives given to you by your instructor, develop at least three alternative ways of bringing about those objectives. Try to be imaginative and suggest very different approaches. You might want to consider nonjudgmental brainstorming, used previously in Module 5, as a technique to stimulate creative approaches in a group situation.

Suppose your objective is to minimize the number of families with incomes less than $5,000. Can you think of three alternative approaches, using respectively job creation, cash payments, and minimum wages? Which would come closest to your objective? Which would be most costly? Which would you prefer, and why? If you are working in groups, after the three alternatives have been developed take a vote to see which group's alternatives are the most imaginative, the most realistic, and the most likely to bring about the desired objective. Let each group justify its own choices. How does the cost of the one most likely to bring about the objectives compare with other alternatives suggested? Is it politically feasible?

Suppose your objective was to minimize the consumption of gasoline in the United States. Can you think of three alternative approaches? Why is political feasibility an important consideration? Answer the questions specified above with respect to the previous set of alternatives.

Calculating Impacts

Assessing the impacts of a course of action is at the heart of a systems analysis. It is this stage that usually limits the rigor of the analysis. If alternatives have been chosen that can be assessed by the use of a known mathematical model, the systems analysis becomes quite exact. Of course, the results obtained by the application of such a model depend upon its appropriateness and correct application. But given the correct application of a model such as those available in queuing theory, linear programming or benefit/cost analysis, the systems analysis is a very powerful tool. Operations research has solved an impressive number of systems problems through the application of these standard mathematical models.

When standard mathematical models are not available, specific computational models may be appropriate. A new approach that has been made possible by the development of large-scale data processing equipment is the use of computer simulation to calculate the impacts of alternative policies. Such simulations have been used extensively in the area of formula allocations, where funds are distributed to states and localities on the basis of some mathematical formula. Title I of the Elementary and Secondary Education Act (ESEA), which was discussed in Module 7, is an example of a formula allocation program. Several alternative formulas can be tested using a computer simulation that estimates the values of certain variables at a particular point in time.

The use of mathematical models and computer simulations requires a level of skill that many of you may not presently have. Nonetheless, you may gain some experience in the use of calculation by examining the alternatives you have previously developed and attempting to make a rough calculation of their respective impacts.

Look back at the three alternatives you specified to bring about a reduction in the number of families with incomes less than $5,000. Where you do not have the information necessary to make the calculations, indicate the information you need. Where would you get such information? Try to get the information and make the calculations. Each group in the class might be assigned this task with respect to several alternatives. Compare the results obtained by each group. Try to gauge the accuracy of your calculations. Can you establish limits within which you are relatively certain that your results are accurate?

Suppose you wanted to assess the respective costs of public and private systems of garbage collection. What calculations would be relevant? How would you calculate the relative costs of a bridge and tunnel? Suppose you had two bids by different companies. How would you know which one to accept?

Suppose you were considering the costs of a free public system of higher education. How would you calculate the costs of such a system? What are the benefits? Could you calculate the costs and benefits of your own investment in college? In the next chapter you will have an opportunity to further investigate a specialized approach for calculating benefits and costs.

Don't be discouraged if the calculation of policy impacts seems a highly technical and specialized area. Attention to this aspect of public policy analysis is relatively recent and appropriate techniques are still being developed. As you gain expertise in a particular policy area, the techniques of policy analysis, including the calculation of the effects of alternative policies, will become more readily apparent.

Assessing Alternatives

The last step in a systems analysis is like the first in an important respect. Sometimes they are both equally obvious, and sometimes they are both equally elusive.

The selection of a criterion is directly related to the statement of objectives. In the example above, the objective was to minimize the number of families with incomes below $5,000. The criterion for assessment, then, is the extent to which each alternative will reduce the number of families with incomes below $5,000. An additional criterion might be the costs of alternative programs.

What might be a good criterion for comparing two alternative weapons systems? What about destruction/dollar? Would such a criterion be useful if the objectives had been stated in terms of contributing to certain strategic objectives, such as guaranteeing the independence of Western Europe from Soviet influence?

If the objectives are in dispute or contradictory, the task of arriving at an acceptable criterion might be considerable. Suppose a job creation program is aimed at reducing unemployment and inflation at the same time. Economists might argue that those objectives are incompatible.

How would you compare two or more approaches to teaching reading in a particular elementary school? What should be the criterion — greatest average performance? Improvement in reading score per dollar invested?

Choosing Criteria

Take a look now at the alternatives you discussed in the section above. When the groups collectively decided that a particular alternative was best, what criterion did they use? What were the possible criteria?

Take a vote in the class to choose the best alternative in some area. Allow several individuals to justify their own choices. Discuss the criteria different individuals suggest for justifying a particular alternative. Now, using this criterion, take a revote. Was there greater agreement after selection of the criterion? There should be. If there wasn't, why wasn't there? What are the marks of a good criterion?

A good criterion should judge the ability of the alternative to reach stated objectives. It should be readily applicable. It should clearly distinguish among alternatives.

The assessment of alternatives is the most important, yet sometimes the most arbitrary, step in the analysis. It is important that the basis for the selection of the criterion be made explicit.

COMMENT ON SYSTEMS ANALYSIS

These steps in carrying out a systems analysis of a public policy question may seem disarmingly simple. Unfortunately, the systems analyst is often plagued by multiple and conflicting objectives. Alternatives may not completely attain the specified objectives. Measures may only approximate actual outcomes. Models may be inexact and similar criteria may lead to different assessments.

Given these difficulties, it is often necessary to view systems analysis as merely a tool in a continuing process of policymaking by successive approximation. As the data obtained from a systems analysis are used in making decisions, revisions in the systems analysis will be indicated. A second cycle of policy implementation and assessment will benefit from the insights of the first cycle and allow for more exact calculations. Objectives may be refined, new alternatives selected, models improved, and assessments made more rigorous. When looked upon as part of a continuing policymaking process, systems analysis, even where inexact, may be invaluable in assisting the policymaker.

Private- and public-sector decision makers have always defined objectives, specified alternatives, calculated impacts, and compared alternatives. What is new about the systems approach is the insistence on an explicit procedure, which consciously includes each of these aspects. Mathematical models continually become more widely used and more detailed, making the techniques of operations research ever more accessible and helpful.

Systems analysis is no panacea. But it can provide analysis, otherwise unavailable to decision makers, improving the "seat of the pants" approach that is often the alternative. By providing a rational framework for decision making, it presents an alternative to merely testing the political winds.

But its limitations must also be considered. Although it can clarify objectives, generate new alternatives, compare alternatives and make assumptions explicit, a systems analysis can never relieve the decision maker of ultimate responsibility for his or her choice. Individual judgment by decision makers who understand its strengths and limitations is critical to successful decision making.

After Robert McNamara successfully introduced systems analysis in the Department of Defense, it occurred to him that it could provide a comprehensive approach to management of all activities in the department. Rather than reserving systems analysis for specific jobs, McNamara sought to incorporate it in the ongoing management of the department and in all significant decision making. McNamara's focus was the budgetary process. Since every subunit in the department sought operating funds each year, McNamara decreed that all requests for funds had to be supported by specification of objectives, alternative approaches, calculations of effects, and choices of the best options. This approach came to be known as a Planning, Programming, and Budgeting System (PPBS). In effect, it applied systems analysis to every major allocation decision in the department. President Lyndon Johnson thought so highly of McNamara's approach that he sought to have it adopted in all federal agencies. The great rush toward PPBS in federal, state, and local governments has been analyzed and discussed elsewhere. However, it does appear that the use of systems analysis in such a comprehensive way almost inevitably ends in defeat. The amount of time and effort required for its meaningful application is just too great.

The next module will consider a specific technique that can be used within a systems analysis to calculate the relative impacts of various alternatives. The technique is benefit/cost analysis and the implicit criterion is net output, the difference between costs and benefits.

NOTE ON PROGRAM AND PERFORMANCE EVALUATION

While systems analysis as a comprehensive approach to the consideration of alternative policies has received increasing attention, the analytic techniques on which it is based are used also during policy revision and new-policy development.

Analytic studies undertaken during policy revision are usually referred to as program evaluations, particularly when they focus on some specific program adopted. Since program evaluations take place during and after the program has been implemented, they can measure the actual impact of policies on society. In this respect, they differ considerably from a systems analysis, which usually relies upon existing knowledge to estimate the expected impacts of public policy. This reliance of program evaluation on empirical data, rather than general knowledge such as a mathematical model, makes it a useful tool in making changes in existing policies and programs.

Program evaluations can focus on some broad policy, for example, the impact of the Comprehensive Employment and Training Act (CETA), or on some specific application, such as the effects of a specific training program funded under CETA. A program evaluation begins with the specific objectives of a particular program and attempts to find out whether they were reached and what costs were incurred in reaching them.

A major task of the program evaluation is to examine relationships between the program or policy under consideration and changes in social conditions. Investigating such relationships may be quite difficult. For example, over some specific period of time, it might be difficult to determine whether employment of CETA trainees resulted from previous background, the training program itself, or changes in the job market. In order to differentiate the effect of a particular program from other factors, comparison or control groups are often introduced.

In theory, whenever a policy or program is evaluated, a control group should be identified. This group of individuals should be equivalent to the group receiving the special treatment, referred to technically as the experimental treatment. Then, at the end of some time period, the changes in both groups are compared so that changes due to extraneous factors are not attributed to the experimental treatment.

Analytic techniques similar to those used in assessing the policy process are used to measure organizational effectiveness. Remember, public policies are carried out by individuals and groups of individuals. The problem of assessing policies may be conceived of as assessing the effectiveness of work groups. Even though policy analysis and systems analysis emphasize policy outputs, the evaluation of work group performance should not be overlooked.

Recall the discussion in Module 2 of scientific management approaches that emphasize measuring work-group performance. You will remember that Frederick Taylor's scientific management theory focused on individual and group performance. Scientific management is based on the belief that organizational activity can be improved with a resulting improvement in performance. The central significance of the Westinghouse experiments was that organizational performance could be improved by altering the conditions and motivations of the individual workers.

Today, scientific management approaches once again emphasize performance evaluation, both of individuals and groups. Management by objectives and performance appraisal are two approaches to incorporating performance indicators within the process of management. Peter Drucker, one of the founders of MBO and generally a wise commentator on the operation of private organizations, has said that public organizations must also be held to high standards of performance. The lack of competitive market conditions and profit and loss statements in public organizations is no excuse for low performance.

Corporations are aware that measures of performance that extend to individual factories and work groups are needed, beyond the overall profitability of the company. Similarly, in public organizations, other measures of performance are available, beyond those focusing on net output.

Organizations may be conceptualized, as they are below, as collections of resources, people, and equipment that carry out work, resulting in both products and services, to bring abut certain purposes. To make these terms more concrete, consider some of the following examples:

	WORK DONE	PURPOSE
Police	apprehend criminals, issue tickets	minimize crimes and law violations
Fire	fight fires	minimize damage caused by fires
Sanitation	collect garbage, dispose of refuse	remove litter from city streets and prevent its accumulation
Education	conduct classes, operate school buildings	teach children reading, writing, and arithmetic
Parks and Recreation	remove litter from parks, run swimming pools	provide recreation and athletic facilities

Just as analytic techniques may be applied to a policy as a whole, they may be applied to organizational units and individuals. In undertaking an evaluation or assessment of the performance of organizational units, three types of measures are most commonly used: workload indicators, efficiency indicators, and effectiveness indicators. A workload indicator measures the amount of work done; examples are cubic yards of rubbish collected or linear feet of bench slats replaced. Efficiency indicators relate the amount of a service output to the amount of resources required to produce it; an example would be cubic yards of rubbish collected per worker-day. Efficiency indicators are sometimes called productivity indicators. Finally, effectiveness indicators measure the extent to which the intended purpose of the services are being met; for example, the extent to which a park is being kept clean.

These different measures are sometimes referred to as performance indicators, since they indicate the extent to which performance is reaching a certain standard. The development and use of performance measures is an important area in the operation of public organizations. Just as systems analysis applies quantitative techniques to measuring policies, performance indicators are used to measure organizational performance.

Clearly, policies and the organizations that produce them are closely interrelated. At every stage, including revision and policy evaluation, the organizational context of policymaking must be understood and accounted for.

Analyses of increasing quantification and sophistication are here to stay in public organizations. Probably no other aspect of the field of public organizations has developed so rapidly. The techniques of systems analysis and the use of performance indicators are important managerial tools.

SELECTED BIBLIOGRAPHY FOR MODULE 8

BRAYBROOK, DAVID, and LINDBLOM, CHARLES. *A Strategy of Decision.* New York: The Free Press, 1963.

DROR, YEHEZKEL. *Public Policymaking Reexamined.* San Francisco: Chandler Publishing, 1968.

CARO, FRANK, ed. *Readings in Evaluation Research.* New York: Russell Sage Foundation, 1977.

EASTON, DAVID. *A Framework for Political Analysis.* Englewood Cliffs, NJ: Prentice-Hall, 1965.

HOOS, IDA. *System Analysis in Public Policy: A Critique.* Berkeley: University of California Press, 1960.

HITCH, CHARLES, and MCKEAN, ROLAND. *The Economics of Defense in a Nuclear Age.* Cambridge: Harvard University Press, 1960.

LERNER, DANIEL, and LASSWELL, HAROLD, eds. *The Policy Sciences.* Stanford, Calif.: Stanford University Press, 1951.

QUADE, E.S. *Systems Analysis Techniques for Planning-Programming-Budgeting, Report P-3322.* Santa Monica, CA: The Rand Corporation, 1966.

RIVLIN, ALICE. *Systematic Thinking for Social Action.* Washington: The Brookings Institution, 1971.

ROSSI, PETER, and WILLIAMS, WALTER, eds. *Evaluating Social Programs.* New York: Academic Press, 1972.

ROUSSEAU, JEAN JACQUES. *The Social Contract.* Chicago: Regnery-Gateway, 1762.

WEISS, CAROL. *Evaluation Research.* Englewood Cliffs, NJ: Prentice-Hall, 1972.

WILDAVSKY, AARON. "The Self-Evaluating Organization," in *Speaking Truth to Power.* Boston: Little, Brown, 1979.

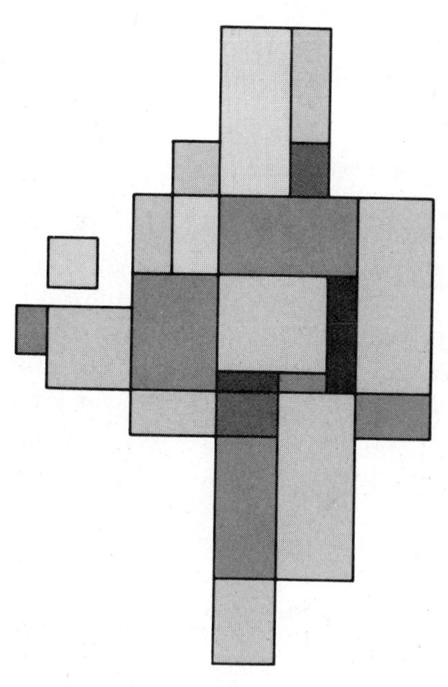

MODULE 9

Calculating the Impact of Policy, Benefit/Cost Analysis

INTRODUCTION

Systems analysis is a broad-based approach to the analysis of public policy. It begins with the specification of objectives and ends with the application of the chosen criteria for comparing alternative courses of action. Between these two steps, a variety of analytic procedures occurs. In many ways, the core of the method is the procedure for calculating the impact of the proposed course of action. For while the clarification of goals and the development of alternative means of achieving them deserve careful attention, it is the calculation of the effects of policy that presents the greatest opportunity for the application of varied quantitative models and techniques.

The most common application of systems analysis is during policy formation, when a policymaker must choose among alternative courses of action. The policymaker seeks to predict the probable effects of these alternatives so that the most productive is chosen. In Yehezkel Dror's terminology, the policymaker seeks to choose that policy with the highest net output. But how can a policy analyst predict today what tomorrow's policy will bring? He or she must rely on knowledge of the way things have happened in the past. The systems analyst is in this sense a historian. A powerful tool is gained when alternatives can be reliably represented using mathematical models, based upon past performance.

Predicting Policy Effects

To what extent can the destructive power of a new weapons system be predicted? Or the ability of a new system to respond to a particular emergency? What will be the generating power of a new plant and how reliable will it be in providing energy to a metropolitan area? What will be the effects, both intended and unintended, of constructing a different type of plant using, instead of water or oil as its source of energy, nuclear or solar power? If a program of education for the disadvantaged is begun, how would you calculate the probable effects in terms of generating higher incomes for those participating? Could you base an estimate on the average present earnings of individuals completing a similar level of education? You might speculate that the more different the new approach is from previous approaches, the more likely that the calculations will be less reliable.

One approach to the conceptualization of the effects of policy is Yehezkel Dror's equation: Net Output = Benefits Minus Costs. For example, the costs of previous weapons systems may provide good guides for the estimation of future costs of similar weapons systems being developed. This does not mean that a particular estimate will be completely accurate. Examples are legion in the national defense area where initial costs are doubled or tripled by the time a project is completed. Can you see any organizational reasons why estimates in this area tend to be lower than actual costs?

If two construction projects, dams, for example, are being contemplated, previous experience again can be used to provide estimates of new projects. Estimates are usually based on history — some analogy to a similar project that occurred previously. Corrections relating to current conditions such as inflation are necessary.

Mathematical Models

Sometimes the results of history can be summarized in a more formal way by the use of a mathematical model. A mathematical model allows for the numerical representation of major factors so that effects can be calculated. Some models, like those used in linear programming or queuing theory, allow for the calculation of an optimal policy mix from an unlimited number of alternative possible combinations.

In its simplest form, a mathematical model can be a single equation, allowing for the calculation of some impact given a certain option. As an example, consider the question of how large a school building to construct. Suppose the number of children a building can accommodate may be given by the equation $X = 25Y$, where X is the number of children and Y is the number of classrooms. The equation incorporates the historical fact that class size in this school district has been approximately twenty-five students over the past five years. Can you think of any circumstances that might make this prediction inaccurate? Can you think of any ways of ensuring that the school does not become obsolete if class size changes? What other facts would be important to you in assessing the proposed capacity of a new school?

How might you estimate the number of students in the neighborhood the school serves? Suppose you obtained estimates from the state education department that statewide, over the next five years, a 15 percent reduction was anticipated in school attendance. Would the equation $Z = .85T$ (Z = projected enrollment, T = current enrollment) be an accurate projection of school enrollment in this neighborhood in five years? How would you use this information in helping to decide about the size of the projected school?

Needless to say, mathematical models are often much more complicated than a single equation. For those of you familiar with simultaneous equations, several equations holding true at the same time, linear programming can be explained as a technique for finding a solution to a series of simultaneous equations. As you develop your interest in public policy analysis, you will probably want to develop your own quantitative skills so that you are better able to understand and apply more complicated models of the public policy process.

BENEFIT/COST ANALYSIS

At this stage, in order to give you a more in-depth understanding of how mathematical models can be useful in calculating the impacts of public policy, you are going to be asked to undertake an exercise in benefit/cost analysis. In its most rudimentary form, benefit/cost analysis asks you to do three things: (1) calculate the benefits of a projected policy; (2) calculate the costs of a projected policy; and (3) compare the benefits and costs. Benefit/cost analysis provides an excellent example of the use of mathematical techniques and the application of an explicit criterion in the assessment of policy alternatives. Its most well-known applications derive from private sector economic concepts and determine whether a particular use of resources, private or public, is a good investment at a given time. Such questions involve calculating rates of return. The rate of return, of course, depends on the amount of the investment and the income that is generated. For example, if a twenty-thousand-dollar investment in real estate yields an annual profit of two thousand dollars (after deducting expenses), we would say that the twenty-thousand-dollar investment yields a two-thousand-dollar or ten percent return.

A central concept in benefit/cost analysis is *discount rate*. The discount rate represents the return that could have been realized if those same resources had been put to some other use. Often the bank rate of interest or the going rate of interest in the investment market may be used as a discount rate. The discount rate reminds us that resources invested in a particular project cannot be used for any other project. The opportunity costs are the foregone benefits that might have occurred if those resources were invested in some other enterprise. Inclusion of accurate discount rates is central to benefit/cost analysis.

Since benefit/cost analysis compares the inputs of a particular program, or the resources utilized by a particular program, with the resources produced, its application requires comparability among inputs and outputs. Ordinarily, such comparability is achieved by expressing costs and benefits in monetary terms. Sometimes such an assignment of values is difficult. The usefulness of a benefit/cost analysis will depend on the reliability of quantification. If it is remembered that benefit/cost analysis is a tool for decision makers to use rather than an automatic process for assessing program alternatives, the dangers of incomplete analysis may be substantially reduced. Benefit/cost analysis can substantially add to the ability of decision makers to make rational decisions.

Benefit/cost analysis can be a powerful tool, for in its pure form, it allows for the comparison of alternative uses of resources of very different sorts. By using the criterion of dollars return for dollars invested, it allows for the comparison of diverse uses of resources. In principle, then, any two alternative uses can be judged against each other, according to the criterion of which brings the greater future income per dollars invested.

Another way of conceptualizing benefit/cost analysis is to say that it measures the outputs or effects of policy against the inputs or resources used to implement the policy. The benefit/cost ration is really a ratio of outputs to inputs. Might benefits and costs vary from year to year? In which year of operation would the benefit/cost ratio be greatest in the problem above, in year 1, 4, or 20? Can you see why it was easier to calculate net output over a twenty-year period?

However, when applying benefit/cost analysis to public policy, serious problems may arise in expressing the costs and benefits in monetary terms. If the benefits of education are new skills, attitudes, or enjoyment of life, these may be difficult to express in monetary terms. But if the benefit of education is supposed to be increased life earnings, this can be readily expressed if life earnings can be calculated or predicted. Similarly, if the benefit is increased revenue from a parking facility, this can be reduced to money terms. Again, it is more difficult to express the convenience of city residents, increased enjoyment, or aesthetic pleasure.

The fact is that many public policies are directed at broad-based social benefits that are difficult to price.

To get a better idea of the way benefit/cost analysis works, consider the following case and answer the questions.

Downtown Parking Authority*

PROPOSED MUNICIPAL PARKING FACILITY

In January, 1968, a meeting was held in the office of the mayor of Oakmont to discuss a proposed municipal parking facility. The participants included the mayor, the traffic commissioner, the administrator of Oakmont's Downtown Parking Authority, the city planner, and the finance director. The purpose of the meeting was to consider a report by Richard Stockton, executive assistant to the Parking Authority's administrator, concerning estimated costs and revenues for the proposed facility.

Mr. Stockton's opening statement was as follows:

"As you know, the mayor proposed two months ago that we construct a multi-level parking garage on the Elm Street site. At that time, he asked the Parking Authority to assemble all pertinent information for consideration at our meeting today. I would like to summarize our findings briefly for you.

"The Elm Street site is owned by the city. It is presently occupied by the remains of the old Embassy Cinema, which was gutted by fire last June. The proprietors of the cinema have since used the insurance proceeds to open a new theatre in the suburbs; their lease of the city-owned land on which the Embassy was built expired on December 31st.

"We estimate that it would cost approximately $40,000 to demolish the old Embassy. A building contractor has estimated that a multi-level structure, with space for 800 cars, could be built on the site at a cost of about $2 million. The useful life of the garage would probably be around forty years.

"The city could finance construction of the garage through the sale of bonds. The finance director has informed me that we could probably float an issue of 20-year tax-exempts at 5% interest. Redemption would commence after three years, with one-seventeenth of the original number of bonds being recalled in each succeeding year.

"A parking management firm has already contacted us with a proposal to operate the garage for the city. They would require a management fee of $30,000 per year. Their proposal involves attendant parking, and they estimate

---

*This case was prepared by Graeme M. Taylor under the supervision of Richard F. Vancil of Harvard University Graduate School of Business Administration on behalf of the U.S. Bureau of the Budget. The case is intended for class discussion only, and certain names and facts may have been changed which, while avoiding the disclosure of confidential information, do not materially lessen the value of the case for educational purposes. This case is not intended to represent either effective or ineffective handling of an administrative situation, nor does it purport to be a statement of policy by the agency involved.

that their costs, exclusive of the fee, would amount to $240,000 per year. Of this amount, $175,000 would be personnel costs; the remainder would include utilities, mechanical maintenance, insurance, etc. Any gross revenues in excess of $270,000 per year would be shared 90% by the city and 10% by the management firm. If total annual revenues are less than $270,000, the city would have to pay the difference.

"I suggest we offer a management contract for bid, with renegotiations every three years.

"The city would derive additional income of around $50,000 per year by renting the ground floor of the structure as retail space.

"It's rather difficult for the Parking Authority to estimate revenues from the garage for, as you know, our operations to date have been confined to fringe-area parking lots. However, we conducted a survey at a private parking garage only three blocks from the Elm Street site; perhaps that information will be helpful.

"This private garage is open every day from 7 a.m. until midnight. Their rate schedule is as follows: 75¢ for the first hour; 50¢ for the second hour; and 25¢ for each subsequent hour, with a maximum rate of $2.00. Their capacity is 400 spaces. Our survey indicated that, during business hours, 75% of their spaces were occupied by "all-day parkers"—cars whose drivers and passengers work downtown. In addition, roughly 400 cars use the garage each weekday with an average stay of three hours. We did not take a survey on Saturday or Sunday, but the proprietor indicated that the garage is usually about 75% utilized by short-term parkers on Saturdays until 6 p.m., when the department stores close; the average stay is about two hours. There's a lull until about 7 p.m., when the moviegoers start coming in; he says the garage is almost full from 8 p.m. until closing time at midnight. Sundays are usually very quiet until the evening, when he estimates that his garage is 60% utilized from 6 p.m. until midnight.

"In addition to this survey, we studied a report issued by the City College Economics Department last year. This report estimated that we now have approximately 50,000 cars entering the central business district (CBD) every day from Monday through Saturday. Based on correlations with other cities of comparable size, the economists calculated that we need 30,000 parking spaces in the CBD. This agrees quite well with a block-by-block estimate made by the traffic commissioner's office last year, which indicated a total parking need in the CBD of 29,000 spaces. Right now we have 22,000 spaces in the CBD. Of these, 5% are curb spaces (half of which are metered, with a 2-hour maximum limit for 20 cents), 65% are in open lots, and 30% are in privately owned and operated garages.

"Another study indicated that 60% of all auto passengers entering the CBD on a weekday were on their way to work; 20% were shoppers, and 20% were businessmen making calls. The average number of people per car was 1.75.

"Unfortunately, we have not yet had time to use the data mentioned thus far to work up estimates of the revenues to be expected from the proposed garage.

"The Elm Street site is strategically located in the heart of the CBD, near the major department stores and office buildings. It is five blocks from one of the access ramps to the new crosstown freeway which we expect will be open to traffic next year, and only three blocks from the Music Center which the mayor dedicated last week.

"As we all know, the parking situation in that section of town has steadily worsened over the last few years, with no immediate prospect of improvement. The demand for parking is clearly there, and the Parking Authority therefore recommends that we go ahead and build the garage."

The mayor thanked Mr. Stockton for his report and asked for comments. The following discussion took place:

Finance Director: "I'm all in favor of relieving parking congestion downtown, but I think we have to consider alternative uses of the Elm Street site. For example, the city could sell that site to a private developer for at least $1 million. The site could support an office building from which the city would derive property taxes of around $200,000 per year at present rates. The office building would almost certainly incorporate an underground parking garage for the use of the tenants, and therefore we would not only improve our tax base and increase revenues but also increase the availability of parking at no cost to the city. Besides, an office building on that site would serve to improve the amenity of downtown. A multi-level garage built above ground, on the other hand, would reduce the amenity of the area."

Planning Director: "I'm not sure I agree completely with the finance director. Within a certain range we can increase the value of downtown land by judicious provision of parking. Adequate, efficient parking facilities will encourage more intensive use of downtown traffic generators such as shops, offices, and places of entertainment, thus enhancing land values. A garage contained within an office building might, as the finance director suggests, provide more spaces, but I suspect these would be occupied almost exclusively by workers in the building and thus would not increase the total available supply.

"I think long-term parking downtown should be discouraged by the city. We should attempt to encourage short-term parking — particularly among shoppers — in an effort to counteract the growth of business in the suburbs and the consequent stagnation of retail outlets downtown. The rate structure in effect at the privately operated garage quoted by Mr. Stockton cleary favors the long-term parker. I believe that, if the city constructs a garage on the Elm Street site, we should devise a rate structure which favors the short-term parker. People who work downtown should be encouraged to use our mass transit system."

Finance Director: "I'm glad you mentioned mass transit, because this raises another issue. As you know, our subways are presently not used to capacity and are running at a substantial annual deficit which is borne by the city. We have just spent millions of dollars on the new subway station under the Music Center. Why build a city garage only three blocks away which will still farther increase the subway system's deficit? Each person who drives downtown instead of taking the subway represents a loss of 50 cents (the average round trip fare) to the subway system. I have read a report stating that approximately two-thirds of all persons entering the CBD by car would still have made the trip *by subway* if they had *not* been able to use their cars."

Mayor: "On the other hand, I think shoppers prefer to drive rather than take the subway, particularly if they intend to make substantial purchases. No one likes to take the subway burdened down by packages and shopping bags. You know, the Downtown Merchants Association has informed me that they estimate that each new parking space in the CBD generates on average an additional $10,000 in annual retail sales. That represents substantial extra profit to retailers; I think retailing after-tax profits average about 3% of gross sales. Besides, the city treasury benefits directly from our 3% sales tax."

Traffic Commissioner: "But what about some of the other costs of increasing parking downtown and therefore, presumably, the number of cars entering the CBD? I'm thinking of such costs as the increased wear and tear on city streets, the additional congestion produced with consequent delays and frustration for the drivers, the impeding of the movement of city vehicles, noise, air pollution, and so on. How do we weigh these costs in coming to a decision?"

Parking Administrator: "I don't think we can make a decision at this meeting. I suggest that Dick Stockton be asked to prepare an analysis of the proposed garage."

As Mr. Stockton, prepare your response to the mayor's request, answering the following questions:

1. List the benefits and costs of the additional parking facility, over the twenty-year period.
2. Assign monetary values to the benefits and costs.
3. What additional information would facilitate your calculation? Where would you get such information? How accurate are your estimates?
4. How would you calculate the foregone opportunities of building the parking facility?
5. What alternative uses of the land are possible and how would you estimate the benefits and costs of these uses?
6. Do the benefits of the project justify the costs?
7. How is the benefit level affected by the charge for parking?

Bring your analysis to class. Together with the other members of your group, develop a common list of benefits and costs and arrive at a common analysis. Be prepared to justify your own position. Remember, a good policy analyst is not only a forceful advocate, but also a good judge of the suggestions of others. Each group analysis should be presented to the class and analyzed. Take a vote and decide which group analysis was the best.

Having participated in group and class discussions that have developed your own understanding of how to calculate benefits and costs, prepare a memorandum of less than three typewritten pages outlining a course of action for the mayor, justified by a detailed calculation of the benefits and costs of three alternatives. Be sure to include a judgment as to the strengths and limitations of your analysis.

Suppose that the mayor has decided that a parking lot shall be constructed in a downtown section of town. He or she then asks you to perform a benefit/cost analysis involving three different sites. How does this alter the nature of the problem presented to you? By specifying that the parking lot will be built and limiting the choice of sites to three, the mayor has considerably simplified your task. In comparing the three sites, describe the types of benefits and costs that might be associated with each.

COMMENT ON DOWNTOWN PARKING AUTHORITY

While the previous case involves a situation closely tied to economic development concerns, the methodology is more general. Many government decisions involve benefits and costs which can be quantified. A knowledge of the likely effects of such projects or decisions ordinarily depends upon expertise in this area. What would the mayor have done if a Downtown Parking Authority did not already exist?

In addition to knowledge of the actual benefits and costs to be considered, knowledge of the methodology of benefit/cost analysis is critical. While benefit/cost analysis can be quite complicated, the basic approach can be understood by most managers.

Often in benefit/cost analysis, simplifying assumptions is necessary in making estimates. Was the use of income generating information based on a current parking facility totally justified? What are its shortcomings? Why use it?

To what extent do nonquantifiable benefits figure into your analysis? How would you quantify the benefits of the aesthetic values of creating a new park? Why is the alternative of a park and underground parking facility particularly amenable, for benefit/cost purposes, in comparison with the parking facility by itself?

Some benefit/cost analysis involves benefits and costs which are more difficult to quantify than those in the above case. How do you quantify the benefits of a training program? Suggestions are made in the research note below.

A NOTE ON BENEFIT/COST ANALYSIS AND OTHER QUANTITATIVE TECHNIQUES

Benefit/cost analysis is becoming a more frequently used tool in the public sector. Where the benefits and costs are apparent and subject to quantitative expression, it can be an invaluable aid. Yet such an analysis is rarely adequate by itself. It must be applied and used wisely by the policymaker.

A benefit/cost problem that in some ways was similar to the Downtown Parking Authority was where to build a third airport in the London area. Not too long ago the British government appointed a special commission to study the problems of this proposal. The commission decided to consult experts, who were asked to undertake benefit/cost analyses of three possible sites for the airport. The actual analysis supposed that the benefit of the construction of the third airport was to be a given. The nature of the cost-benefit analysis was altered so that the objective was to determine the respective costs of the three airport sites. The main costs considered were: (1) airspace movement costs, which related to the air distance of the proposed site from existing airports; (2) passenger user costs, which involved the distances the prospective passengers would have to travel in order to reach the third airport; (3) other costs, including capital costs; and (4) noise costs, affecting local population centers. The commission that requested the benefit/cost analysis followed its recommendations. The government, however, rejected both the recommendation of the commission it had appointed and the recommendation of the research team and decided to choose an alternative site.

This example demonstrates that benefit/cost analysis does not eliminate decision-making responsibilities. However, it certainly can have an influence on the outcome. The final determination, though, rests with the decision maker, who must be able to interpret the benefit/cost analysis in a larger context.

If you are interested in pursuing the analysis of the problem of where to construct London's third airport more fully, you can find a description of this particular case in *1972 Yearbook of Benefit/Cost Analysis*, published by Aldine.

Upward Bound

Benefit/cost analysis is receiving increasing attention as a tool for evaluating education and training programs. According to Gary Becker, in his classic book, *Human Capital,* expenditures for education and training can be conceived of as investments in human capital. The benefits of such programs in terms of increased earnings can be viewed as returns on investments. By calculating the difference in lifetime earnings with and without participation in a particular education or training program, a measure of benefit results. The analysis rests upon the calculation of lifetime earnings, which may be viewed as the sum of annual incomes, referred to in the analysis as income streams.

Using such a perspective, education and training programs can be viewed as efforts to increase the earnings of individuals enrolled in these programs. One such program, Upward Bound, has been analyzed in considerable detail by Walter Garms.* Upward Bound is a federally funded program designed to identify able high school students who would be unlikely to go to college because of a low socioeconomic background or related problems of self-image. Many of those selected have come from minority ethnic groups.

Typically, students are identified in their sophomore year of high school and are given special enrichment work at local colleges during the school year and during the summers. Special efforts are made to place students. In addition, they are given small stipends. Enrollment in college terminates active involvement with Upward Bound.

In order to evaluate the success of the program, Garms chose to compare Upward Bound students with their older brothers and sisters. He found that by and large these students did better than their siblings, but that their siblings often did well, too. In other words, while the individuals selected by the program did come from homes with below-

---

*Walter Garms, "A Benefit-Cost Analysis of the Upward Bound Program," *Journal of Human Resources,* 1971, Vol. VI, pp. 206 – 220.

average deprivation, they were not the severely deprived individuals that were the original target of the program. Even the older siblings in these families had a high rate of college attendance.

In an effort to undertake a more detailed analysis of the benefits and costs of this program, Garms calculated the difference in expected lifetime earnings between the participants in Upward Bound and their sisters and brothers. Why did Garms select any comparison group? Why this particular group?

His calculations are indicated in Table 9 – 1, which is based upon the benefit and costs to individuals. The basic figure in the table is the lifetime income differential, which is calculated for four categories of individuals. It indicates the difference in expected lifetime earnings between those enrolled in the Upward Bound programs and their brothers and sisters who were not enrolled. In addition, the differential is adjusted for discount rates of 5 and 10 percent.

You can see the importance of the discount rate, for in this situation it makes the difference between a substantial return on the investment and a minimal return. In Table 9 – 2, which calculates the benefits and costs from society's point of view, the difference between discount rates of 5 percent and 10 percent differentiates net benefits from net losses. From these examples, you can see how important the discount rate is in affecting the return on investment.

Note also that in all cases the net benefits are lifetime benefits. The annual return on investment would be quite low, even in those cases where the lifetime differentials are substantial.

Do you understand the basic difference between Tables 9 – 1 and 9 – 2? Table 9 – 2 views the problem from society's perspective, while Table 9 – 1 is from the perspective of the individual. What accounts for the larger initial figure for lifetime income differentials in Table 9 – 2? On what basis are taxes included in the Table 9 – 2 figures and excluded from Table 9 – 1? Why is the cost to the government included in Table 9 – 2 and excluded from Table 9 – 1? Which table is more relevant to a legislature revising the policy? Which table is more relevant to an individual wishing to participate in the program?

Would you view Upward Bound as a good investment? Walter Garms concludes that:

> From the social viewpoint, substantial net benefits at the 5 percent discount rate become substantial net costs at the 10 percent discount rate. From the economic viewpoint, Upward Bound is at best a marginal program, and the justification for its continued existence must be sought in presumed benefits which are not accounted for here. In addition, the social benefits shown here are completely dependent upon the existence of excess capacity at the colleges attended by the Upward Bound students. If such excess capacity does not exist, there are no such benefits — only costs.

TABLE 9–1. Analysis of the Upward Bound Program
Benefits and Costs from the Individual's Viewpoint[a]

	WHITE		NONWHITE	
	Male	Female	Male	Female
DISCOUNT RATE 5 PERCENT				
Benefits				
Lifetime income differentials (after taxes)[b]	$5,209	$3,549	$3,943	$5,843
Upward Bound stipend[c]	210	209	224	224
Scholarships and grants[d]	454	394	683	498
Total benefits	$5,873	$4,152	$4,850	$6,565
Cost differentials[e]				
Tuition[f]	370	319	537	378
Extra living costs[g]	260	225	379	267
Total costs	$ 630	$ 544	$ 916	$ 645
Net benefits	$5,243	$3,608	$3,934	$5,920
DISCOUNT RATE 10 PERCENT				
Benefits				
Lifetime income differentials (after taxes)[b]	$ 770	$1,152	$ 354	$1,902
Upward Bound stipend[c]	202	201	214	214
Scholarships and grants[d]	373	324	561	410
Total benefits	$1,345	$1,677	$1,129	$2,526
Cost differentials[e]				
Tuition[f]	308	264	446	314
Extra living costs[g]	215	185	312	220
Total costs	$ 523	$ 449	$ 758	$ 534
Net benefits	$ 822	$1,228	$ 371	$1,992

a. All figures shown as present value at age 16, the approximate age at which a decision is made to include a student in Upward Bound.

b. Differentials are calculated by multiplying the proportion of Upward Bound students in each educational category by the present value of lifetime income for that category, and summing over all four categories. The same is done for siblings, and the difference between those figures is the raw differential. The raw differential is reduced by 25 percent to allow for taxes paid, and the result is again reduced by 25 percent on the assumption that only 75 percent of income differentials are *caused* by education.

c. Stipends averaged $45.36 per month during the summer and $5.60 per month during the school year. For the whole program, stipends ranged from $218 for white females to $233 for nonwhite females. Figures shown are present values of these amounts.

d. Scholarships and grants ranged from $739 to $793 per year for Upward Bound students and were assumed to be identical for siblings. Differentials shown arise because of differential rates of college attendance between Upward Bound students and siblings.

e. Because present values are computed at age 16, the income series automatically shows foregone income as a reduction in benefits, and it is not included separately as a cost. This is also true of the reduced receipts of unemployment and welfare payments by educated individuals.

f. Based on average 1968–69 tuition of $602 for all U.S. institutions.

g. Assumes an average of $425 per year in extra living costs while in college.

SOURCE: Walter Garms, "A Benefit-Cost Analysis of the Upward Bound Program," *Journal of Human Resources,* 1971, Vol. VI, pp. 206–220.

TABLE 9–2. Human Capital and Income Redistribution
Benefits and Costs from Society's Viewpoint[a]

	WHITE		NONWHITE	
	Male	Female	Male	Female
DISCOUNT RATE 5 PERCENT				
Benefits				
Lifetime income differentials (before taxes)[b]	$7,020	$4,777	$5,491	$7,942
Cost differentials[c]				
Upward Bound costs to the government[d]	$1,811	$1,798	$1,922	$1,919
Upward Bound cost to colleges[e]	260	257	275	275
Cost of education[f]	1,057	872	1,424	1,028
Extra living costs[g]	260	225	379	267
Total costs	$3,388	$3,152	$4,000	$3,489
Net benefits	$3,632	$1,625	$1,491	$4,453
DISCOUNT RATE 10 PERCENT				
Benefits				
Lifetime income differentials (before taxes)[b]	$1,066	$1,560	$ 598	$2,609
Cost differentials[c]				
Upward Bound cost to the government[d]	$1,737	$1,724	$1,845	$1,842
Upward Bound cost to colleges[e]	249	247	264	264
Cost of education[f]	852	724	1,183	856
Extra living costs[g]	215	185	312	220
Total costs	$3,053	$2,880	$3,604	$3,182
Net benefits	–$1,987	–$1,320	–$3,006	–$ 573

a. All figures are present values at age 16.

b. Differentials are calculated as in Table 4 [9–1], including the assumption that only 75 percent of differentials are caused by education, but excluding the reduction for taxes paid. The effect of decreased receipts of unemployment and welfare benefits by educated individuals has been removed because in the social context these are transfer payments.

c. As in Table 4, foregone income is included in lifetime income differentials as a reduction in benefits.

d. Excludes cost of stipends paid students, which are transfer payments. Cost calculated from data furnished by OEO.

e. Calculated from data furnished by OEO.

f. Based on total economic cost of education, estimated at $623 per pupil in high school and $1,470 per pupil in college.

g. Extra living cost is estimated at $425 per year while in college.

SOURCE: Walter Garms, "A Benefit-Cost Analysis of the Upward Bound Program," *Journal of Human Resources*, 1971, Vol. VI, pp. 206 – 220.

> Finally, the data point out the possibility that the Upward Bound program is primarily a device for identification of students who would be rather likely to go to college anyway. If this were its only function, all social benefits would also be eliminated, and private benefits would be limited to the value of the Upward Bound stipend.[p. 214]

What items have been excluded from the benefit/cost analysis? Should items such as increased skill levels, or satisfaction, or sense of importance be included in the analysis?

Should a policymaker be concerned with the political impacts of such a program? What are the likely reactions of those excluded from the program? Does the program's effect on the political commitment of individuals deserve a place in the analysis?

CRITICISMS OF BENEFIT/COST ANALYSIS

Some of the most telling criticisms of the application of benefit/cost analysis to public sector problems emphasize the inability of the analysis to deal with certain political dimensions of policy.

Some economists have argued that these political aspects can be incorporated in a benefit/cost analysis if appropriate devices are used. While in theory it may be possible to accomplish this goal, in practice it presents formidable obstacles. It is difficult to quantify the political benefit of gaining or losing the support of some social group, or the aesthetic benefits of a park when compared to a parking facility. In fact, once benefit/cost moves out of the economic marketplace, where all benefits and costs have a monetary value, its execution becomes much more difficult. While it seems likely that the benefit/cost analysis approach will be adopted more widely, and that, especially where costs and benefits can be specified in monetary terms, its use will expand, benefit/cost analysis must be executed with care in addressing public sector problems.

Benefit/cost analysis is just one of the more frequent approaches to quantitative assessment that are used in decision making today. The proliferation of such terms as *operations research, management science, decision science,* and *systems analysis* attests to a variety of approaches. Operations research, which may be taken as a term of reference to the application of mathematical models in rather well specified decision problems, has made considerable strides in private sector problems and some public sector problems as well. Queuing theory, which has been applied to problems of scheduling in the private sector, has also been applied to public sector problems. The general problem of scheduling, whether involving advice in a social security office, classes in a school, or cases on a judicial docket, provides an excellent application for queuing theory. Similarly, linear programming, which involves optimizing resource allocation in quest of some specific outcome(s), also has implications for public sector programs. Whether resources involve health care, transportation, or building construction, public sector problems stand to benefit by the application of these operations research techniques.

Operations research and models such as linear programming are most useful where the decision maker knows the actual situation that will occur and seeks to calculate the effects of that policy using the mathematical model. Even where knowledge is limited to probabilities that certain actions will occur, the decision maker can benefit from quantitative techniques so long as risks that one or another occurrence will take place are considered. The decision maker uses the measures of the probabilities that certain events will occur to calculate the probabilities of future effects. This approach allows for a choice of decision alternatives based on subjective estimates of the probabilities of the occurrence of various events.

Even though public sector decision making often seeks more than a single outcome, such as marketplace profit, the uses for quantitative approaches are legion. And the spreading capabilities of large-scale data processing have accelerated this trend.

Many public sector problems are clearly amenable to such techniques, with the important proviso that objectives must be explicitly stated, as in operations research.

Operations research, then, the application of quantitative methods and techniques in calculating policy impacts, is an integral part of systems analysis in the public sector. While its development is still in its infancy, it promises to greatly facilitate some aspects of public decision making.

SELECTED BIBLIOGRAPHY FOR MODULE 9

BECKER, GARY. *Human Capital.* New York: Columbia University Press, 1964.

Benefit-Cost and Policy Analysis Annual. Chicago: Aldine, 1971 – 74.

BLACK, GARY. *The Application of Systems Analysis to Government Operations.* New York: Praeger, 1969.

BYRD, JACK. *Operations Research Models for Public Administration.* Lexington, MA: Lexington Heath, 1975.

LAZARD, RICHARD, ed. *Cost Benefit Analysis.* Hammondsworth, England: Penguin, 1972.

QUADE, EDWARD. *Analysis for Public Decisions.* New York: Elsevier, 1975.

SQUIRE, LYN, and VAN DER TAK, HERMAN. *Economic Analysis of Projects.* Baltimore: Johns Hopkins University Press, 1975.

STOKEY, EDITH, and ZECKHAUSER, RICHARD. *A Primer for Policy Analysis.* New York: Norton, 1978.

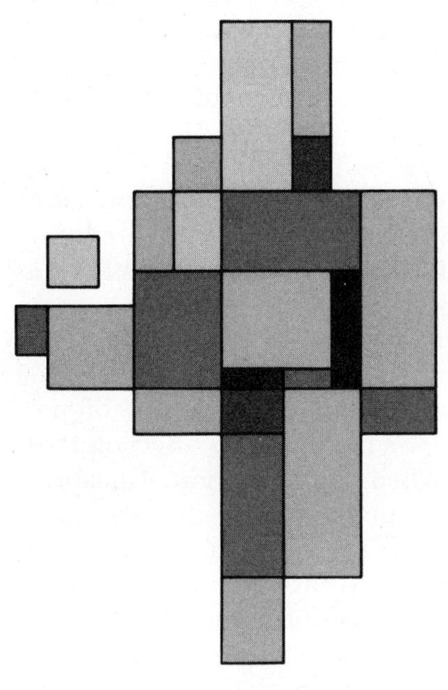

MODULE 10

Less Formal Techniques for Predicting the Future, Social Indicators, Forecasting

INTRODUCTION

Thinking about the future has become a way of life. When Alvin Toffler's widely read book, *Future Shock,* first became popular, people applauded his recognition of a fact they deeply felt, but had not always articulated themselves: that in a rapidly changing world, the pace of change can become overwhelming. The popularity of science fiction is another indication of the extent to which concern about the future has become a pervasive fact of modern life. The once unbelievable predictions of science fiction have become a plausible source for anticipating the future.

This preoccupation with the future has also had its impact on public policymaking. Who anticipated the race to space, or the development of the neutron bomb, or the search for solar energy technologies? Policymakers had to deal with these problems when they occurred. Even more down-to-earth concerns like poverty and unemployment have inspired efforts to predict the future. Attempts by American policymakers during the 1960s and 1970s to grapple with the social problems facing the country led to greater efforts to predict policy outcomes and effects.

While our main concern here is in how to predict the effects of public policies, it should be apparent that policies cannot be abstracted from the environment in which they occur. For example, welfare policy must be understood within an overall economic setting. Transportation policy must be conceived in relationship to population growth and distribution. Agricultural policy must be based upon demands, generated by population trends, and supplies that depend upon the technologies available, as well as worldwide climatic conditions.

Interest in the future has spurred the proliferation of organizations engaged in predictive activities. An inventory taken by the Council of Europe revealed a network of 293 organizations engaged in predicting the future in ten nations of Western Europe alone. Such periodicals as *Futures Technology* and *Social Change* deal regularly with predicting the future.

Techniques such as benefit/cost analysis and others described in the preceding module help predict the anticipated consequences of projected policy within very narrow limits, where the factors affecting these policies are specific and well defined. When the application of quantitative techniques to the prediction of the future is made in a systematic way, it is usually referred to as forecasting. Forecasting techniques have wide applicability in the private sector and may include prediction of the general business climate, the behavior of specific institutions like the stock market, supply and demand of goods, and labor market conditions. A popular treatment of forecasting that you might consult is Louis Bean's *The Art of Forecasting.*

The use of clearly defined mathematical techniques for forecasting is not always desirable. The appeal of science fiction, for example, is not in its mathematical precision, but in its ability to make great, wild leaps into the world of imagination. A similar appeal to open-ended, free-wheeling imagination characterizes the use of scenarios in understanding the future. Scenarios have been described in Module 7 as hypothetical situations. The scenario is probably most closely associated with think tanks and it is particularly closely associated with Herman Kahn of the Hudson Institute. Kahn at first used scenarios to consider national security policy, but later expanded his horizons to include general social policy. His use of scenarios was popularized in his well-known book, *Thinking About the Unthinkable.* The unthinkable in this case was nuclear war. Kahn insisted that planners had to be willing to confront the possibility of a nuclear war and should think about the process by which it might happen and how to respond.

In order to think about this problem and others, Kahn made use of the scenario, which was nothing more than a hypothetical situation cast in realistic terms. A scenario is a progression of events that might occur and that invite the policymakers' response.

Scenarios usually contain considerable detail about a specific situation, but they may also be briefer. They can form the basis of group brainstorming exercises, such as those considered in Module 5. Their point is much the same as that of brainstorming: to create a nonthreatening environment in which individuals can imaginatively confront the future and propose solutions to the important problems of the day.

Scenarios

In order to gain first-hand experience with some futuristic scenarios, divide into groups and be ready to present to the class your responses to the following brief scenarios:

1. Unemployment skyrockets from around 8 percent to 20 percent within two years. What would be the social effects, including public opinion, and some likely responses by the government?
2. The United States finds itself with only ten years of domestic oil supplies left. What should it do?
3. The major cities of the North find the number of welfare recipients has climbed from 10 percent to 15 percent of the population in the last decade and threatens to reach 20 percent by the end of the next decade. The national welfare rate has increased from 3 percent to 5 percent. What collective measures might be undertaken by big-city mayors?

Analyze each of the solutions proposed. Which do you prefer? Why? How would you judge the quality of the decisions? What are the main determinants of the quality of decision making using scenarios and brainstorming? What are the strengths and weaknesses of this approach to decision making under uncertainty and of the techniques suggested in the last chapter?

Both the mathematical techniques discussed in the previous module and scenarios are useful when dealing with problems about an uncertain future. This module will describe two additional approaches to anticipating the consequences of proposed public policy: *cross-impact analysis* and the *Delphi method.* These may be considered intermediary techniques in that they use neither the mathematical sophistication of the techniques described in the previous module nor the open-ended speculative nature of scenarios. The Delphi method relies on the judgments of experts to anticipate the consequences of public policy or future developments in some field. It provides a systematic method for combining expert opinion to arrive at a consensus. Cross-impact analysis is a visual display technique and group-consensus mechanism for isolating the major variables affected by some public policy decision and judging their probable change as a result of that decision.

Having studied the operation of public organizations and the public policy process, you are well aware of the importance of understanding the context of public policy. Every public policy decision has ramifications for many people and many organizations, both public and private. If, for example, the government raises the minimum wage, the incomes of many people are raised. Other jobs may be lost, some inflation may result, and the tax revenues of the government itself will change, as will those of other local and state governments. If a new mass transportation system is built, the result will be jobs for its construction and operation and new relationships between localities, ultimately affecting the places people live and their ability to commute for work and pleasure.

In order to understand the implications of public policy, then, it is critical to describe and understand its context. The cross-impact approach as contained in CROSSPACT below helps explain that policy context. It provides a method of visual display and calculation of the possibly far-ranging impacts of a given policy or group of decisions.

Crosspact

CROSSPACT is a game designed to help policymakers anticipate, consider, and deal with future policies and their consequences. It is based upon the recognition that public policymaking occurs in a complex world resulting from the interaction of social, economic, technological, political, and psychological forces, and that in order to understand public policy and its implications, all these dimensions must be considered. Policymakers must use every available device to ensure that their decisions are the best possible ones, that they achieve their desired impact and minimize any harmful side-effects.

CROSSPACT places policy questions in the larger context in which they occur, so that the decision maker will understand the impact on the entire social system. It operates on questions where precise information may be hard to come by. Instead of calculating a few impacts with great precision, it focuses on all relevant factors that might be affected by the policy and attempts to consider the impact of all these factors.

CROSSPACT outlines an approach to assessing the impacts of a proposed public policy. Once a policy has been identified, the context is set by the enumeration of groups of factors that will be affected by the policy. Usually this phase of the game will be separate from the actual assessment, so that when the assessment begins, everybody will be considering the same factors.

The selection of factors to be assessed is an important part of the game and in turn affects the following stages. As these factors are delineated, the participants are actually outlining the policy context, a mutually acceptable list of factors to be considered in assessing policy impacts. Usually these factors will be divided into categories such as economic, political, social, and governmental. The use of four categories facilitates the visual display, as you will see below.

Having developed a framework for the conduct of the game and the analysis of the policy impacts, the second phase of CROSSPACT is concerned with the actual assessment. Using a visual display device that allows for calculating the cumulative impact of a series of policies or discrete decisions, the game provides a mechanism for reconciling diverse opinions. To add realism, the participants should reflect not only their individual differences, but differences resulting from institutional diversity. Thus, different interest groups, agencies, or levels of government should be represented during this phase, where possible.

PHASE I: SELECTION OF A PROBLEM

In choosing a public policy area for analysis, you may want to consider the following factors:

1. Is the public policy area familiar to many of the students?
2. Is information about it readily available?
3. Is it of current interest?
4. Does it have complicating aspects, involving the interaction of interest groups, different government agencies, and different levels of government, local, regional, state and federal?
5. Is it possible to specify a sequence of at least three interrelated discrete policies or decisions whose cumulative effects can be judged?

In case you are having difficulties selecting an area for analysis, try the following suggestions for New City, located in New State.

A. Transportation Policy: (1) Develop a new underground subway system. (2) Modernize and expand existing aboveground bus facilities, through the use of federal monies, on a 50 percent matching basis. (3) Coordinate bus and subway facilities with suburban areas through creation of a Metropolitan Transportation Authority.

B. Health Policy: (1) Create a new emergency services unit to respond to health and related emergencies. (2) Include within the scope of operation intervention in all health-related emergencies, including bizarre conduct, failing health, and drug-related cases. (3) Establish a warning system to coordinate with police and fire units when necessary.

C. Economic Development: (1) Apply community development funds to the revitalization of the downtown area by reconstruction of old wharves and piers to create business and residential areas. (2) Set aside one-third of the housing for public housing units. (3) Set aside one-third for middle income housing to be subsidized by income from business properties.

D. War on Pornography: (1) Create a "porno zone" for dirty book stores, X-rated movie theatres, "massage" parlors, and prostitution. (2) Outlaw all pornography sales and prostitution within city limits. (3) Tax all pornography at the rate of 50 percent of the sales price.

PHASE II: SETTING THE ANALYTIC FRAMEWORK

Having chosen the policy area for investigation, you will now set the context for the analysis of policy impact. This involves choosing the most important factors that will be affected by these decisions. The appropriate factors will vary as you move from one policy area to another. As a start, to generate your own initial set of factors, you may want to list the following four categories and try to select the ten most appropriate factors within each category: population characteristics, economy, political support, and government revenues. When you are dealing with a problem that spills over from local to regional, state, or national dimensions, you may want to choose factors at several different levels. Be meticulous in the development of factors that are specifically applicable to the policy you chose, for the delineation of the area will in large part determine the overall value of your analysis. To demonstrate what factors might be selected, consider the three decisions about transportation policy contained in "A" above and their effect on New City. These decisions would have impacts on the city itself, the surrounding suburbs, and finally the entire state. Indeed, effects might well spill over into adjoining states, but for purposes of simplification, those effects will not be considered. Changes in the transportation system might well have effects on the makeup of the population, local economic conditions, political support for local leaders, and the flow of government revenues. Can you add other relevant factors?

Important insight into the policy decisions will flow from discussions about which factors to include. Some sample factors for an analysis of transportation policy are listed below.

Population characteristics

- Median income
- Percent over 65 years old
- Percent black
- Median education
- Total population of city

Economy

- Rate of inflation
- Rate of unemployment
- Total income

Political support (of policymakers)

- Unions
- Big business
- Public opinion
- Clientele groups

Government Revenues

- Federal grants
- State income
- Local taxes

Having chosen a number of factors which you believe will most accurately reflect the impacts in a particular policy area, discuss these factors with your group and finally with the entire class. Through some method chosen by the instructor, agree upon a list of twenty to forty factors.

PHASE III: JUDGING THE IMPACT

Each individual should make a tally sheet for each decision. The tally sheet should list on the left side all the factors being considered. Three columns should be indicated to the right of the sheet: in the first column, indicate whether or not that factor is affected; in the second column, indicate the direction of the effect, positive or negative; and in the third column, mark the approximate percentage change. A sample tally sheet is provided as Table 10–1.

TABLE 10–1—Tally Sheet
Decision 1—Develop a New Underground Subway System

	Effect	Direction	Percent
Population Characteristics			
Median income New City	Yes	+	5
Median income New State	Yes	+	1
Median income suburbs	No	−	5
% poverty New City	Yes	−	1
% poverty New State	Yes	−	
% poverty suburbs	No		
Total population New City	Yes	+	5
Total population New State	Yes	+	1
Total population suburbs	Yes	−	3
Economy			
Rate of unemployment New City	Yes	−	5
Rate of unemployment New State	Yes	−	1
Total personal income New City	Yes	+	5
Political Support			
Big business support of mayor	Yes	+	15
Union support of mayor	Yes	+	20
Public opinion rating of mayor	Yes	+	15
Public opinion rating of governor	Yes	+	5
Citizen satisfaction with mass transit	Yes	+	10
Government Revenues			
Total city sales tax revenues	Yes	+	5
State sales tax revenue	No	−	5
Federal grants to city	Yes	+	

Do you agree with the ratings in Table 10–1? Can you cite reasons for supporting an opposite conclusion on any of these items? The discussion surrounding individual items can be quite illuminating and lead toward better information. To what extent will experts have a better understanding of the impacts than you as an ordinary individual? Do you know where you might get better information to allow for more accurate readings of the impacts of these factors? Could you design a data information system that would allow you to judge these factors on a continuing basis?

PHASE IV: CUMULATIVE EFFECTS

A series of three decisions will have cumulative effects. The total effect can be indicated by choosing an arbitrary set of initial values for the indicators and then summing the cumulative effects of the series of decisions. The initial values could also be set by reference to some particular city or other locality at some particular point in time. Or they could be selected by the instructor or the class based upon hypothetical data.

After the initial state of these variables has been set, either by attempting to estimate their level in some hypothetical city or by an arbitrary procedure such as their assignment by the group leader, you are ready to begin the play. Complete the tally sheet, as shown above. Separate tally sheets should be completed for each decision. The cumulative effects of the three decisions can be indicated on a summary sheet. In the first column list the initial values of the variables and in subsequent columns list the changed values resulting from the series of decisions. Table 10–2 shows a sample summary sheet.

The summary sheet includes the initial level of the indicators and records their changes over a series of three decisions. The figures here are fictional, but in the actual play of CROSSPACT may be based upon real governments. Many of these indicators are available through the U.S. Census Bureau for specific governmental units. The indicators for the levels of support for governmental leaders may be difficult to obtain, but periodic public opinion polls are increasingly available. While these support figures are meant to range from 0 to 100 and indicate the general level of support among a certain constituency, they may also be taken to operationalize the percentage positive response to a survey questionnaire seeking the answer to: *Do you generally support or would you give a favorable rating to the following governmental leaders?*

Try to fill out the summary sheet for a locality with which you are familiar. Would you have arrived at similar results? What determines changes in median income levels? Would a more efficient transportation system help the economic development of a city? How? What would be the impact of a more highly integrated metropolitan transportation system? Would individuals with higher-paying jobs in the city tend to relocate outside of the city? How important is the quality of transportation in attracting business and employees into a city? How might the distribution of the poor change after the creation of a metropolitan transportation authority?

While the causes of unemployment and inflation are varied, how might a more efficient transportation system result in decreases in these rates? Both job creation and greater ease in getting to jobs might decrease unemployment. The lowered rates of unemployment would result in greater income in New City.

At least in the short run, it would appear that the mayor and governor will reap substantial political benefits from refurbishing the mass transportation system. When improvements are made within the city the mayor stands to benefit the most. What would happen to citizen ratings for mass transit if the subways and buses proved uncomfortable and unreliable and the new Metropolitan Transportation Authority did not perform well?

How would the improvements in transportation affect government revenue? Increased sales in the city, resulting from decisions 1 and 2, would increase sales tax revenues for the city, but at least part of this increase would come from decreases in other parts of the state. However, the creation of the city-suburbs link might result in greater gains for both city and state. Federal grants for mass transportation would increase as a result of decisions 2 and 3.

If you have the time and the inclination, a further elaboration of the summary sheet described above can be used to provide a more dramatic visualization of the impact of decisions. A display sheet such as shown on page 208 has the advantage of grouping factors and providing a mechanism for the immediate recording of a series of decisions.

The changes in indicators can be made directly on the sheet and the consequences of a series of decisions immediately perceived. This technique of visual display is based upon Armstrong and Hobson's *Nexus*.

TABLE 10–2
Summary Sheet
Decisions 1, 2, 3

	Initial Value	1	2	3
Population Characteristics				
Median income New City	$10,000	$10,250	$11,000	$11,000
Median income New State	$11,000	$11,110	$11,200	$11,300
Median income suburbs	$12,000	$12,000	$12,000	$12,100
% poverty New City	25	23.7	23	23.5
% poverty New State	15	14.85	14.7	14.6
% poverty suburbs	10	10	10	9.8
Total population New City	1,500,000	1,575,000	1,625,000	1,600,000
Total population New State	7,000,000	7,070,000	7,100,000	7,150,000
Total population suburbs	1,000,000	170,000	950,000	1,000,000
Economy				
Rate of unemployment New City	8.00%	7.60%	7.40%	7.30%
Rate of unemployment New State	5.00%	4.95%	4.93%	4.90%
Total personal income New City	15,000,000,000	15,750,000,000	16,500,000,000	16,400,000,000
Total personal income New State	150,000,000,000	151,500,000,000	151,800,000,000	152,250,000,000
Political Support				
Big business support for mayor	70	80.5	85	90
Union support for mayor	60	72	80	85
Public opinion rating of mayor	70	80.5	83	85
Public opinion rating of governor	65	68.5	70	75
Citizen satisfaction with mass transit	50	55	65	75
Government Revenues				
Total city sales tax revenues	7,500,000	7,875,000	8,200,000	8,500,000
Total state tax revenues	50,000,000	50,000,000	50,000,000	53,000,000
Federal grants to city	100,000,000	100,000,000	110,000,000	110,000,000

Legend
1 New Subway
2 Modernize Bus System
3 Metropolitan Transportation Authority

Display Sheet

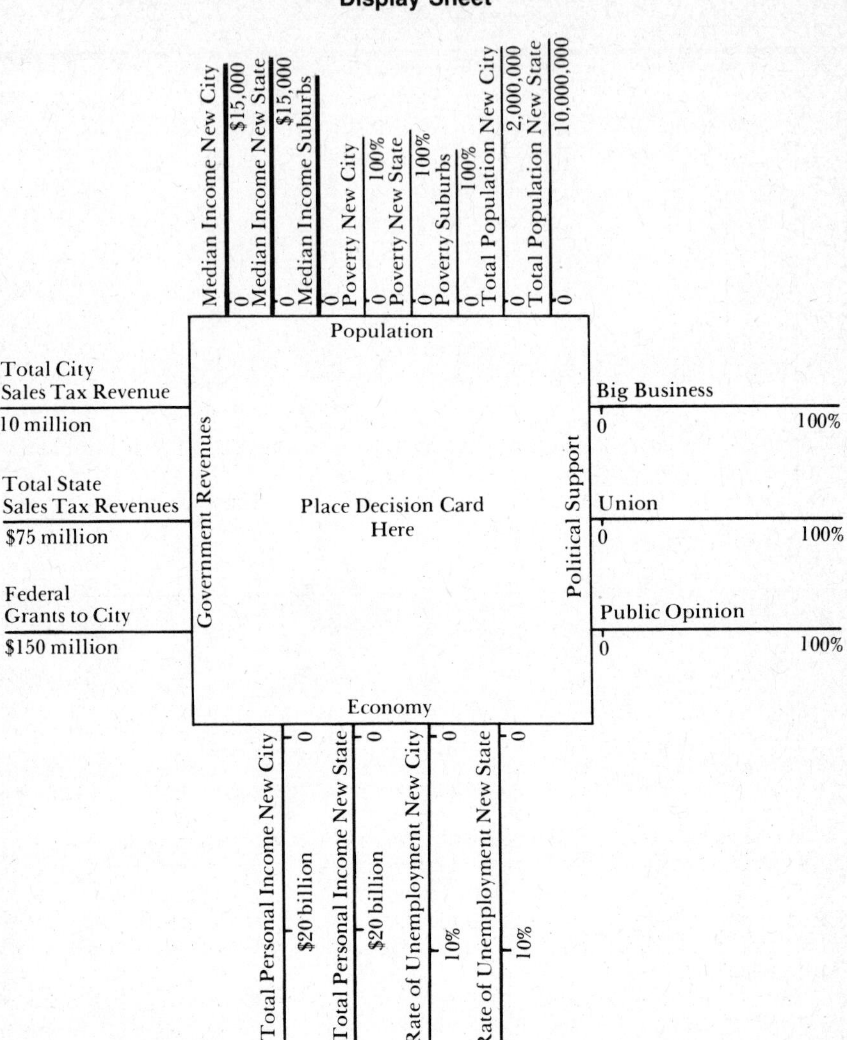

COMMENTS ON CROSSPACT

As you look back on the four phases of CROSSPACT — selection of the problem, setting the analytic framework, judging the impact of a decision, and summarizing the impact of several decisions — the interrelationships among these phases should be clear. Implicit in the game is a very general orientation to decision-making analysis, which holds that in any series of interrelated decisions, a manageable number of factors can be isolated that will indicate the major impacts of those decisions. The major advantage of CROSSPACT as compared to more rigorous decision tools is its ability to comprehend large numbers of factors with wide ranges of uncertainty. It also allows for the inclusion of factors without exact numerical representation. Another major advantage is its use of subjective calculations by the decision maker. Even where the basis for decisions cannot be specified in terms of some mathematical formula, the results of a decision maker's judgment may be included in the analysis.

CROSSPACT is of special utility when individuals with expertise in a particular field are brought together to confront real or hypothetical situations designed to test and improve their judgment. It provides an ideal setting for interaction among individuals who are trying to improve their judgment skills in a particular decision area. Of critical importance is the process of interchange and the way in which differing assessments are justified. Under the guidance of a skilled group leader, CROSSPACT can be an exceptionally gratifying experience.

The Delphi Method

Do you believe in psychics — people who can predict the future? This section is going to make you believe in them, or at least in one kind of psychic — the expert.

Through the ages, people have relied on soothsayers in attempts to divine the future or find guidance for problems. The Greeks consulted the oracle at Delphi, perhaps one of the most well known examples of reliance on individuals skilled in prediction.

Today we call individuals who can "see" into the future better than others experts rather than soothsayers. Thus, astronomers can predict the development of new space travel techniques better than laymen. Similarly, business and public sector executives can predict the needs for training in their fields of endeavor over the next ten or twenty years better than laymen. In other words, experts, relying upon their knowledge, can provide useful predictions where other methods may be useless. These subjective judgments are the basis of the Delphi method.

Before studying the Delphi Method, you might ask yourself what methods you might use for choosing from among the opinions of several experts. One technique for pooling expert opinions would be to bring them together in a collective decision-making situation, such as that described in Module 6. Each expert could be given one vote and then encouraged to make deals with other experts to arrive at a compromise.

The Delphi method is one such method, attributed to researchers who developed the procedure while working at the Rand Institute, a nonprofit research group that was developed and has been supported in large part by the United States Air Force. Although the technique was apparently first used to help Rand researchers pool their best hunches on $2 winners at local race tracks, it was also used for predicting national security needs. Delphis have been widely used to obtain group judgments where lack of information makes other methods of prediction useless. They have also been used for predicting future technological development, the pattern of the stock market, optimal policy, and goals compatible with differing value configurations.

A Delphi is nothing more than a procedure for eliciting opinions from experts, providing feedback to the experts about the opinions of other experts, and then asking them to revise their initial opinions to move toward consensus. The distinctive characteristics of a Delphi are that several stages are used, the experts never have direct contact with one another, and those administering the Delphi never participate in it. It differs from other methods of consensus building in that the participants never have direct contact. This distinctive characteristic has two main advantages. It is a relatively inexpensive and efficient method for soliciting information from individual experts who may be widely dispersed. Along with this rather mundane advantage is the fact that since the experts never directly confront one another and they are never informed who holds what opinions, undue influence on the part of one or a few individuals is eliminated.

After the selection of the panel of experts, the Delphi begins by presenting to the panel a series of written questions for which answers are solicited. The first series of questions often includes some open-ended ones, but the tendency is to prefer close-ended questions, which are more readily tabulated. Those administering the Delphi record the responses, which are then fed back to the experts, who are asked to respond to the same questions in light of others' responses, or perhaps to new questions following from the original set. The responses are reported in summary form. For example, if an answer can be scaled from 1 to 5, the average or median score would be reported.

Next, the experts are asked to answer the second set of questions, which are again added up, and summary data is fed back to them. This process will continue, usually until a predefined consensus is reached — for example, when 80 percent of the responses fall some arbitrary distance from the median.

In order to demonstrate the use of the Delphi technique, assume that each one of you is an expert in a particular subject area. That subject area will be the activities of graduates of Masters Programs in Public Administration (MPA) (or some other educational program) in this country. While in actuality you may not be an expert on this subject, hopefully you will have sufficient information to assume the role of expert for this exercise. Each group member will be considered an expert, and from now until the end of the game, your judgment will be considered expert opinion. The Delphi method will be used to develop a consensus as to the skills needed by graduates of public administration programs over the next ten years.

PHASE I — ARRIVING AT GENERAL AGREEMENT AS TO THE NATURE OF THE QUESTION

If sufficient time is available, a Delphi may well begin with an open-ended questionnaire to selected experts inquiring what they view as the major issues in a particular area or how they would formulate the major problems relating to prediction in a particular area. Depending upon the purposes of the Delphi, it might begin with quite specific questions, such as projections of the availability of human resources for the New York City area over the next ten decades.

Phase I will be eliminated in this exercise and each of the experts will be provided with a list of fairly specific questions to be answered.

PHASE II — THE POLL

In order to judge what activities MPA graduates will be engaged in, it will be necessary for you to have some sense of advancement patterns of individuals and the structure of public organizations ten years from today. For each of the skill areas listed below, mark 1, 2, 3, 4, or 5 to the left of the item. 1 indicates that you consider this relatively unimportant, 3, that you consider it to be moderately important, 5, that you consider it to be a very important activity of administrators graduating from the MPA program fifteen years from today. 2 and 4 are intermediate points.

A. Program management, techniques of developing and administering programs
B. Evaluation techniques of assessing impact of particular programs
C. Budgeting and financial analysis
D. Staff development and training
E. Conflict resolution, group dynamics
F. Computer technology
G. Research methodology
H. Organizational diagnosis and analysis
I. Procedures for administrative efficiency and office management
J. Planning techniques
K. Motivating employees
L. Relations with citizen groups

After each individual has rated each item, each group will calculate the total number of points for each item. Each person must vote on each item. Now, a class total will be calculated for each item and divided by the total number of individuals in the class. That number will now be posted on the board in the front of the class.

PHASE III — THE SECOND POLL

Now, each of the experts will be asked once more to mark 1, 2, 3, 4, or 5 in front of each item, representing the relative importance that each one of these activities will have for graduates of the MPA program fifteen years from today. Following this procedure, the total point value for each item will be calculated and an average value will then be placed on the board.

PHASE IV

The process completed in Phase III may be repeated. Delphi exercises usually consist of an initial solicitation, indicated by Phase I, and two revisions, indicated by Phases II and III.

COMMENTS ON THE DELPHI METHOD

How do you explain the difference between the results in Phase II and Phase III? Which of the results is more accurate? Why?

How does the Delphi method compare with other techniques for arriving at accurate predictions? Is the Delphi method more accurate than face-to-face discussions among experts? Do different panels of experts arrive at similar conclusions? Does the Delphi method increase or decrease the impact of psychological factors, such as unwillingness to abandon publicly expressed opinions and the bandwagon effect of majority opinion?

Can you think of a better technique for predicting the training of graduates of an MPA program? Who might be a better group of experts to utilize?

Exercise

If you would like to try a Delphi from scratch, design ten questions to solicit expert opinion on one of the following questions:

1. The extent of air pollution in a metropolitan area in 1985.
2. The need for mass transit in 1985 in a metropolitan area.
3. The costs of welfare for a metropolitan area in 1985.
4. The need for vocational training in New York City high schools at the present time.
5. The extent of crime in 1985.

Choose a panel of experts and follow the steps outlined above. After you have formulated the questions, arrive at a group consensus, assigning values to each of the specific questions. One group will have an opportunity to administer the questionnaire, performing a Delphi with the entire class as subjects. Afterwards, explain any disparity between the findings of the Delphi and the predictions of the individual group. Which is more accurate and why?

A NOTE ON THE DELPHI METHOD

Research that has been conducted comparing the Delphi method with face-to-face discussions among experts indicate superior results with the Delphi. Also, repeated uses of Delphis indicate that different groups of experts arrive at similar results.*

A specific use of the Delphi technique that may be of interest to you was reported in the July/August 1973 issue of *Public Administration Review.* It was concerned with predicting the future pattern of the discipline of public administration. The Delphi indicated adherence to two competing paradigms of public administration: (1) the conventional approach, and (2) the management and policy sciences approach. Emanuel Wald's article, "Toward a Paradigm of Future Public Administration," concludes that a consensus is developing, indicating increasing importance of the management science and policy science approach as compared to con-

---

*See N. C. Dalkey, *The Delphi Method: An Experimental Study of Group Opinion* (Santa Monica, CA: Rand Corp., 1969); and J. Martino, "The Consistency of Delphi Forecasts," *The Futurist* 4 (1970): 63.

ventional public administration. It finds that increasing reliance will be placed on tools, techniques, and methodology adapted from the social sciences.

How reliable would you view the Delphi method as an approach to predicting future developments in the field of public administration? Do you like the way the future of public administration looks? Is it compatible with your own interests? Or, perhaps more important, are your own interests compatible with the future of public administration?

A NOTE ON SOCIAL INDICATORS AND SUBJECTIVE JUDGMENT

Both the Delphi Method and CROSSPACT make extensive use of subjective judgments. Two of the categories described in CROSSPACT dealt with what may be termed general social conditions. They were included because the policy analyst is always concerned with the impacts of policies on the social system. Will a particular policy increase or decrease inflation? Will it lead to greater income for individuals? How will the policy affect social conditions and the quality of life?

CROSSPACT has the advantage of taking the "clean slate" approach. Participants are asked to consider those factors viewed as most critical to the assessment of policy impacts. But this requires that the selected factors can in fact be calculated. We are not talking about the problems of specifying a mathematical formula to determine value, but about the availability of basic information. Unless we can bring some information to bear on the estimation of a particular factor, it may be useless to include it in our analysis. CROSSPACT does not require exact information, but it does require useful information, which allows distinctions and judgments about policy impacts.

The problem of obtaining information that will permit intelligent decision-making is not unique to CROSSPACT. It is a pervasive fact of policymaking at every stage. Yehezkel Dror has referred to the application of knowledge to questions of public policy as the major task confronting those who would improve the quality of decision making.

Unless we have some knowledge about the existing social conditions and the changes wrought by particular policies, the assessment and estimation of policy impact will die stillborn. It is in part a recognition of this fact that has given rise to the social indicators movement. Proponents of this movement emphasize the importance of recording and monitoring indicators of the health of the society. Unless such social indicators are available, we don't know where we have been or where we are going.

Census Data and Other Sources

But the development of better measures is not our problem right now. Rather, we are concerned with locating and using available information. The major source of population characteristics is the Census of Populations carried out by the United States Bureau of the Census every ten years. Recently, provisions have been made for five-year census updates. These updates have become more important with the development of extensive federal programs, such as revenue sharing, which are allocated on the basis of the number of persons in a particular state or locality. An update may shift millions of dollars among the various states, counties, and cities.

Census reports are ordinarily available for states, cities, and special units known as standard metropolitan statistical areas, which for the most part include cities with populations of 50,000 or more and the surrounding county. You might go to your school library and thumb through the census reports. They include information on median income, for example, which can be used in the play of CROSSPACT. They also include information on housing conditions and labor markets.

Do you know where to obtain information about economic conditions? Try your regional office of the Bureau of Labor Statistics. Can you guess within which federal department this bureau is located? Another federal department that might help is the Commerce Department, which maintains considerable economic data. Federal, state, or local budgets provide a wealth of information about how governments spend their money and where they get it.

Many sources of statistical information that can form the basis of policy analysis now exist. Many organizations develop and maintain their own data sources for their own programs. Government and nongovernment agencies collect and maintain a wealth of information, which can be located through the *Federal Statistical Directory*, the *Directory of Non-Federal Statistics for State and Local Areas,* and *Statistical Abstracts.*

Using Information in Decision Making

The importance of monitoring policy and its impact leads some agencies to incorporate social indicators into their ongoing management information system. Government supervisors responsible for specific programs need to know what effects their policies are having. While contemporary decision makers should be familiar with a variety of techniques to accomplish this, their use must be monitored carefully. Only rarely in public policymaking will an analytic technique yield "the answer" to a decision problem. More frequently it will provide information or data to improve the basis of decision.

Decision making must, in the end, rely on individuals who are thoroughly familiar with the area in which they are operating and who know how to apply analytic skills. While it is true that sometimes knowledge and experience can blind one to the need for new approaches and departures, on the whole knowledge and experience are invaluable to the decision maker. There is no substitute for specific knowledge and experience in a particular area of endeavor.

The Delphi method, by tapping individuals' expertise, acknowledges the importance of individual judgment. This is valuable for another reason. Often policy decisions involve not only judgments as to how the world actually is, but judgments as to how the world should be. In discussions of abortion, pollution, school integration, and nuclear testing, the attitudes of individuals toward what the world ought to be like will influence their policy orientation. Sometimes we refer to this phenomenon as the influence of values on decision making.

Attention to values, which may be on either an individual or a group basis, is often referred to as the normative dimension of public policy. Not only are the actual consequences of policy important, but they should be placed within a context of individual and group views of how the world ought to be. Yet the place of values in social policy is often controversial. The conflict between individual preferences and group values or norms of behavior is often difficult to reconcile.

This dilemma as it faces the individual was initially discussed in Module I and recurred throughout this book. One outstanding example was the Tor operating within the Collpol who had to decide whether to pursue an independent point of view or that of the constituency. In the first case we spoke of a trustee role and in the second instance of a delegate role.

Probably no matter how conscientiously an individual pursues the delegate role, at times a trustee orientation will emerge. Indeed, bureaucrats, who are often selected because of their expertise, tend to emphasize their own knowledge of the public interest and exhibit a trustee orientation.

As you view the conduct of public servants, and when and if you become a public servant, you should be aware of this dilemma. The public servant has an obligation to the public to use expertise wisely and to decide matters of fact and value judiciously.

In an age when individual self-interest too often seems the preferred course, especially for individuals operating in large, often anonymous bureaucratic settings, and in an age when official corruption is widespread, that is a big order. But unless our system of public service can successfully command the loyalty and dedication it requires, the prospects for our future as a nation and a society are not bright.

SELECTED BIBLIOGRAPHY FOR MODULE 10

BAUER, RAYMOND, ed. *Social Indicators.* Cambridge: MIT Press, 1966.

BEAN, LOUIS. *The Art of Forecasting.* New York: Random House, 1970.

FALK, RICHARD. *A Study of Future Worlds.* New York: Free Press, 1975.

KAHN, HERMAN. *Thinking About the Unthinkable.* New York: Horizon Press, 1962.

LINSTONE, HAROLD, and TUROFF, MURRAY, eds. *The Delphi Method: Techniques and Applications.* Reading, MA: Addison-Wesley, 1975.

THEOBALD, ROBERT. *An Alternative Future for America.* Chicago: Swallow Press, 1968.

TOFFLER, ALVIN. *Future Shock.* New York: Random House, 1970.

SECTION IV

PUTTING IT ALL TOGETHER

The preceding modules have covered the main components of the field of public organizations, or what has been referred to, more traditionally, as public administration. The first set of modules dealt with the organizational context of government activity and focused on the individual and the administrative agency. The second set focused on the stages of the policymaking process, the most far-reaching aspect of public organizational activity. The third set of modules dealt with techniques for analyzing policies. The final module will help you integrate all the concepts and skills you have learned.

This module deals specifically with the budget-making process—just one small, though important, aspect of governmental activity. But it also treats budgeting as an example, perhaps the most important example, of a policymaking process.

As you read this module and participate in BUDGSIM, try to put together the insights you have developed throughout the course. Look at budgeting as both an organizational activity and a policy process. Think of how both incremental and rational approaches to the policy process are illustrated in budgeting. Think about the political constraints on budgeting and how the techniques of systems analysis might be used within the budget process.

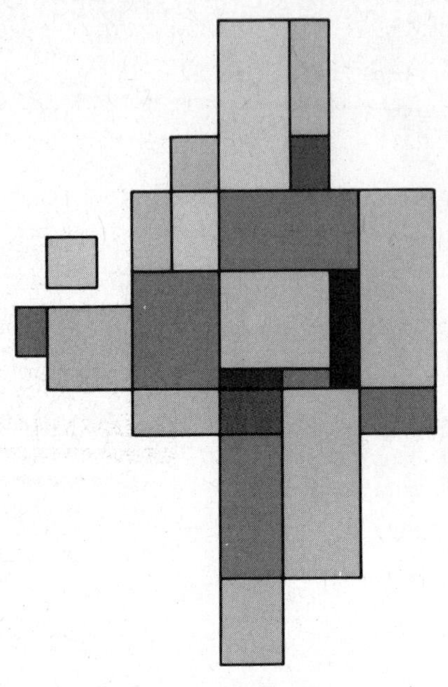

MODULE 11

Public Budgeting: Organizational Activity and Policy Process

INTRODUCTION

A budget is a fiscal plan. It sets forth how someone or some organization is going to spend its money or other resources. When you were a small child, your parents may have said to you, "We're going to give you an allowance of one dollar a week. In return, we would like you to tell us in advance what you're going to spend that money for." While you may question the value of spending time and effort preparing a budget to plan for the expenditure of a dollar a week, the basic budgeting concept is the same as that used in all organizations, both public and private. The parent/child relationship is reflected within organizations by the requirement that budget plans be submitted up the hierarchy.

Balancing the Budget

An organization that depends on an individual, group or organizational unit for its resources or for its budget approval establishes a relationship of accountability. The superior unit can always ask whether the budget plan was actually followed. To clarify our terminology and keep it consistent with current usage, we will refer to money or resources that come to an organization as revenues and money or resources that are spent as expenditures. A budget in these terms is a plan by which revenues become expenditures. When a budget plan provides that revenues equal expenditures, we refer to the budget as balanced. If revenues exceed expenditures, we have a budget surplus. If expenditures exceed revenue, we have a deficit. Remember, a budget is a plan. So even if a budget is balanced, it does not necessarily mean that when the budget is implemented the actual expenditures will equal the actual revenues. If either revenues are less than anticipated or expenditures are greater than anticipated, a budget deficit will occur. Indeed, in government budgeting, you will find that very often a plan for a balanced budget does not result in an actual balance of revenues and expenditures. Since both revenues and expenditures are difficult to predict, participants in the budget process must make estimates. But the budget process itself is a competition for resources. Participants might find ways of using estimates to favor their own position.

One of the differences between public and private organizations is the source of revenues. Private organizations obtain revenues, for the most part, from selling their products and services on the open market. If costs go up, they raise their prices. If they cannot sell sufficient quantities at higher prices, they go out of business. Private organizations are directly responsible for balancing their revenues and expenditures. When their revenues fall, they either increase their revenues through increased prices or greater volume, or decrease their expenditures by cutting costs. Public organizations, on the other hand, exist in a very different world. With the exception of certain public utilities and license bureaus, which generate their own revenue, most public organizations are dependent upon other public organizations for their revenues. The chain of command usually proceeds up the hierarchy within an agency or department to the highest agency or department level, then to the elected chief executive, whether mayor, governor, or president, and finally to the elected legislature.

Each level of government, federal, state, and local, has its own budget and each department or agency, and even many subunits, have their own budgets. The level of budget detail varies among governmental levels and within agencies. In its simplest form, a budget sets forth a total dollar amount of expected revenues and then divides that amount among the various units of government. A budget for a large city might look like the one on page 220.

The Fiscal Year. This balanced budget provides a plan for spending the anticipated revenues during the course of the fiscal year. Most budgets of government units as well as private businesses are geared to a fiscal year, which is not necessarily the same as a regular calendar year. The federal government used to have a fiscal year beginning on July 1 and ending the next June 30. Recently, it has been changed to begin on

Budget Summary—Current Fiscal Year

Anticipated Revenues: $1,538,733,737

	Budgeted
1. Education	$ 588,749,800
2. Fire	80,769,000
3. Housing	10,593,750
4. Employment and Training	27,755,000
5. Parks and Recreation	15,985,600
6. Police	174,216,675
7. Sanitation	59,815,472
8. Social Services	579,848,440
Total Planned Expenditures	$1,538,733,737

Funds derived from state and federal sources are indicated in the program descriptions. The program category involving general government and miscellaneous expenses has been omitted for simplification.

October 1 and end the following September 30. Many state and local units have fiscal years conforming to the old federal dates; some conform to the ordinary calendar year. Usually, all agencies within a single level of government will conform to the same fiscal year. Public corporations such as the Port Authority of New York and New Jersey, which have a more autonomous position, may have a separate fiscal year — in this case, the calendar year January 1–December 31.

Toward the end of one fiscal year and the beginning of the next, legislatures at the federal, state, and local levels are often scrambling to complete action on the upcoming budget. Since all agencies depend on this annual allocation, it is important to them that the legislature has authorized budgetary allocations prior to the beginning of the fiscal year. When conflict arises within the legislature, the resultant delay can cause considerable uncertainty about the level of agency allocations. Planning for the operation of the agency under such circumstances may be quite difficult.

What happens when the legislature approves a deficit budget? Or what happens when a budget is balanced when approved, but estimated revenues are not met or projected expenditures are exceeded? That is, an operational deficit is incurred. Are such situations unusual? At the Federal level, deficit budgets at both the legislative and operational levels are common. Can you think of any reason why the operational deficit is ordinarily greater than the projected deficit? Can you see any difficulties in projecting expenditures for programs such as welfare and social security? Budget deficits at the state and local level are much more serious than budget deficits at the Federal level, which at times are welcomed as a legitimate economic policy. States and localities ordinarily have constitutional prohibitions against deficit spending. Furthermore, they borrow in the commercial market and must remain solvent. They run the danger of going bankrupt if their prospects for raising revenue exceeding expenditures do not look bright for the immediate future. New York City, Cleveland, and Detroit are three cities that have experienced extreme difficulties in recent years because of repeated budgets where expenditures exceeded revenues.

What happens when a city or state goes bankrupt? It means that the individuals working for that government, the contractors providing materials and supplies, and individuals and groups who have loaned money may not receive payments. Then someone must be found in the short run to provide extra funds. Who are likely candidates? The federal government, state governments where cities are going bankrupt, employees through deferred wages or loans from their pension funds, or creditors through deferred payment schedules. Is it likely that a city going bankrupt will be able to convince individual investors to loan it additional funds?

The short run immediate problem of raising monies is only the first problem confronted by a bankrupt government. The longer range problem is how to achieve a balance between expenditures and revenues. This might seem a relatively simple matter — just raise revenues and cut expenditures. The problem, of course, is that if the solution were so simple the government would never have approached bankruptcy. Governments go bankrupt, ordinarily, when long run trends in their revenues and expenditures develop in such a manner that the government is not able to control them to ensure a budget balance. Revenue sources for cities usually include federal and state revenues, real estate taxes, and possibly sales or individual taxes. Expenditures include the salaries of government officials and special programs such as medicare, and in the case of New York City, welfare. If economic conditions are such that inflation causes rising costs for salaries, goods and services, and welfare, while revenues from real estate taxes and state and federal monies are not increasing as rapidly, an imbalance occurs. And if a local government attempts to raise real estate or other taxes, particularly if it is entering a period of decline, it may find the flight of business actually reducing revenues. The solution to bankruptcy is a careful plan that requires sacrifice from everyone and a delicate balance that leads to economic revival rather than continued economic decline.

Fiscal Control

Looking back at the simplified budget presented above, we can see some complications. Funds could be earmarked for smaller organizational units within each agency. Different uses of funds within the agency might be distinguished. In other words, greater detail may be advisable. The degree of detail of allocations is directly related to the questions of accountability, control, and management.

At its most obvious and rudimentary level, budgeting is a fiscal operation. Given the fact that monies are allocated for specific activities, what guarantee is there that these monies will be spent for these activities? This desire for fiscal control leads to a more detailed budget, which breaks down allocations to smaller organizational units within the agency and also distinguishes among different uses within agencies. Very often the distinction is made between funds for personnel (personal services, or PS) and other than personnel (other than personal services, or OTPS), which includes supplies, equipment, and travel.

Depending on the distinction made for organizational unit and category of expenditures, budgets vary within a very broad range of detail. Ordinarily, the smallest unit of the budget focusing on fiscal control is referred to as a line. Budgets that focus on organizational units and types of expenditures for basic fiscal control are often referred to as *line-item budgets.*

Program Budgeting

But a budget can be looked at as more than a statement of how much each organizational unit receives for the purposes of paying personnel and buying supplies. It may be conceived of as a statement of government purposes and policies. The money spent by government is not intended merely to pay people and supply them with paper and pencils. Government monies are expended to carry out specific purposes, as directed in the policies that have been adopted. Monies are spent to implement programs to reach the goals and objectives of government activities.

This dimension of the budget process is captured by the term *program budgeting.* Program budgeting emphasizes program units rather than organizational units as the basic building blocks of a budget. So if the purpose of government is to educate its citizens, all educational programs might be placed together. The program budget can be applied across or within departments, agencies, or any organizational unit chosen.

Used properly, the program budget has some very important advantages. Since it emphasizes programs linked to the goals and purposes of government, it provides a convenient way of assessing whether the purposes of government are being carried out and the extent to which specific programs are furthering these purposes. In this way, it becomes an effective management tool, and indeed a tool of policy analysis. You may remember that it was a variant of the program budget, the Department of Defense's Planning, Programming, and Budgeting System (PPBS), that helped establish the place of systems analysis in government. A Planning, Programming, Budgeting System is just a fancier and more elaborate budget process that incorporates systems analysis approaches within the actual budget process.

During each fiscal year, prior to the submission of the budget by the elected executive to the legislature, each agency is asked to generate a budget proposal. As this request is ordinarily relayed back down the bureaucracy, smaller organizational units in turn submit requests within the organizational hierarchy. The basic approach of PPBS is to require the presentation of the agency budget by program category. Then, using a systems approach, each program must be related to agency goals and objectives and the budget must indicate how the proposed program will bring about the desired goal. Agencies may also be required to suggest alternative approaches to the attainment of program goals and to analyze their relative costs and benefits. PPBS systems are a logical extension of the program budget, and the use of systems analysis in a comprehensive fashion. Unfortunately, they often become overwhelmed by their own detail and too cumbersome to operate efficiently.

Whether a government unit uses a line-item budget, a program budget, or some combination, it should be increasingly clear to you that the budget process is perhaps the most important policy process of government. The budgetary process is the means government uses to determine the basic allocation of its own resources for its various purposes. The separation of revenue and expenditure processes within government means that budgeting and the budget process become the mechanisms that organizational units use to contest their survival. It substitutes for the market mechanism in deciding whether or not individual agencies, bureaus, or departments are going to flourish or atrophy; indeed, whether and for how long they are going to exist. The budget process is the basis for deciding "who gets what" of what there is to get. It is the focus of much of the politics of public organizations. Its mastery and understanding are critical for the prosperity of any public organization.

The Budget Cycle

The budget process, like policy processes in general, can be divided into four stages: policy development, policy formation, policy implementation, and policy revision. The budget cycle occurs over a two-year period. Soon after one fiscal year has begun, the chief executive for a city or other governmental unit circulates budget guidelines to agencies (the highest-level organizational unit) for the preparation of the next fiscal year's budget. Agencies follow suit and distribute guidelines to the units within them that participate in the budget development process. In some agencies the budget may be prepared at the highest levels without involving subunits.

When all agencies have submitted their budgets in the form of budget requests, the process of policy formation begins in earnest. The executive, through the budget office, surveys all the requests, asks the agency heads and their budget officials to justify their budgets, and produces the proposed executive budget. The process of policy formation then reaches its finale in the passage of the budget by the legislature (which at the local level is usually called a council). Often the process of policy formation goes up to and even beyond the start of the next fiscal year, requiring in the latter case special arrangements to allow government to function on an interim basis without a formal budget.

During the second year the process of budget implementation occurs, with agencies spending monies allotted to them and budget officials keeping watch to see that they do not exceed budgeted amounts. Also during the second year the process of policy revision occurs as changes are made in the existing budget, often referred to as budget modifications.

As you participate in BUDGSIM, a simulated budget process for a large city, pay attention to the basic concepts of line-item and program budgeting, but also consider the broader implications. The budgeting process places agencies, executives, legislators, and nongovernmental actors in a competitive situation in which each actor attempts to gain greater resources. Government budgeting is the most important policy process, because it determines governmental priorities and the level of resources devoted to specific purposes. When you understand budgeting in its several aspects, you will have gone a long way toward understanding public organizations, the nature of public policy processes, and the techniques of policy analysis.

BUDGSIM

BUDGSIM is a game about the budget process in fictional New City, with a population of 2,000,000. It is meant to teach potential participants in the budget process how it works and sharpen the understanding of those who already are familiar with it. BUDGSIM does not apply exactly to a specific municipal budget process, but is designed to approximate many city budget processes. Certain aspects may not exactly mirror the processes of your city or the city with which you are most familiar. For example, most cities do not budget education funds, which are raised by separate, independent boards of education. After participating in BUDGSIM, explore the differences between the BUDGSIM model and your own city. Consider what changes in BUDGSIM would make it closer to your own municipal budget process.

BUDGSIM has two distinct phases. During the first, agencies are required to develop a budget and defend it before the mayor's budget examiners. During the second, the agencies attempt to influence the final adoption of the budget by the mayor and the council, which is an elected group of representatives of the ten districts into which New City is divided. During this second phase, the political environment of the budget game will be expanded to include such non-governmental actors as interest groups and influential individuals.

PHASE I — PLAY

Preliminary Instructions

In order to begin Phase I, the class will be divided into groups of five to eleven individuals. In each group at least four agency heads will be designated along with one to three budget examiners.

The agencies and the budget examiners are given the game materials contained in the Appendix to BUDGSIM:

I. Budget preparation guidelines
II. A budget summary for the current fiscal year
III. Agency program budgets for the current fiscal year, including program summaries
IV. Program summaries explaining the categories used in each agency budget

Options in the guidelines should be determined by the mayor (instructor), indicating the rough estimate for the budget and specific program priorities. Then the budget examiners and agency heads should be given their assignments for the next meeting:

a. Budget Examiners: Meet and decide upon a systematic strategy for reaching the overall budget indicated.
b. Agency Heads: Prepare a revised agency budget based on last year's budget, after reading the guidelines which follow.

These assignments should be carried out after the participants have read the items in the Appendix, the Overview, and the Strategy Memo.

After you have completed your proposal for the upcoming fiscal year and provided written justifications, bring it to class. Then you will be asked to present your proposed budget to the mayor's budget examiners while the other agency heads listen.

After the budget examiners have met with and questioned each agency head, they will develop a proposed budget for the upcoming fiscal year, which is referred to as the executive budget, since it is prepared by the elected executive. In preparing this budget, the budget examiners should carry out the guidelines enunciated in the letter to agency heads. They also should be prepared to justify their budget as a rational allocation of resources, given the individual agency request and the mayor's priorities. They should realize that the executive budget must be passed by a council of ten elected representatives from the wards of New City.

The instructor will rate the performance of the budget examiners. If possible, the presentation of the executive budget should occur during the following class to allow for a thorough reasoned presentation. The winning agency is the one that obtains the greatest percentage increase over last year's budget.

Overview

Phase I of BUDGSIM simulates the interaction between agency heads and the chief executive's (mayor or city manager) budget staff. Budget staffs vary widely according to the size of the city. In very large cities individuals will be assigned to specific agencies as budget examiners and will ordinarily follow that agency's budget through its entire cycle. In BUDGSIM a team of one to three budget examiners will be responsible for reviewing all agency budgets and proposing a combined citywide executive budget. It is suggested that to play Phase I at least four agencies be assigned of the eight described below.

Phase I centers around the preparation of agency budgets for the upcoming fiscal year. The process of preparing a combined budget for all agencies is perhaps the most important phase in the budget process. It determines the allocation of funds among agencies and programs. The great detail that these decisions require means that the preparation of the executive budget involves innumerable decisions. As the process of budget formation moves to the legislature, because of resource constraints in terms of both time and personnel only a small number of these allocation decisions are ordinarily reviewed. At the national level, a full-time legislature and a full-time staff help increase the scope of review, but at the local level the power of the executive is often dominant.

The task of proposing a budget for an entire agency is a complex affair. Its complexity discourages departures from incremental changes. It leads to a strong reliance on prior budgets. That is why, in the materials in Appendix A, the agency heads are provided with the current year's budget, which becomes the starting point for next year's budget. But there is a good deal more to budgeting than rewriting last year's budget. New constraints must be taken into consideration. Often wages and salaries are rising. State and federal policies have a strong impact on local budgets. A large portion of the budget for New City consists of state and federal funding. In writing a budget particular care must be taken to anticipate changes in federal and state revenues. Cuts in city funding may result in loss of state and federal matching funds. The chief executive's own priorities may determine the reaction to an individually prepared agency budget.

Finally, the budget presents the opportunity for the agency head to demonstrate competence and leadership in giving new direction to the agency. Successful budgeting is closely related to successful management, for the budget determines the extent of the resources of the agency and how they will be allocated among the goals and objectives being pursued.

Now read the budget guidelines in Appendix A, as modified by the mayor (instructor), and the Strategy Memo.

Strategy Memo

The most important statement in the budget guidelines is its projection for the overall level of the next fiscal year's budget. But this guidance must be interpreted in terms of your own experience and that of the agency. As you prepare your budget, based on the materials in Appendix A, remember that agency heads generally attempt to maximize their share of the budget. In fact, for purposes of BUDGSIM the agency heads are directed to devise a strategy for maximizing their own budgets. Their primary goal is to increase their share of the budget (not including state and federal funds) relative to their current share. This may be judged by comparing the percentage change of an agency's allotment for the next fiscal year as compared to the current year's allotment (excluding state and federal funds). Developing the most costly budget is not, however, the best strategy in attempting to maximize your allocation. Rather, you should try to convince the mayor and the budget examiners that your agency is the most worthy, in terms of demonstrated performance, careful justification of budget requirements, reasonable requests, and compliance with the mayor's priorities. Another factor is the extent to which the items in the budget request are likely to generate political support for the mayor in future campaigns.

In preparing your written budget request for the fiscal year, make sure it is neat, clear, and understandable. At a minimum it should include complete figures for each program category within your agency's program budget for both personal services (PS) and other than personal services (OTPS), including summaries and totals. Be sure to indicate the projected city portion and the percentage change in this portion from the current budget. These calculations should take into account wage increases and changes in federal and state programs. You should also indicate the justification for each program, with particular emphasis upon any new programs and increased funding. This justification should relate the request to the mayor's priorities and possible political consequences.

At least two major initiatives should be described to meet the mayor's priorities. These initiatives may involve the creation of new organizational units or the reformulation of programs, or they may occur within existing organizational and program constraints. Your task is to convince the mayor and the budget examiners that your initiative will further their stated priorities.

In changing the numbers of clerical, professional, and supervisory personnel, you may use the following average earnings figures for each of those positions which are eliminated or added: clerical work, $12,000 per year; professional employees, including teachers, police, and sanitation workers, $20,000 per year; supervisory personnel, $30,000 per year. You may posit last year's distribution among these three categories based upon independent research or reasonable hypothesis. Each change from the previous year's budget should be justified in terms of the mayor's priorities.

In making the above changes, you will be given a great deal of latitude. Since you may not be familiar with any of these program categories, you may draw upon any materials at your disposal.

The task you are being asked to perform is not a research task. If materials are readily available to you, they may be helpful; otherwise, use your imagination. So long as the suggestions you make are reasonable, the mayor's budget analysts will not challenge them. That does not mean, however, that they may not challenge your suggestions on other grounds, particularly as they are related to the mayor's stated priorities.

APPENDIX A

Budget Preparation Guidelines

Dear Agency Head:

As you know, the agency budgets for the upcoming fiscal year must be submitted to the Budget Bureau as soon as possible. This year is a period of (select one)

(budget cutbacks.
only minimal increases.
some budget leeway.)

I have prepared a budget (select one)

A. 10% less than last year's budget;
B. approximately 5% greater than last year's budget;
C. approximately 10% greater than last year's budget.

While allocations to individual agencies will vary according to their ability to contribute to my priorities, please prepare a budget with the overall limits of the budget in mind. I stress the importance of certain priorities for the coming year, which are (select a small number):

1. increased productivity throughout the city;
2. efforts to combat an increasing rate of unemployment in the city;
3. special assistance to the aged;
4. attempts to reduce the incidence of poverty in the city;
5. increased efforts to ease the burden of working women;
6. greater attention to the leisure-time activities of the citizens;
7. special efforts to increase personal safety;
8. increased attention to the elimination of corruption in government;
9. protection of programs that employ minorities and women;
10. elimination of services that will be minimally opposed by powerful labor, business, and community groups.

In order for you to estimate your increased costs over last year, please remember that personnel costs including fringe benefits must be figured at an increase of 5% over last year as a result of collective bargaining agreements in effect.

Attached to your projected budget for the upcoming fiscal year should be a supplementary discussion of each major program item, not including employee fringe benefits. This discussion should explain your rationale for the basic budget projection. Describe any significant changes in funding, personnel, or program. Each budget presentation should describe at least two major efforts to meet my priorities. [Optional: With respect to one of these efforts, whether a new program category or the revision of an existing program category, undertake a systems analysis contrasting your proposed alternative with another plausible alternative.] I am also quite concerned with getting the most for my money. Any cost analysis you can present will be most welcomed.

When you present your budget, please be prepared to leave one typed copy with my Budget Examiner. Thank you for your cooperation.

M. Mayor

The Mayor

Budget Summary—Current Fiscal Year

Anticipated Revenues: $1,538,733,737

	Budgeted
1. Education	$ 588,749,800
2. Fire	80,769,000
3. Housing	10,593,750
4. Employment and Training	27,755,000
5. Parks and Recreation	15,985,600
6. Police	174,216,675
7. Sanitation	59,815,472
8. Social Services	579,848,440
Total Planned Expenditures	$1,538,733,737

Funds derived from state and federal sources are indicated in the program descriptions. The program category involving general government and miscellaneous expenses has been omitted for simplification.

Program Budget Summaries—Current Fiscal Year

1. Education Program Budget

	PS	OTPS	TOTAL
I. Administration	$ 16,798,432	$ 7,896,320	$ 24,694,752*
II. Citywide Instructional Services	109,157,210	53,764,010	162,921,220*
III. Community School District Instructional Services	260,001,600	86,687,080	346,688,680*
IV. Curriculum and Instructional Support	2,732,450	1,116,082	3,848,532*
V. Reimbursable Programs	44,525,023	6,071,593	50,596,616
TOTALS	$433,214,715	$155,535,085	$588,749,800

*Approximately 30% of these monies are attributable to state aid. No state aid is lost by reduction in city monies.
Program V is federal money, which is expected to remain at the same level for next year.

1. Education Program. The Education Department is charged with organizing and supervising all elementary, secondary, vocational, and other schools and classes necessary to meet the education needs and demands of the city. In addition to administering the schools, the Education Department is responsible for a variety of support functions, including maintenance and construction of school buildings, curriculum design, teacher training, personnel administration, budgeting and financial administration, and purchasing.

I. Administration

The administration program is concerned with providing services to both citywide and community school districts that are necessary to the operation of the school system, but do not include educational functions. This program includes payroll, data processing, financial management, supplies and purchasing, school construction, and school maintenance.

II. Citywide Instructional Services

In this program are included all expenses for high schools and special schools that are under the jurisdiction of the citywide Board of Education. These expenses include the salaries of teaching and supervisory personnel and the costs of supplies and equipment for the operation of educational programs. Special Education programs focus on children with physical or mental handicaps, including socially maladjusted and emotionally disturbed children.

III. Community School District Instructional Services

This program includes all expenses for the direct costs of operating schools at the elementary and junior high school levels. These services include the costs of teaching and supervisory personnel, the costs of textbooks and supplies, and the costs of maintenance of the school buildings. Community boards are responsible for these schools.

IV. Curriculum and Instructional Support

This program includes the Bureau of Curriculum Development and specialized subject matter bureaus that develop curriculum materials and provide consultant expertise to centralized and decentralized school units. These central units also provide teacher training and instructional opportunities for staff members interested in personal development and qualifying for additional payment steps.

V. Reimbursable Programs

This program consists of monies obtained from the federal government for specific programs aimed at helping disadvantaged students. The costs for this program include direct instruction, teacher training, and evaluation of these special programs, which are funded totally from federal monies.

2. Fire Program Budget

	PS	OTPS	TOTAL
I. Administration	$ 3,021,480	$ 412,020	$ 3,433,500
II. Fire Operations, Land	48,790,035	995,715	49,785,750
III. Fire Operations, Marine	1,281,840	26,160	1,308,000
IV. Prevention and Special Services	3,310,832	50,418	3,361,250
V. Fire Communication Service	1,511,715	113,785	1,625,500
VI. Employee Benefits	21,255,000		21,255,000
TOTALS	$79,170,902	$1,598,098	$80,769,000

2. Fire Program. The fire department has the responsibility for putting out fires, protecting life and property in the event of fires and disasters, and minimizing the outbreak of fires throughout the city.

I. Administration

Program I includes the central offices of the fire department (including the office of the fire chief), which are responsible for management and information services. Specifically, these offices provide such services as personnel, budget, finance, procurement, repair, in-service training, machine accounting, and data processing.

II. Fire Operations, Land

This program is responsible for protecting lives and property through the extinguishing of fires at any place within the jurisdiction of the city, except those described in Program III below. It includes all the costs of personnel and materials necessary to fight fires throughout the city.

III. Fire Operations, Marine

This program includes all costs for the extinguishing of fires on the waters adjoining New City. It includes the extinguishing of fires on any dock, wharf, pier, warehouse, or other structure bordering upon or adjacent to the Port of New City. It includes the costs of personnel services and the maintenance of equipment and materials.

IV. Prevention and Special Services

This program is aimed at reducing the possibility of the outbreak of fire through fire prevention and community relations. It includes the costs of efforts to determine the causes of suspicious fires through investigation and follow-up procedures.

V. Fire Communication Service

This program includes the costs of operating, maintaining, improving, and extending the fire alarm telegraph service throughout the city to provide public facilities for the transmission of alarms of fire and to direct the response of assigned fire-fighting apparatus to fire locations. It provides a complete communication system including two-way radio communication between fire headquarters units and all field fire-fighting apparatus. It is also concerned with programs to reduce the possibility of false alarms.

VI. Employee Benefits

This program includes an allocation for pensions and fringe benefits pursuant to the collective bargaining agreement operative in this agency.

3. Housing Program Budget

	PS	**OTPS**	**TOTAL**
I. Administration	$ 819,913	$ 670,837	$ 1,490,750*
II. Code Enforcement and Special Improvement	3,429,170	423,830	3,853,000*
III. Housing Construction and Development	2,691,750	83,250	2,775,000**
IV. Relocation	1,018,407	50,343	1,068,750**
V. Fringe Benefits	1,406,250		1,406,250*
TOTALS	$9,365,490	$1,228,260	$10,593,750

*15% of these funds derive from city sources.

**These funds derive solely from noncity sources.

3. Housing Program. This agency is responsible for the city's programs for housing, rehabilitation, urban renewal, publicly assisted middle-income housing, and code enforcement.

I. Administration

This program includes the general management of all program activities and the development of new and revised housing policies. It includes administrative programs related to personnel, budget, finance, accounting, data processing, investigations and audits, training programs, and labor relations. Fifteen percent of these funds are charged to the city tax levy budget; the rest are derived from state, federal, and capital funds.

II. Code Enforcement and Special Improvement

This program provides for enforcement of the housing maintenance code, including emergency services, in accordance with regulations required for the acquisition of state and federal grants-in-aid. It provides for the supervision of special improvement programs, including federally assisted code enforcement, receivership, housing repair maintenance, and landlord repair contracts. Fifteen percent of these funds are derived from tax levy sources; 35 percent from state sources; 10 percent from federal sources; and the rest from capital funds.

III. Housing Construction and Development

This program includes the coordination, supervision, and administration of federally supported urban renewal programs and state-supported middle-income housing. It encourages the formation of nonprofit housing sponsorship and directs and controls housing rehabilitation efforts and measures designed to encourage new methods of construction. These funds are derived from the federal government, capital funds, and special grants.

IV. Relocation

This program supports residential and business tenant relocation. It includes the costs of coordinating the relocation of individuals, families, and firms displaced by urban renewal activities, construction of public improvements, and emergency vacate situations. Studies relating to relocation, including the analysis of demand groups and their needs, social services required for relocatees, and program costs, are also included. These funds are derived equally from federal sources and capital funds.

V. Fringe Benefits

This program includes an allocation for pensions and fringe benefits pursuant to the collective bargaining agreement operative in this agency.

4. Employee and Training Program Budget

	PS	OTPS	TOTAL
I. Administration	$ 2,012,049	$ 601,001	$ 2,613,050**
II. Job Counseling	5,537,290	3,252,060	8,789,350*
III. Public Service Jobs	3,500,000	500,000	4,000,000*
IV. Job Placement and Development	6,698,910	1,377,790	8,076,700*
V. Data Collection, Research, and Evaluation	796,550	153,650	950,200**
VI. Employee Fringe Benefits	3,325,700		3,325,700***
TOTALS	$21,870,499	$5,884,501	$27,755,000

*These are federal funds determined by objective formulas.

**30% of these funds derive from city sources.

***85% federal funds, 15% city funded.

4. Employment and Training Program. This program provides for training and placement of individuals not employed, particularly those from low-income backgrounds. Substantial funding is made available through the Comprehensive Employment and Training Act. Other activities for upgrading job skills also are included.

I. Administration

This program includes general management of all program activities and expenditures and the development and revision of policies. It also includes activities related to personnel, budget, finance, accounting, data processing, general services, investigations and audits, training, and labor relations. The estimated federal contribution is 70 percent.

II. Job Counseling

Provides counseling to enable the unemployed to use available employment services to gain confidence in their ability and to improve their employment status. Includes basic literacy education to permit further skilled training and vocational training in skill-shortage occupations. This program is funded on a 100% reimbursable basis by the federal government.

III. Public Service Jobs

Provides public service jobs with built-in career training for unemployed individuals. Totally federally funded.

IV. Job Placement and Development

Provides protected work environments to permit the unemployed to develop the work habits and vocational skills necessary for permanent employment.

Provides for determining existing job vacancies, inducing the use of relevant hiring standards, redesigning existing jobs to create additional entry level jobs, and promoting the development of career ladders. Totally federally funded.

V. Data Collection, Research, and Evaluation

Provides for the development of a data base relating to job opportunities in the city area. Also provides for the research and evaluation of other programs. Federal contributions estimated at 70 percent.

VI. Employee Fringe Benefits

This program includes an allocation for pensions and fringe benefits pursuant to the collective bargaining agreement operative in this agency. Federal contribution estimated at 85 percent.

5. Parks and Recreation Program Budget

	PS	OTPS	TOTAL
I. Administration	$ 685,776	$ 67,824	$ 753,600
II. Parks Maintenance and Operation*	7,388,602	913,198	8,301,800
III. Design, Engineering, and Construction	650,000	3,200	653,200
IV. Recreation	3,429,282	258,118	3,687,400
V. Cultural Affairs, Landmarks	240,000	207,200	447,200
VI. Fringe Benefits	2,142,400		2,142,400
TOTALS	$14,536,060	$1,449,540	$15,985,600

*Presently an additional $1.5 of employment and training funds is spent here, but indicated in the Employment and Training budget.

5. Parks and Recreation Program. This agency supervises the planning, development, construction, maintenance, and operation of the city park system and has general responsibility for recreation and cultural affairs.

I. Administration

This program includes the formulation, revision, and reviewing of all policies and programs; the recommendation, acquisition, and development of properties for expansion of parks; and general services, including personnel, audit, and management analysis.

II. Parks Maintenance and Operation

Maintains and operates all park facilities, including personnel, supplies, materials, and equipment.

III. Design, Engineering, and Construction

Plans additions to existing parks and the creation of new parks. Prepares working drawings and supervises private contractors in the construction of work involved. These funds are allocated to the capital budget.

IV. Recreation

Initiates, directs, and supervises recreation programs, including the assignment of personnel and the allocation of supplies and equipment.

V. Cultural Affairs and Landmarks

Manages and develops cultural affairs programs for the city. Designates for preservation of buildings, structures, districts, and other works of historical or aesthetic importance.

VI. Fringe Benefits

For the payment of interest and the redemption of bonds or amortization installments on outstanding debt on departmental capital items.

6. Police Program Budget

	PS	**OTPS**	**TOTAL**
I. Administration	$ 6,503,000	$1,400,950	$ 7,903,950
II. Patrol and Prevention	71,259,264	2,969,136	74,228,400
III. Investigation and Apprehension	17,500,377	541,248	18,041,625
IV. Traffic Control	8,543,999	219,076	8,763,075
V. LEAA—Special Programs	5,500,000	500,000	6,000,000*
VI. Employee Fringe Benefits	59,279,625		59,279,625
TOTALS	$16,586,265	$5,630,410	$174,216,675

*100% federal funds.

6. Police Program. The police department is charged with protecting persons and property throughout the city. It carries out extensive patrol activities, is responsible for rapid intervention in response to requests for assistance, and undertakes the investigation of criminal acts. It is also responsible for facilitating the operation of vehicular and pedestrian traffic.

I. Administration

This program provides centralized services for local police units, including personnel, pension, medical, printing, accounting, payroll, equipment and supplies, engineering, records, electronic data processing, and motor transport. The program also includes the costs of licensing procedures for taxicabs and guns and maintaining staff facilities at the police academy. It also includes community relations, press relations, a civilian complaint review board, and general costs of maintaining a centralized administration responsible for the direction of the police department.

II. Patrol and Prevention

This program includes the costs of patrol operations and administration, communications operations and maintenance, and also the costs of maintaining precinct receptionists.

III. Investigation and Apprehension

To identify, discover, and apprehend suspected and known criminals and to control criminal activity. To assist in the resolution of noncriminal problems such as missing persons and fatal accidents and to provide internal security for the police department. Includes a range of specialized departments, many of which function out of the central police headquarters. Some of these specialized units include homicide squads, burglary squads, river-front squads, and youth agents. This program also includes the borough and precinct detectives and technical services such as laboratory, ballistics, and bomb squad.

IV. Traffic Control

Includes programs directed at traffic safety, enforcement of traffic regulations, school crossing guards, congestion relief, and the tow-away program, and it also includes special squads, including the taxi squad and the special events squad.

V. LEAA—Special Programs

Includes a variety of special programs subject to approval by state and federal agencies; 100 percent federal monies.

VI. Employee Fringe Benefits

This program includes an allocation for pensions and fringe benefits pursuant to the collective bargaining agreement operative in this agency.

7. Sanitation Program Budget

	PS	OTPS	TOTAL
I. Administration	$ 3,519,733	$ 572,979	$ 4,092,712
II. Automotive and Plant Maintenance	4,268,334	1,578,698	5,847,032
III. Street Cleaning and Refuse Collection	25,375,023	517,857	25,892,880
IV. Snow Removal	852,522	26,366	878,888
V. Waste Disposal	6,738,759	918,921	7,657,680
VI. Pensions and Fringe Benefits	15,446,280		15,446,280
TOTALS	$56,200,651	$3,614,821	$59,815,472

7. *Sanitation Program.* The sweeping, cleaning, sprinkling, flushing, washing, and sanding of streets; the removal and disposition of ashes, street sweepings, garbage, refuse, rubbish, and wastes; the removal of ice and snow from the streets; the removal of encumbrances from streets and storages and the disposal of such encumbrances; the operation, maintenance, and use of incinerators; construction, alteration and repair, maintenance and operation of all sewers.

I. Administration

This program includes all costs of administration and direction. It includes the review of policy and programs, management and project planning, and legal services. Supervision of labor and public relations and the conduct of department trials are included. It also provides general services, including payroll, personnel, auditing and accounting, data processing, statistical records, and training of new employees.

II. Automotive and Plant Maintenance

This program includes the repair and maintenance of motor equipment, power plants, and various machinery operated by the administration. It also includes maintenance and repairs on buildings, garages, section stations, and incinerators, and painting motor equipment, properties, and street signs.

III. Street Cleaning and Refuse Collection

Sweeps, cleans, and flushes approximately 500 miles of paved streets. Collects and removes refuse, rubbish, and ashes from residential, public, and special use buildings. Empties department litter receptacles. Gathers and removes fallen leaves. Provides for clean-up of storm and other debris. Removes street sweepings, encumbrances, dead animals, and offal.

IV. Snow Removal

Removal of snow and ice and the year-round related preparatory functions. Budgeted figures are based upon the average experience of the last five budget years.

V. Waste Disposal

Provides for the disposition of approximately two million tons or eleven million cubic yards of waste materials per year, necessitating the maintenance, operation, and use of incinerators, truck land fills, marine loading stations, marine unloading plants, tractors, bulldozers, cranes, hauling wagons, drag lines, and other hauling equipment. Reclaims waste swamplands for public benefit by land-fill operations.

VI. Pensions and Fringe Benefits

This program includes an allocation for pensions and fringe benefits pursuant to the collective bargaining agreement operative in this agency.

8. Social Services Program Budget

	PS	**OTPS**	**TOTAL**
I. Administration	$12,908,646	$ 3,027,953	$ 15,936,599
II. Public Assistance	36,702,598	487,620,247	524,322,845*
III. Auxiliary Services for Those on Public Assistance	10,219,113	647,769	10,866,882**
IV. Food Stamps	1,827,560	2,741,339	4,568,899***
V. Special Services for Children and Adults	2,988,597	3,370,119	6,358,716
VI. Employee Fringe Benefits	17,794,499		17,794,499
TOTALS	$82,441,013	$497,407,427	$579,848,440****

*$355,000,000 of OTPS category represents grants to Families with Dependent Children. Federal reimbursement covers 50%, state reimbursement represents 25%. A 5% increase in this program is projected for the next fiscal year.

**80% federal matching local grants.

***100% federal monies.

****This figure breaks down as 30% city, 30% state, and 40% federal.

8. Social Services Program. The Department of Social Services is responsible for the administration of welfare programs and related services. A large portion of the budget funds go directly to recipients as cash payments. The total costs of social services are split among the federal, state, and local governments roughly in the following percentages: city, 30 percent; state, 30 percent; federal government, 40 percent.

I. Administration

This program includes the costs of directing the entire department and establishing major policies. Maintains liaison with other city, state, and federal agencies. Maintains press and public relations and directs departmental publications. Reviews departmental work, controls procedures and forms, and conducts administrative studies. Handles all personnel matters, including relations with staff organizations and departmental staff training. Conducts fiscal accounting and statistical operations. Manages, maintains, and operates all departmental buildings and equipments. Prepares plans and specifications for building additions.

II. Public Assistance

Through social service centers, renders financial aid to persons in need of aid to dependent children and home relief. Administers veterans' cases. Provides medical care and dental care required by public assistance recipients and processes authorizations for hospital care services to the medically indigent. The portion of monies designated for AFDC are 50 percent reimbursable from the federal government and 25 percent reimbursable from the state government.

III. Auxiliary Services for Those on Public Assistance

Handles legal matters pertaining to public assistance recipients and rights of employees. Conducts special investigations involving special case load situations. Administers various auxiliary and community service programs including day-care centers for persons sixty years of age and over, rehabilitation, employment, and homemaking programs for families with children and older handicapped adults. Also deals with community organizations and conducts social research. This program is reimbursable at 80 percent from the federal government. During the next fiscal year the federal portion could be increased by up to 20 percent if city funds are available.

IV. Food Stamp Program

Administers the program for qualified public assistance and eligible non-public assistance households. This program is totally reimbursable from federal government funds.

V. Special Services for Children and Adults

Provides coordinated facilities dealing with varied problems of homeless men and women. Administers the services for the care at public expense of children and unmarried pregnant women or unmarried mothers outside their own homes. Handles the recruitment, study, and approval of foster homes for children. Administers care and treatment of dependent and neglected children committed to municipal child-care institutions for temporary shelter. Allocates New City funds to day-care centers operated by nonprofit agencies and community groups. Provides enriched preschool experience, including health, education, and social services for children from needy homes.

VI. Employee Fringe Benefits

This program includes an allocation for pensions and fringe benefits pursuant to the collective bargaining agreement operative in this agency.

COMMENT ON BUDGSIM – PHASE I

Would Phase I have been easier if you had had greater familiarity with the agency you represented, or with the budget bureau if you were a budget examiner? Of course. But by being thrust into an unfamiliar role you may have learned a great deal you didn't know before. It is one thing to read about the budget process, it is another to participate in budgeting. How would you characterize the budgeting process? What is the central interaction pattern between budget examiners and agency representatives? In trying to maximize your agency's budget, did you ask for more than you intended to get? Why?

What factors determine the effectiveness of the participants in the budget process? What makes for results in budgeting? How does BUDGSIM differ from the real world? Do agency heads always attempt to maximize their budgets? Why do some agencies attract large amounts of state and federal funds? Why is developing new programs tailored to the mayor's priorities a good strategy for increasing an agency's budget? To what extent are accuracy and truthfulness in the budget process rewarded?

Was your budget very different from last year's budget? What factors minimize changes from last year's budget?

PHASE II — PLAY

At the conclusion of the budget hearing in Phase I, the budget examiners were instructed to present a detailed budget during the next class. Individual roles for Phase II should be selected at the same time.

During Phase II, the proposed executive budget will be presented to an elected council for review and adoption. The process described here is a specific instance of policy formation. You may want to review Modules 5 and 6 before proceeding to the play of BUDGSIM, Phase II.

The participants in this phase of BUDGSIM will represent council members, the mayor and assistants, agency heads, interest groups, and influential individuals. While the number of participants in each category will vary from game to game, a suggested distribution for a class of thirty might be: council members, twelve; agency heads, eight; influentials, two; interest groups, five; mayor and assistants, three. It is suggested that an attempt be made to adapt to local conditions by selecting interest groups and influential individuals from the local scene. Some suggestions are described below.

The play begins with each participant—with the exception of the mayor and assistants and newly designated agency heads — filling out the Individual Proposed Budget form based upon projected changes in the proposed executive budget. In making changes, indicated by the percentage change in an agency's budget (not including state and federal revenues), a total of 100 percentage points of change should be indicated. For example, % change in police allocation = 60; % change in fire allocation = 40. In making such changes, participants should assume a particular role. If they are legislators they can vote their conscience or their constituency (see POLFORM). Participants then attempt to have their own point of view incorporated in the budget that is finally adopted by the council. The mayor and assistants attempt to retain the existing budget, while the agency heads attempt to gain maximum increases for their individual agencies.

After the mayor and assistants present the executive budget to the council, council members will be allowed to ask one to three questions each, as time permits. The total period for presentation and questions should not exceed thirty minutes. After the initial presentations, the mayor and assistants, the agency heads, interest groups, and influentials will all attempt to promote their own preferred budgets by influencing the votes of council members. During these meetings, the mayor and assistants seek to make changes in the executive budget to satisfy the objections of individual council members, so that at the end of a 30-minute period a majority will vote to pass the entire budget in a single vote. In the event that a deadlock arises and the mayor is unable to obtain a majority in the council, an impasse will be declared and an additional fifteen-minute interaction period will take place. The mayor will again attempt to revise the budget to gather the support of a majority of the council.

While the mayor is attempting to influence the council members, the agency heads are lobbying with the council members to increase their own budgets. They are also attempting to find allies among the interest groups and influential individuals to back their positions.

Interest groups and influential individuals, meanwhile, are attempting to make sure that the revised policy will reflect their own perspectives, as recorded at the beginning of Phase II. They each have 100 influence points, which they may give to council members in return for their support on some item of importance to them. A written binding contract is suggested, which can be enforced by the game leader. It will specify that an individual will support a certain change for a number of influence points, either by refusing to vote for a budget without that item in it, or by promising to fight for inclusion of that item in the budget and not receiving the points unless the item is included. If an interest group or influential individual contracts for more than 100 points, all their contracts are invalid.

Scoring for Phase II of BUDGSIM reflects the objectives of each group: the council members to accumulate influence, the mayor and assistants to minimize change in the budget, the agency heads to increase their own allotments, the council members and the interest groups and influential individuals to obtain changes in accord with their indicated preferences.

Score for council members:

3 × (sum of percentage changes initially indicated that are incorporated in the final budget), plus total influence points obtained

Score for mayor and assistants (they all get the same score):

100 minus sum of percentage changes in all agency budgets

Score for agency heads:

3 × % increase in agency budget

Score for interest groups and influentials:

5 × (sum of percentage changes initially indicated that are incorporated in the final budget)

The form for your individual proposed budget and descriptions of interest groups and influentials appears in Appendix B. Try to adapt these descriptions to the realities of politics in your municipality.

APPENDIX B

Individual Proposed Budget

Program	Proposed Executive Budget	% Change	Preferred Budget
Education			
Fire			
Housing			
Manpower			
Parks & Recreation			
Police			
Sanitation			
Social Services			
Total Funds			

INTEREST GROUPS AND INFLUENTIALS

New City Chamber of Commerce:

This group represents the large-and medium-sized businesses of New City. In general, they are interested in increasing the business opportunities in New City, while limiting governmental expenditures. A major strategy is to seek low taxes while keeping service levels for commercial interests high. Needless to say, these goals may result in shortchanging some human services provided by the city. But they see the long-run gains in economic prosperity as more than making up for temporarily reduced government services. In BUDGSIM, the goal of the Chamber of Commerce is to reduce the city portion of each agency budget by at least 10 percent and the education and social services budget by 20 percent.

New City Labor Council:

The New City Labor Council is a powerful federation of trade, industrial, and public service unions. It represents about 200,000 of the 2,000,000 residents of New City. While its leaders cannot dictate how their members vote, their public endorsements and control over union political funds make them a potent force in local politics. In general, the New City Labor Council is interested in maintaining the levels of public service employment while increasing the salaries of workers. However, since the Labor Council represents the working middle class, it is somewhat wary of expenditures for welfare. In recent years, the Labor Council has become concerned about the future prosperity of New City, the problems of safety in the streets, and the scarcity of jobs. Their large proportion of middle-class workers who have been moving to the suburbs is only partially committed to the city and fears continued demographic change, which they see as resulting in their loss of control over jobs and neighborhoods in New City. In BUDGSIM the Labor Council will seek a 15 percent increase in the city portion of each agency to increase wages and to provide new jobs, with the exception of no change in social services and a 10 percent increase in employment and training.

Black Citizens United:

A black self-help organization, including approximately 25,000 of the 500,000 blacks in New City. Consisting of two-thirds blacks with under $8,000 annual income and the rest with $8,000 – $20,000, the organization attempts to speak for the black community. While conceived of as a militant organization, it enjoys considerable support throughout the black community. It is particularly concerned with city services including education, housing, manpower, and social services. It also seeks adequate levels of police, fire, and sanitation services. Object for BUDGSIM will be to secure 30 percent increases in education, housing, and social service budgets and 10 percent increase in employment and training.

New City Civic Associations:

Many parts of the city have organizations of local homeowners or apartment dwellers who represent their particular communities. The interests of civic associations that are very closely tied to neighborhoods may be captured in the notion of neighborhood quality. Civic associations are ordinarily dominated by property owners and small-size business establishments, which seek to preserve the particular character of their neighborhoods. In New City, most of the civic associations represent the older, more established groups. The new ethnic groups tend to be underrepresented in this group and, in fact, may view the civic associations as tending to exclude them. The civic associations and their membership are very often individuals committed to their neighborhoods and are eager to maintain their own positions in those neighborhoods. They are very concerned with maintaining services to their neighborhoods and with an overall atmosphere of prosperity. The civic associations would be very much in favor of maintaining traditional services such as fire, police, and sanitation. They would also be concerned with parks and recreation, and education, to a lesser extent. Housing and social services would elicit mixed reactions from civic associations, depending upon their location. In this particular budget controversy, the New City Civic Associations will attempt to increase the allocations to fire, police, housing, and education by 25 percent each.

New City Taxpayers' Association:

In many ways mirroring the position of the Chamber of Commerce is the Taxpayers' Association, which represents individual property owners and small business owners. The Taxpayers' Association is dominated by individuals who pay substantial direct taxes. Since property taxes are the major source of revenue for local governments, taxpayers' associations ordinarily are made up of individual property owners and small businesspeople who are hit by the burden of real estate taxes. These individuals are generally concerned, too, about local sales taxes, where these exist. Taxpayers' Associations seek to limit government spending, which has the direct effect of limiting tax burdens. In this particular budget situation, the New City Taxpayers' Association will seek a decrease of 20 percent in the proposed budget for education, employment and training, parks and recreation, and social services.

Morey Estate:

Morey Estate is the largest real estate owner in New City. He is concerned with two basic aspects of the budgetary process and wishes to minimize the taxes he must pay. He also wishes to provide adequate services, maintain the prosperity of New City, and, hopefully, further the city's real estate. Morey Estate seeks 25 percent cuts in education, employment and training, and social services, and a 25 percent increase in housing allocated to the category of housing construction and development.

Gum Vendor:
Gum Vendor, a local entrepreneur eager to obtain gum vending contracts with the city, will try to convince an agency to revise its budget to include a gum vending program for private contract.

Big Boss:
Big Boss is the leader of the majority party in New City, concerned with maintaining his or her flow of patronage in city agencies. As such, Big Boss is willing to work with city agencies to help them obtain influence with the mayor in return for a commitment from the agencies to follow his or her advice on job appointments. How many jobs can Big Boss control by making deals within the budget process?

Little Boss:
Little Boss realizes that the ability to maintain power within his or her party is also dependent upon patronage powers. Even though Little Boss's party is out of power, he or she is eager to maintain access to certain jobs within city agencies and is willing to enter into deals with agency heads to protect their agencies with what political influence he or she has in return for the rights of patronage within those agencies. How many jobs can Little Boss obtain through manipulation of his or her influence in the budget process?

COMMENT ON BUDGSIM – PHASE II

After the game is completed, compare the scores of the individuals in your group. Do they accurately reflect those individuals who played the game best? Do real-life rewards go to those who play the game best? What differences can you uncover between BUDGSIM and real life? Does the budget process in your municipality have any important distinguishing characteristics that might be incorporated into BUDGSIM? Is Phase I or Phase II most likely to incorporate a systems analysis?

What was the outstanding difference in BUDGSIM Phase II? Did the introduction of bargaining and negotiation completely change the budget process? Can rational arguments about specific programs still be used in Phase II? How did the dynamics of the process change from the point of view of the agency heads?

What would be the impact on the process if only the mayor could make changes in the budget, while the council still had the power to approve or reject? Would that increase or decrease the power of the mayor?

Do you see any similarities between BUDGSIM Phase II and POLFORM Phase II? Do interest groups attempt to intervene in budgeting at the municipal level? Would they have better access to the mayor or the city council? What would that depend upon?

How does an agency decide what budget to submit to the mayor? Are there bargaining processes that occur at the agency level? Do you see any way in which interest groups might help agency heads? How can legislators know if particular expenditures are justified? To what extent does the outcome of the budgeting process depend upon the specific relationships between agency heads, the mayor, the council, and interest groups?

ON BUDGETING AND OTHER THINGS

Having participated in the play of BUDGSIM, you should now understand some of the complexity of the budget process. As the budget is built from the requests of smaller governmental units to those at the agency level and finally to choices among different agencies, individuals are called upon to decide among alternative allocations of programs and governmental units that they may only vaguely understand. For example, consider the plight of a legislator on the House Appropriations Committee who must be able to compare expenditures in the nuclear energy field with those for solar energy. Or manned bombers against unmanned bombers. Or increased unemployment benefits against job creation. Or consider the difficulties of deciding between expenditures for energy development and conservation, or between defense and unemployment initiatives. These matters are extremely technical, and the decision-making processes become extremely complex.

Budgeting is a process involving the interaction of individuals in an organizational setting. Conflict is inevitable, for budgeting constitutes resources allocation — some get more resources and some get less. The position of individuals within the organization becomes closely related to their ability to secure resources through the budgeting process. Budgeting is an expression of competition for limited resources among the agencies and within agencies.

Securing additional personnel may in the first instance mean increasing a unit budget. Ample justifications must be made to the appropriate officials. Budgeting may involve a reallocation among categories. It also may result in additional funds with which to support staff; it thus may perform a central role in motivating staff. It also is an ideal mechanism through which to present certain approaches to management control.

Think back to Section I and the topics of personnel, motivation, leadership, communications, and superior-subordinate interaction. The budget process is central to many of these interactions and provides a context in which to practice your newly acquired skills.

Budget officials find it difficult to optimize the use of resources, for deciding among various alternatives might involve long and unreliable calculations. Like other policymakers, those making the budget must often accept satisficing solutions. They must often draw analogies from one aspect of a program to another. For example, the use of real estate in a new space program might be investigated by budget personnel familiar with correct practice in real estate. They may assume that if the real estate component is well worked out, the larger program will be similarly justified.

Another simplifying rule is the concept of *fair share,* whereby agencies previously funded will be considered to be roughly responsible for a certain proportion of the total budget. While their actual expenditures may vary, the fair share is the approximate amount of the total budget they have received in the past.

Having participated in the play of BUDGSIM, do you now have a better understanding of why budgeting is so often characterized as incremental? Do you understand why next year's budget will reflect the previous year's budget? The budget is shaped by the individuals who make it up and reliance on last year's budget is a practical way of minimizing the work and effort needed to produce a budget. Since budget making often takes place under extreme time pressures, the incentives to be guided by the previous year's budget are considerable. But perhaps the most compelling impetus toward incremental budgeting is the necessity for building a coalition of nongovernmental and governmental supporters of the budget. Since ultimately the budget must be supported by an elected executive and passed by an elected legislature, it must be able to muster widespread political support. If the budget is drastically different from that of the previous year, it risks alienating those suffering cuts. These individuals and groups will oppose the budget and may endanger its passage.

Can you see any dangers in incremental budgeting? What if some program that was funded last year just isn't working? Or what if some agency needs to be completely overhauled? Incrementalism allows for only minor departures from the status quo. It means that it may take many years to eliminate wasteful activities or to build new programs. Can you see any alternative to incremental budgeting?

Zero-base budgeting is an attempt to offset the incremental tendencies within the budget process. According to the principles of zero-base budgeting, a program or agency should not be continued merely because it existed the previous year. During the process of constructing the budget, each program and agency must be justified. No assumption will be made that the agency or program is needed next year just because it appears in the current year's budget.

Can you see any similarity between zero-base budgeting and PPBS? Both systems attempt to evaluate each agency and program to determine their usefulness and effectiveness. Both systems call for some substantive evaluation. They transform budgeting from a purely fiscal exercise to a management review process. They both can also generate a large amount of paperwork. If you think back to the module on systems analysis, you will recall that a systems analysis requires considerable effort. Imagine if each and every government program each year were subjected to a complete systems analysis. Zero-base budgeting, like PPBS, is a very ambitious undertaking.

President Carter's preoccupation with zero base budgeting was not unlike President Johnson's advocacy of PPBS. The power of the presidency is enormous. Was President Carter more successful than President Johnson in adopting a comprehensive, rational approach to budgeting?

It is perhaps fitting that this introductory text should end with a description and analysis of budgeting, for by our reckoning, budgeting is at the heart of public policy and administration. It is the allocation of public values in the form of government resources. So while budgeting comes at the end of this text, it is in many ways the beginning of public policy and administration. For without resources, public organizations are like a penniless creditless businessperson — nowhere. Perhaps that is something to think about the next time the tax bite seems particularly onerous. President Reagan again has demonstrated the power of the presidency to influence budgeting in obtaining major cutback agreements in his first months in office.

Budgeting illustrates as well as any other aspect of the policy process the political competition among administrators, executives, legislators, and nongovernmental actors. It also illustrates the problem of decision making under pressure. When the new fiscal year is upon them, decision makers must pass a new budget. Only occasionally will they put back the hands of the clock in a make-believe charade that, after all, the deadline has not passed and the new fiscal year has not begun; sometimes that is the only way a budget can be passed.

Budgeting also beautifully illustrates a policymaking process that needs improvement and in which attempts at improvement are constant. Program budgeting, PPBS, and, more recently, zero-base budgeting are attempts to introduce more thoroughgoing analysis into a process that is too often incremental and lacking in serious review. Decision makers struggling to meet deadlines too often are forced to settle for the policies or budgetary allocations of yesterday in order to make today's deadlines.

Yet, as we strive to improve the processes of policymaking, to better utilize available knowledge, as Yehezkel Dror so often exhorts us to do, let us not forget that it is people who carry out those processes. Public organizations must be able to compete successfully with private organizations for the most talented individuals. They must be able to retain, promote, and motivate the best and the brightest. Otherwise, hopes for a more efficient and better public service will never be realized.

If you are preparing for a career in the public service, do not think lightly of it, for the demands of working in large public bureaucracies are great and life can be frustrating. But the personal and psychic rewards also can be great. And you will have the chance to make government work a little better for all of us. Those of you who are not entering government service can help, too. By demanding the highest standards of government and its employees, you help create better government. But be aware that the government operates in the context of a larger society and to expect government and its employees to be different in work habits and dedication from the society as a whole is to be unrealistic.

Public organizations are no more nor less than groups of individuals like yourself trying to carry out sometimes unclear and contradictory goals in a complicated and frustrating world. Better government performance is all our jobs and the rewards are for all of us.

SELECTED BIBLIOGRAPHY FOR MODULE 11

BRAZER, HARVEY. *City Expenditures in the United States.* New York: National Bureau of Economic Research, 1959.

BURKHEAD, JESSE. *Government Budgeting.* New York: Wiley, 1956.

CAMPBELL, ALAN, and SACHS, SEYMOUR. *Metropolitan America: Fiscal Patterns and Governmental Systems.* New York: Free Press of Glencoe, 1967.

ENTHOVEN, ALAIN, and SMITH, K. WAYNE. *How Much is Enough?* New York: Harper and Row, 1971.

LYNCH, THOMAS. *Public Budgeting in America.* Englewood Cliffs, NJ: Prentice-Hall, 1979.

IPPOLITO, DENNIS. *The Budget and National Politics.* San Francisco: W. H. Freeman, 1978.

MUSGRAVE, RICHARD. *Fiscal Systems.* New Haven: Yale University Press, 1969.

SHARKANSKY, IRA. *Spending in the American States.* Chicago: Rand McNally, 1968.

WANAT, JOHN. *Introduction to Public Budgeting.* North Scituate, MA: Duxbury Press, 1978.

WILDAVSKY, AARON. *The Politics of the Budgetary Process.* Boston: Little, Brown, 1964.

INDEX

A-95 review, 84
accountability, 12, 129–30
ad hoc groups, 112
administrative game, 11
Administrative Procedures Act of 1946, 129
affirmative action, 27, 55
agenda building, 111, 116–117, 127
Allison, Graham, 132
amenities, 131
authority, charismatic, 35
Argyris, Chris, 22

Bachrach, Peter, 111
Bailey, Stephen, 143
balanced budget, 219
Baratz, Morton, 111
Barnard, Chester, 68, 72, 123
Bauer, Raymond, 106
Bean, Louis, 200
Becker, Gary, 192
Bennis, Warren, 22
Bentley, Arthur, 112
Berne, Eric, 28, 58
bloc-grant programs, 142
boards, 122
Braybrooke, David, 164
Brown v. *Board of Education,* 115
Brownlow Commitee, 49
budget (definition), 218
Budget, Office of Management and, 12, 66, 83–84
budget cycle, 223
budget guideline, 223, 228
bureau, 11
bureaucracy, 2, 35
bureaucratic autonomy, 9
Burke, Edmund, 128

categorical grant programs, 142
Census of Populations, 213
civil rights, 115
Civil Rights Act of 1964, 109, 139
civil service, federal, 47, 51–56
Civil Service Commission, U.S., 26, 48–49
Civil Service Reform Act of 1978, 49, 50
Classification Acts of 1923, 1949, 51
classification systems, 31, 50–51
clientele groups, 10, 12, 85–87, 118
coalition principles, 131
commissions, 122
competitive examinations, 50–51, 55
Comprehensive Employment and Training Act of 1973, 173, 179
contextual analysis, 25
control, 68, 222
control group, 180
councils of governments (COGs), 83
courts, 6, 124
crossimpact analysis, 201

decision (definition), 103
deficit budget, 220
Delphi technique, 201, 208, 212
Deutsch, Karl, 101
direction, 67
discount rate, 186
disjointed incrementalism, 164
direct services, 4
division of labor, 37
Dror, Yehezkel, 165, 183, 212
Drucker, Peter, 70, 180

Easton, David, 109, 120, 167
Elementary and Secondary Education Act of 1965, 142–148, 161
elite, 10, 111
employee relations, 31
Equal Employment Opportunities Commission, 27
exam, competitive, 50–51
exam, PACE, 52
exam, unassembled, 51
executive, 6, 11, 84, 103, 110, 122–124, 140, 224
executive budget, 224
executive order, 139
expenditures, 218

fair share, 244
Fayol, Henri, 35, 37
federal departments, 7
federal regions, 7
Federal Telecommunications System, 76
feedback, 70
fiscal control, 221–222
fiscal federalism, 142
fiscal year, 219-220
forecasting techniques, 200
formula grants, 142

game, 27–28, 58
Garms, Walter, 192
gate-keepers, 110–111
General Accounting Office, 12
General Schedule, 52–54
Gergen, Kenneth, 106
goals, 9, 27, 39, 41, 70, 76–78, 152, 158
grant programs, 142, 161
Great Society, 140
Gulick, Luther, 38

Hatch Act, 95
Herzberg, Frederick, 22
human relations approach, 38, 40
Humphrey, Hubert, 110

incrementalism, 164
independent regulatory commissions, 7
intergovernmental relations, 142
intergovernmental transfers, 142
interest groups, 111–112

job analysis, 37
job descriptions, 25, 58
job satisfaction, 22
Johnson, Lyndon B., 110, 139, 179
judicial decisions, 139
judiciary, 6, 11, 103, 124

Kahn, Herman, 200
Kaufman, Herbert, 69–70
Kennedy, John, 140

Lasswell, Harold, 120
leadership, 66–68
leadership style, 62, 67
legislators, 11, 84
legislature, 6, 11, 103, 110, 122, 140
lifetime earnings, 192
Likert, Rensis, 63
Lindblom, Charles, 113, 164
line-item budgets, 222
line organization, 30

McGregor, Douglas, 39
McNamara, Robert, 178–179
Management by Objectives, 70–71, 76, 180
management, scientific, 38, 180
Manpower Development and Training Act of 1962, 171
Maslow, Abraham, 22
matching funds, 226
mathematical models, 175, 178, 184–185
Mausner, Bernard, 22
Mayo, Elton, 39
media, 112
merit system, 48, 50
Merit Systems Protection Board, 49, 50
monitoring, 68–71, 213
Mosher, Edith, 143
Mosher, Frederick, 49

National Training Laboratory (NTL), 73
needs, hierarchy of, 22
net, output, 165, 184
Nixon, Richard, 110
nondecisions, 111

objectives, 76, 152, 170–171
observational method, 39
operations research, 168–169, 175, 197
opportunity costs, 186
optimizing solutions, 164
organizational changes, planned, 22
organization development, 73
organization theory, 34

participative management, 70
party leaders, 111
performance indicators, 181
Pendleton Act of 1883, 47
Personnel Management, Office of, 44–50
personnel officer, 26, 28
planning implementation, 149-155
Planning, Programming, Budgeting System (PPBS), 179, 223, 245
policy (definition), 103
policy memoranda, 106
policy planning, 149
policy process, the, 106
policy-makers, 116, 124
policymaking, 165
policymaking, executive, 123
Pressman, Jeffrey, 140
private corporations, 9
procedures, 131
program budgeting, 222
program evaluation, 179–181
public corporations, 9
public opinion, 11

Quade, E. S., 167
queuing theory, 196-197

rationalism, 164
redistribution, 4
red tape, 37, 81–82, 84
regulation, 4, 104
revenues, 218
revenue sharing, 142
Roethlisberger, F. J., 39
role, 2, 25, 41, 58, 61, 128
role orientation, 61, 128
Rosen, Anne, 59
Rousseau, Jean Jacques, 163

satisficing decisions, 164, 244
Sayles, Leonard, 64, 124
scenario, 155, 201
Schmidt, Warren, 62
school systems, 12–13
Schubert, Glendon, 163
self-actualization, 22, 67
self-help groups, 3
Selznick, Philip, 68, 106
Senior Executive Service, 54
Sherman, Harvey, 15
Simon, Herbert, 40, 113, 123, 164
social indicators, 212–215
Snyderman, Barbara, 22
staff function, 30
systems, political, 109
systems analysis, 167, 183

T-group, 73
Tannenbaum, Robert, 62
Taylor, Frederick, 35, 37, 180
teambuilding, 72–75
Toffler, Alvin, 199
Truman, David, 112, 141

unions, 32

Voting Rights Act of 1965, 109, 139

War on Poverty, 140
Weber, Max, 35, 37
welfare bureaucracy, 13
White, Leonard, 52
Wildavsky, Aaron, 140
workflows, external, 65
work group, 65, 73

X, theory, 39

Y, theory, 39

zerobased budgeting, 245